Forgotten Places

Rural America

Hal S. Barron
David L. Brown
Kathleen Neils Conzen
Cornelia Butler Flora
Donald Worster
Series Editors

Forgotten Places
Uneven Development
in Rural America

Edited by Thomas A. Lyson
and William W. Falk

 University Press of Kansas

© 1993 by the University Press of Kansas
All rights reserved

Published by the University Press of Kansas (Lawrence, Kansas 66049), which
was organized by the Kansas Board of Regents and is operated and funded by
Emporia State University, Fort Hays State University, Kansas State University,
Pittsburg State University, the University of Kansas, and Wichita State
University

Library of Congress Cataloging-in-Publication Data

Forgotten places : uneven development in rural America / edited by
    Thomas A. Lyson and William W. Falk.
        p.   cm.
    Includes bibliographical references and index.
    ISBN 0-7006-0592-4 ISBN 0-7006-0593-2 (pbk.)
    1. Rural poor—United States.   2. Rural development—United
States.   I. Lyson, Thomas A.   II. Falk, William W.
HC110.P6F67   1993
338.973'009173'4—dc20   92-43847

British Library Cataloguing in Publication Data is available.

Printed in the United States of America
10 9 8 7 6 5 4 3 2 1

To Our Mentors
Harry K. Schwarzweller and Arthur G. Cosby

Contents

Preface

THE IMPETUS FOR this book came from our colleague Gene Summers, a professor of rural sociology at the University of Wisconsin. After Gene was elected president of the Rural Sociological Society for 1990, he took as his charge a complete reexamination of rural poverty in the United States, something that had not been done for nearly thirty years. Toward this end, he organized the Task Force on Persistent Rural Poverty. With funding from the Kellogg Foundation and from the four U.S. Department of Agricultural Regional Centers for Rural Development, a large group of sociologists, economists, and other social scientists spent over two years delving into the causes of rural poverty in the United States today.

Forgotten Places was one of our contributions to the larger Task Force effort. Our purpose in commissioning the chapters for this book was to shed light on the territorial dimensions of rural poverty. In selecting the contributors, we sought out leading researchers in the fields of rural economic development and social welfare. We believe that their efforts represent the best original thinking and scholarship in an area of national concern that has been ignored for too long. We hope that the material in this book will begin to stimulate debate among policymakers, program planners, and government administrators over what can be done to bring the millions of Americans who live in depressed rural backwaters of the United States into the mainstream.

As editors, we received support for this undertaking from several sources. The Cornell University Agricultural Experiment and the Maryland Agricultural Experiment Station provided financial support for this project through the auspices of USDA/CSRS Regional Research Project S-229 (The Changing Structure of Local Labor Markets in Nonmetropolitan Areas: Causes, Consequences and Policy Implications). Additional support was provided by a grant from the Aspen Institute for a project titled "Diversified Rural Livelihood Strategies among Low Income Farm Households in the Northeast." Administrative and clerical support through the Department of Rural Sociology at Cornell and the Department of Sociology at the University of Maryland was provided by Tracy Aagaard and Cass O'Toole.

Tom Lyson, Ithaca, New York
Bill Falk, College Park, Maryland
December 1992

1 | Forgotten Places: Poor Rural Regions in the United States

Thomas A. Lyson and William W. Falk

OVER THREE DECADES ago, Michael Harrington documented the desperate plight of people living in depressed rural regions of the United States. His book *The Other America* helped fuel President Kennedy's efforts to improve the lives and opportunities of people living in Appalachia. And Harrington's findings were used to justify many of President Johnson's War on Poverty programs. Since Harrington wrote his seminal book, six presidents have entered and left the White House. Most of the federal programs and policies that were put in place to combat poverty and regional underdevelopment in the 1960s have now been dismantled. Washington seems to have forgotten the Other America Harrington wrote about.

It is both ironic and disconcerting that amid prolonged periods of economic growth in the United States since World War II, there are still rural regions of the country that continue to stagnate and in some cases decline. It is all the more troubling that many millions of people who live in these areas lack access to decent jobs, housing, and the types of social services that are taken for granted in much of urban America. In the Black Belt of the South, for example, there is not one county in which per capita income equals the national average. And in many Black Belt counties, per capita income is less than half of the national average. Infant mortality rates are higher, life expectancy lower, illiteracy more prevalent, and welfare benefits minimal.

The majority of the counties in Appalachia have per capita incomes well below the national average. And the more isolated the county, the greater the gap with the rest of the nation. Similarly, the Lower Rio Grande Valley is not only economically disadvantaged vis-à-vis the nation as a whole, but the large concentrations of Latinos in the Valley form an ethnic subculture that identifies as much with Mexico as with the United States.

The Black Belt, Appalachia, and the Lower Rio Grande Valley are not the only predominantly rural regions that lag behind the rest of the country on quality of life and standard of living measures. The Ozarks, the Cutover Region of the Midwest, the timber communities in the Pacific Northwest, and many parts of northern New England have failed to ride the rest of the economic tide of prosperity that washed over the country in the 1980s. Even within relatively affluent and prospering regions, such as California, one can find rural areas that have not kept pace with the region as a whole. All of these are truly forgotten places.

Placed within a broader theoretical context, the dismal economic conditions found in many rural regions today can be seen as part and parcel of a historical process of uneven development in the United States. For reasons that have social, economic, and political roots, different regions of the country have manifested different trajectories of growth and development. Some regions have been able to exploit their own natural and human resources or the resources of other regions, and they have prospered over the years (see Markusen, 1987). Parts of the rural Northeast, Middle Atlantic States, and southern California are good examples of these types of areas. Other rural regions, however, have not been in a political or economic position to serve as anything but internal colonies whose natural and human resources have been exploited by firms located in other places.

There are, of course, reasons for rural stagnation other than internal colonialization. The economic plight of the timber communities in the Pacific Northwest has as much to do with the politics of regional development as it does with economic exploitation. Likewise, the economic problems plaguing the Lower Rio Grande Valley are the result of an intertwining of cultural, political, and economic causes.

The contributors to this book document and examine the plight of people living in nine lagging rural regions in the United States today. All of the chapters were specially commissioned. Each addresses a similar set of fundamental questions: Why have these regions languished in the economic doldrums during an era of economic growth and prosperity? What social, economic, and political forces have contributed to uneven development and poverty in many rural areas of the United States?

In this book we focus attention on large rural regions of the United States that most people know little about. Although these regions are criss-crossed with interstate highways and many Americans may have passed through them at one time or another as they ventured across the country, few people take the time or have the interest to experience or learn about them. Most of these regions are not desolate places, though urbanites might portray them as such. They are, instead, inhabited by people who often live outside the mainstream of American society. Many are unable to secure the types of employment that would allow them to achieve a middle-class level of living. Middle-class job opportunities are scarce relative to the number of qualified workers, that is, there is a mismatch between labor supply and demand.

We believe that many rural workers and their families are unable to improve their life chances because of structural factors beyond their control. They constitute a reserve army of underemployed and unemployed workers who, by historical circumstances and tradition, find themselves anchored to communities where their families settled generations ago.

For some of these families, migration out of lagging regions has been one pathway toward the economic mainstream. And indeed, the legions of poor blacks and Appalachians who left their rural homes in the 1960s and 1970s to seek a better life in the North and West show that migration can serve as a social safety valve. Yet despite the millions who have migrated out of rural poverty over the past forty years, millions more remain. They constitute the rural underclass that concerns us.

Neoclassical economists tell us that over time labor will migrate to places where there are jobs and jobs will move into areas where there is surplus (i.e., cheap) labor. Given enough time, the free flow of labor and capital across regions should erase any economic inequalities. For a while during the post–World War II period, a case could be made that the system was working. The rural poor left their homes for jobs in the industrial cities of the Midwest and Northeast or for the booming California metropolitan areas. At the same time, branch plants of large national and multinational corporations began setting up shop in rural regions, especially in the South (Lonsdale and Seyler, 1979).

However, beginning in the 1970s and continuing into the 1980s and 1990s, it became clear that regional economic divergence rather than convergence was the norm (Lyson, 1989). The Cutover Region of the Upper Midwest, Central Appalachia, and the Lower Rio Grande Valley did not attract employers to the same extent as the rural South. Even there development was uneven (Falk and Lyson, 1988). The Black Belt counties, for example, failed to share in the economic development of much of the region in the 1970s and 1980s.

From the perspective of neoclassical theory, such forgotten places are the product of unique historical circumstances. Today, lagging rural regions are best viewed within a larger global economy. The socioeconomic gap between rural America and urban America has begun to widen. The solid, well-paying, middle-class jobs in northern factories are vanishing (Harrison and Bluestone, 1988). The occupational structure is fragmenting into well-paying jobs for highly skilled, well-educated, technologically sophisticated workers and low-paying, low-skill, service jobs. Migration no longer offers the same opportunity for people in forgotten places to improve their economic lot as it did even a generation ago (Wilson, 1987). Within lagging rural regions, branch plants are closing their doors and moving to Third World locations where wages are even lower and workers less organized than in the economic backwaters of the United States (Lyson, 1989). The forgotten places in this book are being by-passed in the newly forming global economy.

THE BOOK IS ORGANIZED as a series of case studies. Each case study focuses on one predominantly rural region of the country that has been characterized by slow economic growth, comparatively low quality of life, and minimal prospects for improvement. These regions are illustrative rather than definitive of the types of underdevelopment that can be found in the United States. Many other lagging rural regions could have been included. These regions can be conceptualized as "forgotten places." They have been forgotten by policymakers in Washington. They have been forgotten by the mass media. They have been forgotten by most Americans who have never seen and know very little about them.

To address the issue of uneven regional development and the lack of opportunity in rural America, our authors focus on the following lagging regions:

    1. *Central Appalachia:* the mountain counties spanning a five state region of Kentucky, West Virginia, Virginia, North Carolina, and Tennessee

    2. *Black Belt South:* a band of counties with a large concentration of black residents running from East Texas across the Deep South states of Louisiana, Mississippi, Alabama, Georgia, and up the East Coast through South Carolina, North Carolina into Virginia

    3. *Mississippi Delta:* mainly the Lower Mississippi Delta that includes a band of counties running along the Mississippi River from Memphis to the Gulf of Mexico

    4. *Missouri Ozarks:* the Ozark counties of southern Missouri that connect with the 'northern' Ozarks, which run through Arkansas and northern Louisiana and into Kansas and Oklahoma

    5. *Lower Rio Grande Valley:* a band of counties running along the Rio Grande River in South Texas on the border with Mexico

    6. *Cutover Region of the Upper Midwest:* primarily focused

on the Upper Peninsula of Michigan and especially one county (Ontonogan) in the western UP

7. *Northern New England:* nonmetropolitan counties primarily in the upper New England parts of Maine, Vermont, and New Hampshire

8. *Timber Region of the Pacific Northwest:* rural counties in northern California, Washington, and especially Oregon whose economic base rests on logging and the timber industry

9. *Rural California:* nonmetropolitan counties located primarily in the northern and eastern parts of California

These particular regions were selected to be illustrative rather than definitive of the types of underdevelopment that can be found in the United States. There are, of course, many other lagging rural regions that could have been included as case studies, such as the Indian reservations in the Dakotas or the Four Corners area in the Southwest. However, our own interests and previous field work experiences led us to limit our inquiry to these nine regions.

To the extent possible, we asked the authors to identify any noteworthy locally based attempts to enhance economic development. The purpose here was to begin to identify and assess unique and innovative programs that are operating in the regions to improve living conditions. The work of the Appalachian Alliance and Southerners for Economic Justice are two examples of these types of efforts. We also asked the authors to provide an assessment of what is likely to happen within these regions in the future. We thought it would be useful and informative to have the authors speculate about what they believe will happen in their regions in the 1990s and beyond.

In the last chapter, we return to the themes of uneven development and the loss of opportunity in rural America. We summarize the dominant theoretical perspectives embedded in the substantive chapter and we discuss how different policy prescriptions might improve opportunities for rural workers and their families.

We hope that these presentations of economically lagging regions in the United States will serve to focus debate on the future of rural America. It is important to remember that 70 million Americans live outside the nation's large metropolitan centers. Tens of millions of these people remain tucked away in regions that are socially and economically cut off from the mainstream of American society. It is time for the nation once again to focus attention on these forgotten places.

References

Falk, William W., and Thomas A. Lyson. 1988. *High Tech, Low Tech, No Tech: Recent Occupational and Industrial Changes in the South.* Albany, N.Y.: State University of New York Press.

Harrington, Michael. 1963. *The Other America.* New York: Macmillan.

Harrison, Bennett, and Barry Bluestone. 1988. *The Great U-Turn.* New York: Basic Books.

Lonsdale, Richard E., and H. L. Seyler. 1979. *Nonmetropolitan Industrialization.* New York: John Wiley and Sons.

Lyson, Thomas A. 1989. *Two Sides to the Sunbelt: The Growing Divergence between the Rural and Urban South.* New York: Praeger.

Markusen, Ann R. 1987. *Regions: The Economics and Politics of Territory.* Totowa, N.J.: Rowman and Littlefield.

Wilson, William J. 1987. *The Truly Disadvantaged.* Chicago: University of Chicago Press.

2 | Uneven Development in Appalachia

Dwight Billings and Ann Tickamyer

SINCE THE WAR ON POVERTY publicized the economic distress found in much of the Appalachian region, the term "Appalachia" has symbolized poverty, exploitation, and regional underdevelopment. War on Poverty programs and related economic development policies coincided with a substantial decline in Appalachian poverty rates. Nonetheless, the success of these efforts is open to question. The region still lags far behind the rest of the nation on most economic indicators. For example, the dramatic drop in central Appalachian poverty rates from 54.1 percent in 1960 to 22.7 percent in 1980 contrasts with the corresponding U.S. figures of 22.1 percent and 12.4 percent. The assault on poverty brought the region to the state of the rest of the nation of twenty years earlier (Tickamyer and Tickamyer, 1987). It is not yet possible to determine definitively 1990 Appalachian poverty rates, but preliminary evidence suggests that the region continues to lag substantially behind the rest of the country and that many of the economic gains of the 1970s were reversed in the 1980s (Couto, 1992).

The ongoing problems of Appalachian poverty and uneven development have been the source of great controversy among scholars, policymakers, and grass-roots organizers. We continue this tradition by examining both the material conditions of Appalachian economic development and the terms of debate that have emerged from efforts to understand it. Our purpose is twofold: to construct a realistic account of Appalachian regional development issues and to deconstruct the rhetoric that has accompanied such analyses in the past.

What is Appalachia?

Images of Appalachia have taken on almost mythic proportions in popular perception, the media, and even policy circles (Shapiro, 1978). These images vary from highly pejorative to intensely partisan, often on the basis of the same attributes. The region is variously depicted as a cesspool of grinding poverty and human misery, a throwback to pre-industrial and pioneer standards of self-sufficiency and strength, the quintessential example of internal colonial exploitation, a testimonial to the endurance of the human spirit, a "hillbilly" backwater, and the repository of the quaint customs of a "strange land and peculiar people" (Shapiro, 1978:v).

Although much of the inflated rhetoric can be attributed to the hyperbole associated with contemporary political and economic struggles over the allocation of resources to and from the region, it is not unique to recent history. As early as the mid-nineteenth century, portions of the region had been singled out as different from mainstream America (Precourt, 1991). The myth of Appalachian "otherness" grew from accounts missionaries, local color writers, ethnographers, and social workers, and it continues unabated (Shapiro, 1978; Tice and Billings, 1991).

The variety of images hints at a diversity that is not often acknowledged in popular stereotypes and that directly contradicts the homogenizing impact of the Appalachian label. The true diversity lurking behind the myth of Appalachia results in a number of confusing and even contradictory claims about the region. The record shows great variation in territorial boundaries, economic conditions, and cultural norms. At least one observer has suggested that there are as many Appalachias as there are writers on the subject. Others have questioned the very existence of a unique regional entity identifiable as Appalachia (Billings, 1974).

The difficulties in defining Appalachia are clearly demonstrated in the most fundamental task of delineating its boundaries. There are numerous territorial definitions of Appalachia, based on such wide-ranging criteria as topography, geography, history, demography, culture, and popular images (Raitz and Ulack, 1984). The current official definition of Appalachia is the outcome of the Appalachian Regional Development Act of 1965, creating the Appalachian Regional Commission (ARC). By current ARC definition, there are 397 Appalachian counties in thirteen states, ranging from New York in the north to Mississippi and Alabama in the south. At both northern and southern extremes, official ARC designation defies common understanding and historical convention. It is generally recognized that this definition of Appalachia was the result of a political process requiring territorial compromises in exchange for political support. Portions of at least four states—New York, Ohio, Pennsylvania, and Mississippi—never previously defined as Appalachian ultimately were included in the ARC designation as part of the price of support for the critical legislation (Bradshaw, 1988).

At the same time that official Appalachia has gained territory, the stereotype has consolidated around a much smaller portion of the region. A core of central Appalachian counties near the coal-mining regions of Kentucky, Tennessee, Virginia, and West Virginia most closely corresponds to the Appalachia of stereotype. These counties are physically remote and isolated by geography and, to an arguable extent, culture. Their economies have been ravaged by dependence on the boom-and-bust cycles of the coal industry that has dominated the area since the turn of the century. Previously these were areas of subsistence agriculture. Neither type of economic base provides the means for sustained economic growth and development, and this area still has the worst social and economic conditions of all of Appalachia.

Although the coal industry has sometimes been used to give a material grounding to a definition of Appalachian regionalism (Markusen, 1987), even in this core area coal is not the only economic activity. Other forms of resource extraction (timbering, agriculture) and a variety of low-wage manufacturing are also prevalent. If North Carolina mountain counties are added to the core group—as is consistent with traditional definitions of Appalachia stemming from assumptions about historic settlement patterns and cultural homogeneity—textiles, tourism, and second-home development also become key parts of the local economy.

The ARC divided counties covered by their mandate into northern, central, and southern regions. When disaggregated in this fashion, it is the central Appalachian region that most closely resembles the stereotype of persistent poverty and underdevelopment and that consistently has social indicators far below those of other areas of the country. In many instances, northern and southern areas are closer to national standards of poverty, income, and employment or more closely resemble their regional standards than central Appalachia. Thus, much of northern Appalachia must be characterized in terms of forms of deindustrialization common to the mature industries of the northeastern and north central United States. Similarly, portions of southern Appalachia participate in both New South economic growth and development and Old South patterns of racial tensions and economic exploitation. Even central Appalachia is not uniformly dominated by coal interests either historically or currently.

The underlying diversity inherent in the region is underscored when it is recognized that many Appalachian development issues are *rural* problems although the region contains or is contiguous to a number of major metropolitan areas. These include some of the most dynamic urban areas in the country, such as Atlanta and Washington,

D.C., as well as numerous smaller but nonetheless growing centers of urban influence. Conditions in urban and in rural Appalachia often bear little resemblance to each other.

The difference between urban and rural Appalachia is illustrated by comparing 1980 poverty rates of metropolitan and nonmetropolitan counties in the three subregions within the five states of Kentucky, North Carolina, Tennessee, Virginia, and West Virginia. Nonmetropolitan poverty ranges from 19.9 percent in central Appalachia to 12.7 percent and 12.4 percent in northern and southern Appalachia, respectively. The corresponding metropolitan rates are significantly lower at 12.4 percent, 8.8 percent, and 10.7 percent (Tickamyer and Tickamyer, 1987).

Diversity within Appalachia undermines many of the definitions of the region. To the extent that there is an Appalachian region, it must be understood as neither a naturally occurring territory whose boundaries can be defined by physical terrain or economic activity, nor a mental construct existing in the identities and identifications of its inhabitants. We have argued elsewhere that the current definition of Appalachia is the outcome of the intersection of the logic of capitalist development with the discursive practices of both local residents and outsiders to the region (especially the latter) whose various agendas constructed a quasi-mythical regional identity (Billings and Tickamyer, 1990). These include the local color writers and settlement workers alluded to previously, the political machinations of ARC formation, the mobilization of indigenous and outside War-on-Poverty workers, and the creation of an academic discipline of Appalachian studies.

The problem of defining Appalachia is compounded by the difficulty in finding information about the region. The basic unit for defining the region is the county. Thus, compiling data on Appalachia depends on the availability of comparable county-based statistics. Much of the information on poverty and income for counties is reliably available only from the decennial census. The result is a very long lag in obtaining current information on economic conditions of area residents. Some states produce intercensal estimates of income and poverty, but these are of varying quality and comparability. Other county level statistics which are available at regular intervals between censuses, such as employment and unemployment figures, must be specially tabulated across the 397 counties or whatever subportion of the region is desired. There is no official source of Appalachian data that regularly produces social indicators of the region's social and economic well-being. The two closest approximations are the occasional reports produced by the ARC and by the Appalachian Center of the University of

Kentucky. Neither source has a regular schedule or series, nor is either necessarily confined to a uniform definition of Appalachia for data-reporting purposes.

For all these reasons, it is difficult to discuss Appalachia per se or to adopt a uniform definition of the region. Since the Appalachia of both popular and scholarly concern most often corresponds to portions of central Appalachia, we will concentrate our analysis on this portion of the region. However, the lack of readily available comparable data necessitates piecing together evidence using different subsets of the region. Dependence on secondary sources and the desire to take a broad view of regional social and economic development issues require a great deal of tolerance of variation in the definition of Appalachia.

Current Economic Conditions

However Appalachia is defined, large portions of the region are characterized by persistent poverty and economic decline. High poverty and unemployment rates, low per capita income, and job losses are the typical findings from studies of the region. Dependence on transfer payments, including social security, Medicare, and disability payments (including blacklung compensation), is another indicator of economic vulnerability, especially in those areas where transfer payments comprise 20 percent or more of total per capita income. Such transfer payments comprise 20.5 percent of total income in northern Appalachia and 23.9 percent of income in central Appalachia. Transfer payments contribute 15.0 percent of total income in southern Appalachia, the subregion that most nearly approximates the national norm of 14.5 percent (Couto, 1992).

High poverty rates are among the most graphic indicators of regional economic distress. In the mid 1980s, the Appalachian Center of the University of Kentucky issued a report on poverty in central Appalachian counties spanning a five-state region of Kentucky, West Virginia, Virginia, North Carolina, and Tennessee (Tickamyer and Tickamyer, 1987). This report provides a good background for describing central Appalachian socioeconomic conditions, and the five-state area included in this report makes a convenient definition of the region of interest.

The statistics cited in the poverty report were tabulated from the county level summary data of the 1980 census, based on 1979 income information. According to this report, 9.6 percent of U.S. families and 10.6 percent of persons had incomes below the poverty threshold. In the five states included in the report, 11.8 percent of families and 14.9 percent of persons were poor. Within the Appalachian counties of these five states, poverty rates were 13.7 percent and 17.0 percent. Finally, in nonmetropolitan Appalachian counties within these states 15.6 percent of families and 19.1 percent of persons were poor. In other words, the more closely statistics conform to core Appalachian counties, the higher the poverty rates. Rural Appalachian county poverty in the five states is almost double the rate for the entire United States. County poverty rates are based on census income information, which is not yet available for the 1990 census. In the 1980 census, ARC counties have much higher poverty rates than the states in which they are located. Rural ARC counties average approximately one percentage point higher poverty rates than do all ARC counties (Table 2.1).

Statewide and U.S. estimates have been published for 1990. Although the evidence from the poverty report and from the 1980 ARC-state comparisons show that state figures will be significantly lower than specific Appalachian county poverty rates, they at least permit some assessment of trends. There has been relatively little change; poverty remains high for most of these five states (see Table 2.1). The exceptions are North Carolina and Virginia which are noteworthy for having decreased their poverty rates during this decade. Virginia's, which was slightly lower than that of the United States in 1979, is now substantially lower than the national figure. These two states illustrate the diversity of economic conditions found in the region. Even in these two states, however, it is likely that that county level data would replicate the pattern of higher poverty rates for Appalachian counties within each of these states.

Additional evidence confirms ongoing Appalachian economic distress (see Table 2.1). Unemployment rates are higher in ARC counties. Again, North Carolina and Virginia have lower rates than the national one. In North Carolina this extends to ARC counties as well but not to rural ARC counties. Per capita incomes in 1979 and 1985 are lower in ARC counties, although the gap is larger in some states than in others. When 1979 income is converted to 1985 dollars, it can be seen that real income has declined in most ARC counties. This is also true of the entire United States, but the decline is larger in Appalachia.

On occasion, states produce county poverty estimates for intercensal years. These vary greatly in quality, and so must be judged carefully, but they, too, demonstrate continuing Appalachian poverty. One such estimate was produced by the Urban Studies Center of the University of Louisville in Kentucky in 1988. Kentucky has forty-nine Appalachian counties, and it is part of the core of central Appalachia

Table 2.1. Core Appalachian State Socioeconomic Indicators

	Poverty Rate (%)			Per Capita Income ($)		
	1979	1989	Unemployment Rate (%), 1986	1979	('79 in '85$)	1985
Kentucky	17.6	17.3	9.3	5,973	(8,852)	8,614
ARC	28.3	—	14.2	4,450	(7,253)	6,972
rural ARC	29.0	—	14.4	4,355	(6,454)	6,096
North Carolina	14.8	13.0	5.3	6,132	(9,088)	9,517
ARC	16.4	—	6.9	5,445	(8,070)	8,404
rural ARC	17.5	—	7.1	5,252	(7,784)	8,091
Tennessee	16.5	16.9	8.0	6,212	(9,206)	9,290
ARC	20.1	—	11.1	5,186	(7,685)	7,567
rural ARC	21.0	—	11.8	4,976	(7,374)	7,221
Virginia	11.8	11.1	5.0	7,475	(11,078)	11,894
ARC	14.7	—	11.1	5,505	(8,158)	7,996
rural ARC	14.7	—	12.4	5,470	(8,107)	7,881
West Virginia	15.0	18.1	11.8	6,142	(9,102)	8,141
ARC	15.0	—	11.8	6,142	(9,102)	8,141
rural ARC	18.6	—	12.2	6,005	(8,899)	7,989
5-state average	15.1	15.28	7.9	6,387	(9,465)	9,491
ARC	18.9	—	11.0	5,434	(8,053)	7,816
rural ARC	20.2	—	11.6	5,212	(7,724)	7,456
United States	12.4	13.5	7.0	7,295	(10,811)	10,797
ARC/5 states	1.3	—	1.4	.9	.9	.8
ARC/United States	1.5	—	1.6	.7	.7	.7

Source: U.S. Bureau of the Census, *County and City Data Book 1988* (Washington, D.C.: Government Printing Office, 1988).

that is most often identified with the region. Thus, these estimates can be used to obtain a mid-decade portrait of Appalachian versus non-Appalachian poverty.

We can compare poverty rates for Appalachian counties in Kentucky, all Kentucky counties, and the United States in 1979 and 1986, the last year county estimates were constructed (see Table 2.2). Poverty rates are consistently higher in 1986 for all units, and as expected, Appalachian poverty is much higher than that of the state or the nation. It should be noted, however, that the ratio of the rate of Appalachian poverty to Kentucky and U.S. rates remained the same across this period. The Appalachian poverty rate is approximately one and two-thirds times Kentucky's and two and one-third times the United States'. Comparisons of rates of unemployment and per capita income show similar results.

We can also distinguish Appalachian counties on the basis of dom-

Table 2.2. Appalachian Kentucky Socioeconomic Indicators by Economic Base

	Poverty Rate (%)		Unemployment Rate (%)		Per Capita Income ($)		
	1979	1986	1979	1986	1979	('79 in '85$)	1985
Coal only	29.4	36.5	13.9	16.5	4,286	(6,352)	5,787
Manufacturing	24.9	26.5	10.8	12.3	5,920	(7,291)	6,972
Coal and manufacturing	25.7	29.1	10.9	13.6	4,828	(7,155)	6,424
No coal/no manufacturing	31.5	31.7	12.9	14.4	4,020	(5,958)	5,810
Appalachian Kentucky	28.3	31.0	12.3	14.2	4,450	(7,253)	6,972
Kentucky	17.6	18.2	8.5	9.3	5,973	(8,852)	8,614
United States	12.4	13.6	7.1	7.0	7,295	(10,811)	10,797
Appalachian/ Kentucky	1.6	1.7	1.4	1.5	.8	.8	.8
Appalachian/ United States	2.3	2.3	1.7	2.0	.7	.7	.8

Sources: C. Koebel and M. Price, Annual Estimates of Poverty for Counties in Kentucky 1979–1986 (Louisville, Ky.: Urban Studies Center, University of Louisville, 1988); U.S. Bureau of the Census, 1980 Census of Population, vol. 1. General Social and Economic Characteristics of the Population, Kentucky (Washington, D.C.: Government Printing Office, 1983); U.S. Bureau of the Census, County and City Data Book 1988 (Washington, D.C.: Government Printing Office, 1988).

inant economic activity to determine the impact of different types of economic activity on measures of economic distress. Coal production is often identified as the definitive economic force behind Appalachian development problems (Markusen, 1987), and data confirm that counties with large-scale coal production have the highest poverty and unemployment rates (Table 2.2). Manufacturing counties have the lowest rates and the rates of counties with neither coal nor manufacturing are almost as bad as those dependent on coal. The ranking of coal-producing counties and counties without either coal or manufacturing is reversed on per capita income. All Appalachian counties have lost income between 1979 and 1985, but counties with coal activity have fared the worst. Regionwide studies suggest a similar pattern (Tickamyer, 1992).

High regional poverty may be due either to overrepresentation of groups known to be especially vulnerable to poverty or to high poverty rates for all residents or both. Minorities, children, the elderly, and households headed by single women are all high-risk poverty groups.

None of these groups is overrepresented in central Appalachia, and some have unusually small populations. African Americans, for example, are 11.7 percent of the U.S. population but only 2.4 percent of rural central Appalachia. Households headed by single women are 13.9 percent of all families nationally but only 11.5 percent in rural central Appalachia counties. When these households also have children, the difference is even greater. For the United States it is 16.2 percent of all families; for central Appalachia it is just 10.5 percent (Tickamyer and Tickamyer, 1987).

Thus regional poverty cannot be explained away by concentrations of high risk groups. Instead, poverty rates are greatly elevated for nearly all persons, including those who are at higher risk. Sources of poverty must be found elsewhere, most typically in the structure of the local economy, type of employment opportunities, and links to the larger economy. These factors will hit some groups harder than others, in particular, minorities and women, but the lack of opportunities that create economic hardship are implicated for all groups (Tickamyer and Tickamyer, 1991). We will examine three of the factors most often cited as sources of Appalachian poverty: labor market factors, human capital factors, and regional factors.

The primary source of income for most people is wages and salary earned from working in the labor force. Local labor market factors determine the opportunities for gaining income. As described above, much of central Appalachia is characterized by high unemployment rates and low income. Jobs are typically of the low-pay, low-skill, kind and there is great instability in the demand for labor.

Many central Appalachian counties are heavily dependent on the coal industry for employment and income. Although mining employment tends to have higher wages than other industries, it is a highly volatile industry, with frequent periods of unemployment for its workers as well as a small and diminishing total work force. Other types of employment available in Appalachia are low-wage manufacturing and agricultural employment. These are also in decline (Tickamyer and Tickamyer, 1987; 1991).

Decline is not uniform across the region. Appalachian counties in Kentucky, Virginia, and West Virginia lost jobs during the 1980s; in addition to mining, employment losses were in apparel and other textile products, shoes, furniture and other wood products, chemicals, fabricated metals, machine tools, transportation equipment, and agricultural products. In contrast, portions of North Carolina and Tennessee gained employment in the period from 1980 to 1986. Employment gains were associated with tourism and retirement, special manufacturing, and a variety of services associated with proximity to metropolitan areas. For the entire ARC region (including northern and southern areas), employment grew at a rate of 2.2 percent from 1980 to 1986, very slow compared to the national figure of 9.8 percent (Kublawi, 1991).

Growth areas within Appalachia are associated with proximity to the growing service economies of large metropolitan areas, leisure and retirement communities, or with "New South" industrial development. Virginia, North Carolina, and Tennessee all exhibit this type of growth to one extent or another. Appalachian Kentucky and West Virginia, however, have stagnated or declined in the manner of the de-industrialization and restructuring that characterize many mature industries (Couto, 1984; Gaventa, 1987; Fisher, 1990). Coal employment has steadily declined, and the low-wage manufacturing that formed the main alternative to it in many rural counties has sought even lower labor costs offshore.

Human capital has also been blamed for high poverty rates and poor employment opportunities. Individuals with little education or skills to bring to the labor market are unlikely to prosper. Central Appalachian residents have extremely high dropout rates. In 1980 59.5 percent of nonmetropolitan central Appalachian residents over the age of twenty-five had not completed high school, compared to 50.6 percent of the residents of non-Appalachian portions of these states and 33.5 percent of U.S. residents (Tickamyer and Tickamyer, 1987). Schools are frequently poorly funded, feudally managed, and the site of debilitating fights over patronage politics (Duncan, 1992). The region is also characterized by high levels of working age disability. The figure is 16.1 percent for central Appalachia compared to 11.9 percent for the five-state region, 10.7 percent for non-Appalachian portions of these states, and 8.5 percent for the entire nation (Tickamyer and Tickamyer, 1987). Appalachians are at a disadvantage in competing for jobs in the labor market, especially for those that require high levels of education and training. Of course, these are exactly the jobs that are in short supply in much of the region. The relationship between labor-market opportunities and human capital is much debated.

The third source of Appalachian underdevelopment rests in regional factors. In particular, in Appalachia, the connections between depressed labor market opportunities and the qualities of the labor force must be sought in the political and economic history of the region. Current social and economic distress are grounded in the historical development of the region and can only be understood by examining the development of a pattern of regional underdevelopment.

Regional Development Issues

Observations made of different Appalachian communities and sub-regions suggests very dissimilar pictures of the region prior to the modern period of urban, industrial, and commercial development. Thus, on the one hand, a case study of preindustrial life in a geographically isolated section located on the border of East Kentucky and West Virginia (the Tug River valley), describes that locality's farm economy as having been entirely subsistence-oriented prior to 1900 (Waller, 1988). By this depiction, Appalachia at the turn of the century still resembled much of the southern "upcountry" as it would have appeared in 1850 when "the [economic] relations of production were mediated principally by ties of kinship rather than the marketplace" (Hahn, 1985:181). On the other hand, Cades Cove—an Appalachian community only forty miles from Knoxville, East Tennessee's largest commercial center—has been described as "oriented to the larger regional market economy" since well before the Civil War and thus "tied . . . closely . . . to the broad mainstream of American political and social culture throughout the century" (Dunn, 1988:67, 12). Similarly, the western North Carolina mountains before the Civil War have been described as "a thriving, productive, and even [economically] progressive society" where slave-holding and commercial agriculture predominated (Inscoe, 1989:12).

Clearly, the disparities between accounts of preindustrial Appalachia as an isolated, subsistence local economy existing independently of national and even regional marketing structures and, conversely, as a commercially oriented, regional economy integrated into wider economic networks suggest that historical generalizations beyond limited geographical areas in Appalachia are highly suspect. Nonetheless, one of the best accounts of preindustrial life in central Appalachia has been provided by James S. Brown (1950, 1988; 1952a, 1952b) and his associates (Schwarzweller, Brown, and Mangalam, 1971) in a twenty-five-year longitudinal study of the "Beech Creek" neighborhoods of rural East Kentucky.

With family incomes averaging only $800 per household and per capita annual expenditures of only $84, Beech Creek was already impoverished when Brown first observed the community in 1942, before hard-surface roads had penetrated the area. The tiny farms Brown observed each averaged less than 10 acres in crops. Nine of the 29 sample farms that Brown studied exhaustively averaged fewer than 30 total acres of improved and unimproved land—a figure similar to that of the surrounding county. The 29 Beech Creek farms combined to only 275 acres in cultivation, 226 of them in corn. Productivity was low, averaging only 10 to 20 bushels of corn per acre. Although some good bottom lands remained, many portions "[had] been cultivated since the early days and [were] so exhausted by continual cropping and erosion that [by 1942 they were] rocky, unproductive, and thin" (Brown, 1988:24). "Evidence of erosion [was] everywhere—slips, slides, gullies, rock-choked stream beds, washed banks, and bare, scarred fields" (Brown, 1988:28). Yet subsistence farming continued to play a central role in the lives of Beech Creek families.

"In 1942, the farm was still the chief source of income for the Beech Creek family" (Brown, 1988:30). Brown's analysis of thirty family budgets revealed that the total value of farm products for all families was only $12,405, more than two-thirds of which ($8,660) was consumed at home. Less than one-third was sold for a combined total of only $3,745 of income that was shared by all thirty families. This small amount of cash represented one-fourth of the families' entire cash income. The rest came from nonfarm employment in forestry—which paid as low as $1.75 per day—Civilian Conservation Corps (CCC) and Works Projects Administration (WPA) jobs, government subsidies, and pensions. A small portion of income was derived from family members working "outside" in southern Ohio factories, indicating that extra-regional migration and employment were already becoming important factors in the life of Beech Creek.

Thus, by World War II, Beech Creek farms were far from the islands of self-sufficiency that were once stereotypic of remote, nonindustrialized sections of the Cumberland Plateau. "The data on expenditures," according to Brown (1988:31) revealed both "the decreasing self-sufficiency and the relative poverty of the Beech Creek farm family." Brown observed that "when lumbering came to the area and made more money available [around the turn of the century], [Beech Creek people] gave up such domestic crafts as weaving and shoemaking and bought clothing and shoes. Eventually they spent large proportions of cash income for flour, sugar, lard, and meat, which they had formerly produced" (1988:33). By 1942 numerous Beech Creek families were even forced to supplement their home consumption of corn with additional purchases.

The economic situation that Brown described was not unique to Beech Creek. Other communities in the Cumberland Plateau region experienced similar difficulties in those years. A reconstruction of data on family farms flooded by the Tennessee Valley Authority in the Norris Basin section of East Tennessee shows that many farms in that region of the Cumberland Plateau were already impoverished by the 1930s (McDonald and Muldowny, 1982). Similarly, the first federally sponsored survey of Appalachia, conducted by the U.S. Department of Agriculture (USDA) in 1935, reported that in the heartland of central Appalachia, the Allegheny-Cumberland plateaus, self-sufficient or subsistence farms—which constituted 58.4 percent of all farms in the region, the highest proportion of non-commercial farms in the United States at the time—were "for the most part incapable of supporting a farm population" (USDA, 1935:2).

A number of scholars have argued that the key to understanding Appalachia's history of economic and political development, and thus the region's poverty, lies in the juxtaposition of this declining system of subsistence agriculture and industrialization (Pudup, 1990, 1991; Salstrom, 1991). In a historical analysis of rural southern poverty, Billings (1988; also Billings, Blee, and Swanson, 1986) has argued that subsistence agriculture failed to generate sufficient local capital for indigenous entrepreneurs to undertake the huge costs of developing an industrial infrastructure in Appalachia. The capital costs for improving transportation alone in the mountainous sections were enormous. Thus, the impetus and resources for development came largely from outside. Industrialization, which began around 1900, was based on the region's rich natural resources, especially timber and coal. Railroad, timber, and mineral companies purchased huge tracts of land, opened up isolated areas, and built company towns devoted to the extraction of natural resources (Eller, 1982). Absentee owners accumulated vast amounts of land in the region, and their agents and representatives dominated local political affairs (Gaventa, 1980).

The low levels of economic accumulation in the farm sector, high levels of human fertility, soil depletion, and land shortages that set limits on Appalachian agricultural capacity and capital accumulation also produced great strain in the subsistence system of production and contributed to the development of an underemployed labor pool that could be utilized cheaply (Billings and Blee, 1990). Thus, in addition to the region's abundant natural resources, low wages in Appalachia, especially in comparison with other coal mining regions such as the northern fields of Pennsylvania, Ohio, and Illinois, provided additional incentives for industrial development (Corbin, 1981). Corporate land acquisitions further exacerbated land shortages by removing land from cultivation. For example, Harlan County, in the eastern Kentucky coal fields, experienced a decline in average farm size from 260 to 74 acres between 1880 and 1930 and an increase in nonowner-operated farms from 25 to 60 percent of total farms between 1880 and 1910. Total farm acreage in the county dropped from 220,000 acres in 1880 to just over 58,000 acres in 1930 (Banks, 1980).

Throughout Appalachia, then, impoverished mountain farmers were available to work at low wages in the region's mines, timber camps, and textile mills. Many others left to find work in mills and factories beyond the mountains. When the timber resources were exhausted, and when mechanization, overcapacity, overproduction, and competition with other fuels reduced employment in the mines by several hundred thousands of workers in the 1950s, deindustrialization prompted displaced workers to follow previously displaced farmers out of the hills and into industrial cities in the Midwest (Seltzer, 1985). More than 3 million people migrated from southern Appalachia between 1940 and 1970. Hardest hit was the subregion of central Appalachia where, for example, eastern Kentucky lost almost one-third of its entire population between 1950 and 1960 (McCoy and Brown, 1981).

Theories of Appalachian Poverty and Policy Applications

Appalachia's rural poor have been "discovered" and rediscovered many times throughout the twentieth century. How they have been perceived has been shaped by the practical standpoints from which they have been observed. At the turn of the century William Goodell Frost first put impoverished mountaineers on the nation's cognitive map by referring to them in fund-raising drives for Berea College as "Appalachian Americans." For Frost and the audiences to which he spoke, naming was explaining (Shapiro, 1978). The definition of Appalachia as an identifiable American region with a distinct and homogeneous subculture that was out of step with the assumptions of national progress— a definition Shapiro calls the "myth of Appalachia"—sufficed to explain economic backwardness in the southern mountains. Early reform efforts reflected this understanding, adapting settlement house programs and other urban-based strategies to the task of bringing the rural Appalachian poor into the majority culture (Whisnant, 1983).

When rural poverty was "rediscovered" by policymakers and social scientists in the early 1960s, the inherited wisdom that Appalachia was characterized by a unique subculture seemed to explain the region's remarkably high incidence of poverty. With poor families totaling more than half the population in many central Appalachian counties in the late 1960s (Couto, 1984), the depiction of Appalachian culture as an almost regionwide subculture of poverty made sense to many social scientists, policymakers, and popular writers (Ball, 1968; Looff, 1971; Weller, 1965). Although the culture of poverty model has been justly criticized for blatant stereotyping and for placing the blame for poverty upon the poor themselves (Billings, 1974; Fisher, 1976), it served to underline the extent to which intergenerational experiences of living in poverty were likely to blunt faith in personal efficacy (Duncan and Tickamyer, 1988). Most of the programs initiated during the War on Poverty thus sought to break the hold of this subculture on the population it imprisoned, in efforts such as Head Start, community action, educational television programming beamed into the region by the nation's most sophisticated satellite technology, and roadbuilding (Whisnant, 1980). Appalachian Volunteers (AV's) and Volunteers in Service to America (VISTA) workers, in cooperation with the Council of the Southern Mountains, were dispatched into the Appalachian region to mobilize and inspire the local populace to bring themselves and their communities out of poverty (Horton, 1971).

Many of these approaches were combined in and coordinated by the Appalachian Regional Commission, which was created in 1965 but grew out of the 1963 President's Appalachian Regional Commission (PARC). ARC projects now totaling many millions of dollars have been spent to improve transportation, education, and health care and to stimulate economic development through tourism and infrastructural investments, especially in localities designated as potential "growth centers." Critics such as David Whisnant (1980:129), however, claim that the "root confusion" that runs from PARC policy theory through ARC projects lay in the "mistaken assumption" that Appalachia was, in PARC's terminology, a "region apart" that had not sufficiently entered the national "free enterprise orbit." In sharp contrast, however, Whisnant contends that "in fact [the region's] problems derived primarily . . . from its integration into the national economy for a narrow set of purposes: the extraction of low cost materials, power, and labor, and the provision of a profitable market for consumer goods and services."

Another critic sums up the ARC experience as follows:

In total perspective, no one can say all of ARC has been a waste. Its problem has been that its potential has always been far above its results, or even its endeavors. It could have done something about mine safety, about strip mining, about land monopolies, about state and local under-taxation of corporations, about governmental accountability, about local leadership development, about the maze of fumbling Washington bureaucracies that deal with the region and, in short, it could have behaved as if its constituency were Appalachia, as if its mission were to end porkbarrel, and as if it really believed its own studies were worthy of implementation. It seldom has. It has been an agency apart from its own mission, frequently apart from its own better judgment. (Branscomb, 1977:28)

Even more harshly, an important regionwide citizen's group, the Appalachian Alliance, concluded in 1978 that "putting ARC in charge of the interests of the people of the mountains is like putting Dracula in charge of the blood bank" (Appalachian Alliance, 1978:28).

By encouraging the maximum participation of the poor themselves in antipoverty efforts, to overcome fatalism and alienation, the War on Poverty soon came up against a major obstacle—the political and economic powerlessness of those who had been trapped in poverty for generations. Fear and powerlessness understandably limited the horizons and expectations of impoverished Appalachians (Gaventa, 1980). The policy of organizing poor rural Appalachians to demand jobs, social services, decent educations, and environmental reform quickly confronted the reality of entrenched local power structures and absentee corporate owners who monopolized land, politics, and mineral resources (Glen, 1989). Consequently, scholars and activists—like their counterparts in the Third World whose analyses they embraced—advanced a new theory to explain why Appalachia was rich in natural resources whereas its population was poor. Appalachia, they claimed, was a "colony" (see articles in Lewis et al., 1978; Appalachian Alliance, 1978; 1979). "The people of Appalachia know they are poor, and for a long time a lot of them have thought they knew why: they don't own their land, they don't control its use, and they don't share in the wealth it produces" (*Southern Exposure*, 1982:32).

The theoretical model that understood Appalachia as an internal colony of the U.S. national economy stimulated important political struggles in Appalachia that continue to have impact today. One particular configuration of organizations that arose under its impact deserves special attention. In 1977 the Tug River flooded along the border of Kentucky and West Virginia, leaving thousands homeless. Angered at being forced to live in crowded flood plains because of absentee ownership and frustrated by the government's inability to find alternative sites for relocation, local activists called for support from other regional groups to form a federation of grassroots organizations known as the Appalachian Alliance. In addition to providing an important regionwide forum and publishing educational materials (Appalachian Alliance, 1978; 1979; Horton and Einstein, 1982), the Alliance helped to launch the Appalachian Land Ownership Task Force (1983) that coordinated the efforts of indigenous researchers to investigate land ownership and taxation in eighty counties across the region (Beaver, 1983).

Although the Appalachian Alliance is no longer active, the task force's documentation of vast amounts of minimally taxed land and mineral resources owned by absentee firms spearheaded tax reform efforts in Tennessee and Virginia as well as challenges to mineral leasing practices in North Carolina. The information was also used in a successful court battle in West Virginia that ruled the inequitable school funding methods in that state unconstitutional (Appalachian Land Ownership Task Force, 1983). Even more importantly, the project empowered indigenous researchers who remained in their home counties, providing them with new knowledge and skills to battle local political elites. In Kentucky, they helped form the Kentucky Fair Tax Coalition, now Kentuckians for the Commonwealth (KFTC). Numbering more than 4000 members statewide, KFTC has helped to reform unmined mineral tax policy and won passage of a constitutional amendment prohibiting the use of the notorious "broad form deeds" that formerly allowed mineral owners to mine surface owners' property without permission or compensation. It has also sponsored leadership development programs, continues to monitor the state legislature, and pushes for environmental, social, and political reforms (Szakos, 1990).

Thus, the principal contribution of the colonial model has been to call attention to the impact of nonlocal corporate ownership and investments on local taxation, political dependency, and alternative forms of economic development as well as to show how the denigration and stereotyping of Appalachian culture in culture-of-poverty theory has gone hand-in-hand with the exploitation of Appalachia's land and resources (Walls, 1976). But the adherents of the colonial model have probably erred in isolating absentee ownership per se as the principal cause of regional poverty. Such an approach ignores the fact that several central Appalachian states—most notably, Kentucky—contain significant sectors of indigenous coal ownership and extraction that are notorious for low wages, job insecurity, and the lack of health and safety benefits for employees in comparison with larger, absentee-owned corporate firms (Seltzer, 1985). The colonial model also ignores the fact that other coal mining regions, most notably Illinois, are even more absentee-owned than Appalachia yet have significantly more equitable tax policies (Smith et. al., 1978).

In addition to opposition to absentee ownership and control, Appalachians have also waged other important struggles for social and economic justice (see Tice and Billings, 1991; Fisher, 1992). Appalachian miners, for instance, won recognition of "black lung" as a bona fide disease and achieved passage of the first federal program for the compensation of an occupationally induced disease in the United States (Smith, 1987), a victory that touched off health and safety reform and compensation in other industries, especially in the nearby southern textile industry (Judkins, 1986). "Black lung" compensation is undoubtedly one of the most significant transfer payments currently helping to ameliorate poverty in coal field communities. Further, in struggles such as the Pittston Strike, miners have defended their jobs from the consequences of corporate restructuring.

Women have fought alongside men for economic justice (Maggard, 1988) and women's organizations have responded to the increasing "feminization" of poverty by facilitating the participation of women in new economic arenas. For example, the Coal Employment Project supported the entry of women into coal mining, and the Southeast Women's Employment Project extended women's participation in other "nontraditional" jobs (Hall, 1990). Further, a community-based organization in West Virginia, Women and Employment, formed a chapter of Women's World Banking to provide capital for small-scale, alternative development projects, such as day care, that utilize the entrepreneurial skills many Appalachian women have developed through their participation in flea markets and other forms of informal economy (Weiss, 1990).

Finally, Gaventa, Smith, and Willingham (1990:279) document largely "unknown" but "rich and impressive experiences of grassroots communities [in Appalachia] responding to economic change and decline in ways that can be instructive and inspiring to those concerned with economic organizing and empowerment across the nation." They describe various efforts throughout the region to think about economic development in new ways, such as linking job creation to local social-service needs, that respond to capital flight and represent alternatives to the dead-end pursuit of firms seeking to locate.

Future Prospects

Despite important efforts in Appalachia to struggle against poverty, fight for economic justice, and plan for new opportunities, the prospects for economic improvement and thus for lowering rates of poverty in central Appalachia do not seem bright. Economic projections for eastern Kentucky in 1981, for instance, predicted a 14.5 percent rate of employment growth between 1978 and 1985 with mining and manufacturing contributing about half the increase in jobs (Stober et. al., 1981), but as we have shown above, Appalachian Kentucky, along with Virginia and West Virginia actually lost jobs during this period. Nonetheless, many communities continue to pin their hopes on traditional sources of employment in extractive and manufacturing industries, and when these hopes diminish, other economic stimulants, such as tourism, are also sought. Long-term prospects for growth in manufacturing and mining, however, are not good. And the experience from those portions of the region where tourism has expanded, most notably North Carolina, suggests that "one of the major problems with a strategy for economic development based on travel and tourism is that the jobs so generated will have earning rates well below average" (O'Connor, n. d.:14). Further, it is especially difficult to predict success for tourism in the most environmentally ravaged section of central Appalachia, the coal fields.

A study by John Gaventa (1987:28) of workers—most of them middle-aged women—displaced from a unionized manufacturing firm in East Tennessee, suggests that the current phase of deindustrialization in central Appalachia will only further weaken the already seriously distressed regional economy.

> Of 174 laid-off workers, slightly more than half had obtained a new job. Of these workers who had obtained jobs, the largest proportion (35%) had obtained "service" jobs—as cleaners, guards or custodians in workplaces or in private homes, as food service workers, or as child or health care workers in workplaces or peoples' homes. Even for the ones who have been able to get some work, over half (53%) are working at part-time jobs. All but one of the workers report that they have taken pay cuts. Average wages have dropped from $5.79 at Allied to $3.70, a loss of $2.09 an hour. Thirty-nine percent are working at minimum wage of $3.35 or less an hour, and over half are working at $3.45 or less an hour. For 90% of the workers there is no union at their new jobs, and thus one can expect that they have also taken a loss in benefits and job protection.

Such studies, in fact, suggest that even the modest gains against poverty achieved during the past decade may be hard to sustain in central Appalachia in the decade to come.

References

Appalachian Alliance. 1978. *Appalachia 1978: A Protest from the Colony.* N.p.
————. 1979. *National Sacrifice Area.* N.p.
Appalachian Land Ownership Task Force. 1983. *Who Owns Appalachia: Land-ownership and Its Impact.* Lexington: University Press of Kentucky.
Ball, R. 1968. "A Poverty Case: The Analgesic Subculture of the Southern Appalachians." *American Sociological Review* 33 (6):885–95.
Banks, A. 1980. "Land and Capital in Eastern Kentucky, 1890–1935." *Appalachian Journal* 8:8–18.
Beaver, P. 1983. "Participatory Research on Land Ownership in Rural Appalachia. Pp. 252–66 in A. Batteau (ed.), *Appalachia of America.* Lexington: University Press of Kentucky.
Billings, D. 1974. "Culture and Poverty in Appalachia: A Theoretical and Empirical Analysis." *Social Forces* 53 (2):315–23.
Billings, D. 1988. "The Rural South in Crisis: A Historical Perspective." Pp. 13–29 in L. Beaulieu (ed.), *The Rural South in Crisis.* Boulder, Colo.: Westview Press.
Billings, D., and K. Blee. 1990. "Family Strategies in a Subsistence Economy: Beech Creek, Kentucky, 1850–1942." *Sociological Perspectives* 33 (1):63–88.
Billings, D., K. Blee, and L. Swanson. 1986. "Culture, Family and Community in Preindustrial Appalachia." *Appalachian Journal* 13 (2):154–70.
Billings, D., and A. Tickamyer. 1990. "Development and Underdevelopment: The Politics of Region." Paper presented at the annual meeting of the Rural Sociological Society, Norfolk, Virginia.
Bradshaw, M. 1988. *Regions and Regionalism in the United States.* Jackson: University Press of Mississippi.
Branscome, J. 1977. *The Federal Government in Appalachia.* New York: Field Foundation.
Brown, J. (1950, 1988). *Beech Creek: The Social Organization of an Isolated Kentucky Neighborhood.* Ph.D. diss., Harvard University. Berea, Ky.: Berea College Press.
————. 1952a. "The Conjugal Family and the Extended Family Group." *American Sociological Review* 17:297–305.
————. 1952b. "The Family Group in a Kentucky Mountain Farming Community." *Kentucky Agricultural Experiment Station Bulletin no. 588.* Lexington, Ky.: University of Kentucky College of Agriculture.
Corbin, D. 1981. *Life, Work, and Rebellion in the Coal Fields.* Urbana: University of Illinois Press.
Couto, R. 1984. *Appalachia: An American Tomorrow.* Knoxville, Tenn.: A Report to the Commission on Religion in Appalachia.
Couto, R. 1992. "Appalachia: Work, Poverty, and Social Capital in America." Paper presented at the AMERC/CORA "Briefing on Appalachia" Conference, 7 April 1992, New York City.
Duncan, C. 1992. "Persistent Poverty in Appalachia: Scarce Work and Rigid Stratification." Pp. 111–32 in C. Duncan (ed.), *Rural Poverty in America.* Westport, Conn.: Greenwood.
Duncan, C., and A. Tickamyer. 1988. "Poverty Research and Policy for Rural America." *American Sociologist* 11:243–59.

Dunn, D. 1988. *Cades Cove: The Life and Death of a Southern Appalachian Community, 1818–1937.* Knoxville: University of Tennessee Press.
Eller, R. 1982. *Miners, Millhands, and Mountaineers: Industrialization of the Appalachian South, 1880–1930.* Knoxville: University of Tennessee Press.
Fisher, S. 1976. "Victim-Blaming in Appalachia." Pp. 185–94 in B. Ergood and B. Kuhre (eds.), *Appalachia: Social Context Past and Present.* 3d ed. Dubuque: Kendall/Hunt.
———. 1990. "National Economic Renewal Programs and Their Implications for Appalachia and the South." Pp. 263–78 in J. Gaventa, B. Smith, and A. Willingham (eds.), *Communities in Economic Crisis: Appalachia and the South.* Philadelphia: Temple University Press.
———, ed. 1992. *Fighting Back in Appalachia: Traditions of Resistance and Change.* Philadelphia: Temple University Press. Forthcoming.
Gaventa, J. 1980. *Power and Powerlessness: Quiescence and Rebellion in an Appalachian Valley.* Urbana: University of Illinois Press.
———. 1987. "The Poverty of Abundance." *Appalachian Journal* 15 (1):24-33.
Gaventa, J., B. Smith, and A. Willingham. 1990. *Communities in Economic Crisis: Appalachia and the South.* Philadelphia: Temple University Press.
Glen, J. 1989. "The War on Poverty in Appalachia: A Preliminary Report." *Register of the Kentucky Historical Society* 87 (1):40–57.
Hahn, S. 1985. "The Unmaking of the Southern Yeomanry: The Transformation of the Georgia Upcountry, 1860–1890." Pp. 179–203 in S. Hahn and J. Prude (eds.), *The Countryside in the Age of Capitalist Transformation.* Chapel Hill: University of North Carolina Press.
Hall, B. 1990. "Women Miners Can Dig It, Too!" Pp. 53–60 in J. Gaventa, B. Smith, and A. Willingham (eds.), *Communities in Economic Crisis: Appalachia and the South.* Philadelphia: Temple University Press.
Horton, B. 1971. "The Appalachian Volunteers." Masters Thesis, Department of Sociology, University of Kentucky.
Horton, B., and F. Einstein, eds. 1982. *Appalachia in the Eighties: A Time for Action.* New Market, Tenn.: Appalachian Alliance.
Inscoe, J. 1989. *Mountain Masters, Slavery, and the Sectional Crisis in Western North Carolina.* Knoxville: University of Tennessee Press.
Judkins, B. 1986. *We Offer Ourselves as Evidence: Towards Worker Control of Occupational Health.* Westport, Conn.: Greenwood Press.
Koebel, C., and M. Price. 1988. *Annual Estimates of Poverty for Counties in Kentucky 1979–1986.* Louisville, Ky.: Urban Studies Center, University of Louisville.
Kublawi, S. 1991. "The Economy of Appalachia in the National Context." Pp. 215–21 in B. Ergood and B. Kuhre (eds.), *Appalachia Social Context Past and Present.* 3d ed. Dubuque, Iowa: Kendall/Hunt Co.
Lewis, H., L. Johnson, and D. Askins, eds. 1978. *Colonialism in Modern America: The Appalachian Case.* Boone, N.C.: Appalachian Consortium Press.
Loof, D. 1971. *Appalachia's Children: The Challenge of Mental Health.* Lexington: University Press of Kentucky.
Maggard, Sally. 1988. Eastern Kentucky Women on Strike: A Study of Gender, Class, and Political Action in the 1970s. Ph.D. diss., Department of Sociology, University of Kentucky, Lexington.

Markusen, A. 1987. *Regions: The Economics and Politics of Territory.* Totowa, N.J.: Rowman and Littlefield.

McCoy, C., and J. Brown. 1981. "Appalachian Migration to Midwestern Cities." Pp. 35–78 in W. Philliber and C. McCoy (eds.), *The Invisible Minority: Urban Appalachians.* Lexington: University Press of Kentucky.

McDonald, M., and J. Muldowny. 1982. *TVA and the Dispossessed.* Knoxville: University of Tennessee Press.

O'Connor, F. n.d. "Western North Carolina's Economy: The Role of Tourism and Travel." Cullowhee, N.C.: Western Carolina University Center for Improving Mountain Living.

Precourt, W. 1991. "The Image of Appalachian Poverty." Pp. 173–84 in B. Ergood and B. Kuhre (eds.), *Appalachia: Social Context Past and Present.* 3d ed. Dubuque, Iowa: Kendall/Hunt Co.

Pudup, M. 1990. "The Limits of Subsistence: Agriculture and Industry in Central Appalachia." *Journal of Historical Geography* 15 (2):139–62.

———. 1991. "Social Class and Economic Development in Southeastern Kentucky." Pp. 235–60 in R. Mitchell (ed.), *Appalachian Frontiers.* Lexington: University Press of Kentucky.

Raitz, K., and R. Ulack, with T. Leinbach. 1984. *Appalachia: A Regional Geography.* Boulder, Colo.: Westview Press.

Salstrom, P. 1991. "The Agricultural Origins of Economic Dependency, 1840–1880." Pp. 261–83 in R. Mitchell (ed.), *Appalachian Frontiers.* Lexington: University Press of Kentucky.

Schwarzweller, H., J. Brown, and J. Mangalam. 1971. *Mountain Families in Transition: A Case Study of Appalachian Migration.* University Park: Pennsylvania State University Press.

Selzer, C. 1985. *Fire in the Hole: Miners and Managers in the American Coal Industry.* Lexington: University Press of Kentucky.

Shapiro, H. 1978. *Appalachia on Our Minds: The Southern Mountains and Mountaineers in American Consciousness, 1870–1920.* Chapel Hill: University of North Carolina Press.

Smith, B. 1987. *Digging Our Own Graves: Coal Miners and the Struggle over Black Lung Disease.* Philadelphia: Temple University Press.

Smith, J., D. Osterdorf, and M. Schechtman. 1978. *Who's Mining the Farm?* Herrin, Ill.: Illinois South Project.

Southern Exposure. 1982. "Who Owns Appalachia: A Special Section on Land and Taxation." *Southern Exposure* 10 (1):32–52.

Stober, W., M. Hackbart, D. Walls, C. Straus, and J. Kim. 1981. *Employment Patterns and Projections: Toward an Economic Development Strategy for Appalachian Kentucky.* Lexington: University of Kentucky Appalachian Center.

Szakos, J. 1990. "People Power: Working for the Future in the East Kentucky Coalfields." Pp. 29–37 in J. Gaventa, B. Smith, and A. Willingham (eds.), *Communities in Economic Crisis: Appalachia and the South.* Philadelphia: Temple University Press.

Tice, K., and D. Billings, 1991. "Appalachian Culture and Resistance." *Journal of Progressive Human Services* 2(2):1–18.

Tickamyer, A. 1992. "The Working Poor in Rural America." Pp. 41–61 in C. Duncan (ed.), *Rural Poverty in America.* Westport, Conn.: Greenwood.

Tickamyer, A., and C. Duncan. 1990. "Poverty and Opportunity Structure in Rural America." *Annual Review of Sociology* 16:67–86.

Tickamyer, A., and C. Tickamyer. 1987. *Poverty in Appalachia: Appalachian Data Bank Report #5.* Lexington: University of Kentucky Appalachian Center.

Tickamyer, A., and C. Tickamyer. 1991. "Gender, Family Structure, and Poverty in Central Appalachia." Pp. 307–15 in B. Ergood and B. Kuhre (eds.), *Appalachia: Social Context Past and Present.* 3d ed. Dubuque, Iowa: Kendall/Hunt Co.

United States Bureau of the Census. 1988. *County and City Data Book 1988.* Washington, DC: Government Printing Office.

———. 1988. *1980 Census of Population,* Vol. 1, *General Social and Economic Characteristics of the Population, Kentucky.* Washington, D.C.: Government Printing Office.

United States Department of Agriculture. 1935. *Economic and Social Problems and Conditions of the Southern Appalachian.* Washington, D.C.: USDA Miscellaneous Publication no. 205.

Waller, A. 1988. *Feud: Hatfields, McCoys, and Social Change in Appalachia, 1860–1900.* Chapel Hill: University of North Carolina Press.

Walls, D. 1976. "Central Appalachia: A Peripheral Region within an Advanced Capitalist Society." *Journal of Sociology and Social Welfare* 4 (2):232–47.

Weller, J. 1965. *Yesterday's People.* Lexington: University Press of Kentucky.

Weiss, C. 1990. "Organizing Women for Local Economic Development." Pp. 61–71 in J. Gaventa, B. Smith, and A. Willingham (eds.), *Communities in Economic Crisis.* Philadelphia: Temple University Press.

Whisnant, D. 1980. *Modernizing the Mountaineer.* New York: Burt Franklin and Co.

———. 1983. *All That Is Native and Fine: The Politics of Culture in an American Region.* Chapel Hill: University of North Carolina Press.

3 | The Reported and Unreported Missouri Ozarks: Adaptive Strategies of the People Left Behind

Rex R. Campbell, John C. Spencer, and Ravindra G. Amonker

THE OZARKS REGION is bounded on the west by plains typical of Kansas, on the north by the Missouri River valley, on the east by the Mississippi River valley, and on the south by the Arkansas River valley. Some definitions include the Ouachita Mountain region south of the Arkansas River. The region represents a distinct geographical area within the central portion of the United States characterized by very old, poor and rocky soils, abundant water and forest, and a rugged topography. It is beautiful. It does not have the well-groomed look of Pennsylvania's Amish country or the "purple mountain majesty" of Colorado, but the forested hills and hollows and clear, gravel-bottomed streams are appealing to visitors.

The Missouri Ozarks is the largest and most diverse portion of the region.[1] A total of 50 of Missouri's 114 counties lies, at least in part, in the Ozarks. Most of the area is certainly rural and will undoubtedly remain so for a long time to come, but it is no longer isolated. The Ozarks winter is short, and roads are rarely bothered by snow. People travel up to eighty miles one way to Springfield, a burgeoning city of a quarter of a million inhabitants located in the heart of the Ozarks, for shopping, entertainment, and even work. Television is widely available and broadcast reception is good. Metropolitan newspapers are delivered daily in most communities. Kansas City, St. Louis, Little Rock, Memphis, and Tulsa are within half a day's drive, and the country music resort area around Branson, Missouri, is growing very rapidly. It alone brings some four million visitors into the heart of the Ozarks. The tourists in turn bring outside ideas, money, and products into the region.

The region is endowed with major rivers fed by numerous clearwater streams. Today, it contains several man-made lakes, such as Lake of the Ozarks, Lake Taneycomo, Stockton Lake, Bull Shoals Lake, and Pomme de Terre Lake. These have brought about dramatic changes in recreational usage and retirement (Costello, 1975; Hunt, 1974; Rafferty, 1984; Rodes et al., 1974).

Yet, for decades the Ozarks has been a classic example of under-development.[2] Human resources and natural ones—timber, minerals, soil nutrients in foodstuffs—have moved from the Ozarks to urban centers. In many areas of the Ozarks, the out-migration of the educated young and not-so-young has resulted in declining populations and a high incidence of poverty. State and local industrial development programs have tried to stimulate economies by attracting branch factories. In recent years, few factories have moved to nonmetropolitan areas. When communities have been able to attract job-producing industries, they have had to provide incentives, such as granting tax abatements and customizing utilities that often cost more than industry added to the community, especially when attendant environmental and social costs are taken into account. The results of the decades of exploitation of human and natural resources are apparent: poverty is widespread and indeed in some communities most households are poor.

Adaptive Behavior to Poverty

Ozarks subculture has encouraged many of the remaining families to develop strategies of adaptation.[3] These help to provide necessary resources to supplement their limited cash income and mitigate the effects of poverty. These adaptive strategies and tactics are important for two reasons. First, they are vital to residents' well-being and integral to their way of life. Second, they provide opportunities for development through import substitution and improving quality of life by building on existing social and natural resources.

Ozarks individuals and families have three choices when faced with a lack of cash income opportunities: (1) they can migrate to other regions that offer better income opportunities, as many people for four or five generations, especially the young, have done; (2) they can exist in poverty at a bare subsistence level, with inadequate food, clothing, or shelter, which some continue to do, still living like families described by Harold Bell Wright and others fifty or more years ago; or (3) they can use traditional strategies for subsistence or develop new ones to produce food, shelter, and other necessities. In a word, they can adapt. These choices are not mutually exclusive; often individuals or families may do all three. They may leave the Ozarks for some time and return (often with some cash or transfer payments, i.e., unemployment benefits); they may adapt where possible; and they may be in absolute poverty during difficult times when the other two are inadequate or unavailable.

Those who have chosen to adapt have two general strategies. First, they must learn to live with limited cash flow—that is, they must lower or limit their expectations for spending. This follows the old American adage, "make do or do without." Sometimes this means giving up only conspicuous consumption. Often it means taking risk: doing without insurance, avoiding medical care, using questionable equipment on dangerous jobs, and driving less-safe vehicles.

Second, they must learn to produce in the social or informal economy. This wide range of activities includes home production and consumption, trading, sharing, and reusing wherever possible. We will describe some of these later in this chapter. The level of success in the social economy, like success in the formal economy, depends on the possession of personal skills and material resources and thus, varies widely from person to person, from family to family, from community to community.

Economic and Social Characteristics of the Ozarks

The earliest European industry in the Ozarks was lead mining and refining (the native Americans mined lead in the Ozarks also). Decline in demand caused by the elimination of lead in paints and gasoline and automation of the remaining mines has reduced mining to a minor source of regional employment. The decline in mining employment has not caused high out-migration, however. Many ex-mining families have combined survival tactics and, in contrast to other Ozarks families, social programs such as food stamps to "get by."

The timber industry has followed a similar "boom and bust" cycle. Cutting of the virgin timber around the turn of the nineteenth century for lumber and railroad ties created an important but short-lived industry. Poor and droughty soils on the hills have meant that the regrowth of predominantly hardwood trees is slow.

Known for its man-made lakes, its scenic beauty and less hurried way of life, the area has become a major tourist and retirement destination, however. Ozarks recreational or retirement areas around lakes are among the few open-country population growth areas in the United States. Growth potential has been well identified by developers, who offer housing sites, homes, shopping strips, and varied services. Lower land prices, taxes, and cost of living, coupled with limited restrictions, less congestion and pollution, and scenic beauty are attractions (Amonker and Pinkerton, 1991).

Consequently, most new jobs in the Ozarks are in service sectors. Growth of the retirement industry has provided some better-paying jobs in the construction trades, and new residents buy goods and services, which creates other jobs. Also, the older population creates a demand for additional health care facilities and services that bring additional resources to the community. The tourist industry requires large numbers of cooks, waitresses, motel maids, sales clerks and grounds keepers. Pay scales for these usually part-time, often seasonal, dead-end jobs are near the minimum-wage rate. In this development process, natives have been relegated for the most part to marginal, low-paid jobs. Most major resorts and businesses are owned and controlled by outside corporations or by "new money" brought in by retirees and investors. The current boom in the country music industry in Branson is a good example of outside money coming into the area. A close resemblance exists between the control of industries and profits in the Ozarks and such control in Third World countries.[4]

Agriculture in the Ozarks has always been marginal, and row crops are generally limited to creek and river bottoms. The hills and plateaus grow grassses for dairy and beef cattle. The national trend toward mechanized agriculture is not well adapted to the Ozark terrain. Many Ozarks families remain on small farms long after neoclassical economists have declared them unviable. Many of the same survival tactics are used by these small-scale farm operators: low-cost, low-capital, and labor-intensive operations are important components of their continued operations, and farm income may be supplemented by nonfarm earnings.

During the late 1960s and 1970s, a considerable effort was made to develop large scale livestock operations by clearing land of timber and planting grasses. This "boomlet" faded rapidly with the subsequent decline in cattle prices. Timber clearing started again in the late 1980s when cattle prices improved, but the lower cattle prices of the early 1990s seem likely to again halt this practice.

In the 1950s, mobile and mostly labor-intensive industry began to move into the Ozarks. Relatively low-paid and semiskilled jobs in the shoe, clothing, and assembly industries became important sources of income in many Ozarks households. The location of branch plants in the Ozarks resulted in very few higher-paid management employees, however. In recent years many of these factories have moved to Third World countries to take advantage of even lower wage rates. Ozarkers will work hard for relatively low pay, but they cannot compete for wages with Chinese or Mexican laborers, especially for the lowest-skilled jobs. Some anecdotal information suggests higher skill-levels of Ozarks workers may make them competitive with laborers in countries such as Mexico.

The region's patchwork society is apparent in disparate residential structures that dot the countryside in many areas. Here is a shabby stucco storefront converted into a shabby-looking house with plastic film windows and visible decay. Across the road is a newly built three-story house with expensive western cedar siding and artistic stonework that would be a proud addition to a Rocky Mountain ski resort. A few miles down the road a grand colonial brick house faces a nearly derelict mobile home that has tarpaper additions protruding from it like barnacles on a submarine hull. Carefully manicured lawns clash with front yards filled with dogs and derelict cars sitting on blocks. Some homes and whole communities look as though they have been transplanted from the suburbs of St. Louis or Chicago, as indeed they have been. Others, more isolated, maintain the hardscrabble appearance of absolute poverty. A single rural neighborhood may consist of retirees from major urban areas, working farmers, lifestyle migrants from urban middle class backgrounds, and poor "hill folk."

An examination of recent economic indicators provides a more comprehensive picture of the current conditions in the Ozarks. The poverty[5] and unemployment rates of the region have been slightly higher than the state rate. In 1980, the proportion of families with incomes below the poverty level in the Ozarks was 11.1 percent compared to the state average of 9.1 percent.[6] Of the Ozarks' fifty counties, forty had a higher proportion of families with incomes below poverty level than the state average of 9.1 percent. Of these, nine counties had almost one in five families living in poverty.

Although the unemployment rate for the Ozarks counties declined from 8.8 percent in 1980 to 7.1 percent in 1990, it remained 1 percent higher than the state rate. Nine counties of the region had unemployment rates in excess of 10 percent. During the decade, rates as high as 25 to 30 percent were recorded in a few mining counties. We must keep in mind that unemployment rates do not include underemployment, which is very high in most parts of the Ozarks. Nor does it include "discouraged" workers who are not actively seeking employment. In small communities people know when jobs are available. They do not need to go to the unemployment office to find that there are no jobs.

Analysis of data of various types of income also indicates that median per capita income and median household effective buying power were significantly lower in the counties of the Ozarks than in other Missouri counties. In 1989, the median per capita income of the Ozarks ($12,025) was $4,000 lower than the Missouri median. Only four counties of the Ozarks had median per capita incomes close to the state average (Bureau of Economic Analysis, 1990).

In 1990, median household effective buying power of the Ozarks counties ranged from a low of $12,391 to $31,852. In the lowest income county 40 percent of the households had an effective buying power of less than $10,000. In the highest income county, almost one-fourth of the households had more than $50,000. This contrast clearly illustrates the increasing heterogeneity of the region. Even in the poorest county, almost 4 percent of the households exceeded the $50,000 figure and in the richest county, 11.7 percent had effective household buying power of less than $10,000 (Sales and Marketing Management, 1991).

A very important change is the rapid growth in people who say they are self-employed in the nonfarm proprietorships. In Missouri in the decade from 1979 to 1989, nonfarm self-employed proprietors increased 64 percent while total employment was increasing only 18 percent. Hobbs (1992) found that in areas of rapid population growth both the salary and the wage categories and nonfarm proprietors category increased. In areas of some population growth, there was a modest increase in the number of salary and wage earners and considerable increase in the number of nonfarm proprietors. Areas of population loss had a decline in the number of salary and wage earners which was more than offset by an increase in the number of nonfarm proprietors. It is our hypothesis that a significant and probably large part of those representing the increase in people reporting proprietorships are actually marginally employed. They may be working part-time in construction, driving their own trucks, or engaging in a wide variety of other part-time occupations and listing themselves as "self-employed."

It is our contention that the distribution of low-income households in the Ozarks is more geographically uniform than the distribution of upper-income households. Areas with more total numbers of households have larger numbers of middle- and upper-income households, but about equal numbers of low-income households. In looking at these statistics, we should note that in urban areas, income levels are more geographically segregated and thus, statistics make poverty more visible there than in rural areas with economically mixed populations.

Transfer payments, especially retirement including social security, are the most important single source of income in many Ozarks communities. Welfare programs such as Aid to Families with Dependent Children (AFDC) and food stamps are an important part of many household incomes. However, the typical Ozarks family will strongly resist use of such "welfare programs." Social security and unemployment benefits are seen as "earned" and, thus, more acceptable. In 1990, 10.3 percent of the population in the Ozarks received food stamps, compared to 9.3 percent in the rest of Missouri. AFDC participation rates run counter to other assistance rates. In 1990, 7.3 percent of children under 18 in the Ozarks received assistance, compared to 11.0 percent for the remainder of Missouri. The lower rate is the result of a relatively older population and vigorous social disapproval of government assistance Ozarkers consider "welfare."

The Ozarks also has a higher proportion of people with literacy problems than the rest of the state. In 1980, the proportion of people in Missouri over twenty-five years of age who had literacy problems was 10.9 percent, and only ten counties in the Ozarks had lower percentages. In several counties, almost one out of five people over twenty-five years of age had literacy problems. Again, a large portion of this can be explained by the long term selective out-migration of the young and educated.[7]

The educational attainment of Missouri's population has increased significantly over the years. Between 1940 and 1980, the median number of school years completed by persons 25 years and over increased by nearly 4 years to 12.4 years (U.S. Bureau of the Census, 1983). The educational level of the Ozarks population was slightly below the state average. In 1980, median school years attained by the Ozarks population was 11.7 years, compared with the state average of 12.4 years. Furthermore, in ten counties the median number of school years completed was less than 11. The highest median was 12.6 years (U.S. Bureau of the Census, 1983). The difference in educational levels can be explained in part by older average ages.

The subculture of the Ozarks has never emphasized education, and a majority of the people have not had resources to attend college if they desired to do so. The result has been relatively high dropout rates and low college-attendance rates. In 1980, among persons 25 years and over in Missouri, 63.5 percent had graduated from high school and 13.9 percent were college graduates; in the Ozarks 63 percent were high school graduates and 9.8 percent were college graduates. In 1980, of the Ozarks' 50 counties, 44 had proportions of high school graduates lower than the state average of 63.5 percent, and 46 had proportions of college graduates lower than the state average.

Because of lack of employment opportunities for college-educated people in most communities, a college degree means out-migration. Schools and government agencies offer the largest sources of employment in the typical small community. State and federal jobs are normally filled by people from outside the region and offer limited opportunity for native sons and daughters.

The Ozarks population has fluctuated with economic conditions in the region. The trends have been influenced both by the national economy and by regional changes, but population changes have not been uniform throughout all parts of the Ozarks, producing large variations in population densities.

The European settlement of the Ozarks started nearly three centuries ago. Among the earliest settlers of the region were those of French heritage, followed by Scotch-Irish and Germans. Most early immigrants came from the Appalachian Mountains and southern states (Gerlach, 1976). Population growth in the Ozarks during the early period of settlement was relatively slow. The Civil War disrupted settlement and resulted in many of the early settlers fleeing the Ozarks because of numerous battles and skirmishes. The thirty-five years after the War saw renewed settlement, and by the 1900 census, 904,000 people resided in the fifty counties of the region. In many counties, the largest population was reached during the decades from 1900 to 1920, when cutting of timber reached a peak. By 1920 most of the region had been cut over, and subsistence farming and hunting became mainstays.

The region experienced erratic population change from 1900 to 1960, but since that time, there has been a significant increase in population. Gradual development of the tourism industry and establishment of light manufacturing fostered growth. From 1960 to 1990, population of the region increased by 44.7 percent, compared to a Missouri increase of 17.5 percent. By 1990 total population of the fifty counties of the Ozarks totaled 1,495,000 (see Table 3.1).

Population increases and decreases have varied widely both among counties and over time. Population declines in recent decades have been associated with the closing of mines, the closing of factories, and the loss of farms in areas where off-farm jobs are not available to supplement farm income. Of the Missouri region's fifty counties, forty-two (84 percent) gained pouplation and eight (16 percent) lost population during the 1980–1990 decade. Suburban counties and several recreational or retirement counties situated around lakes had population increases exceeding 20 percent. Improvement in highways, especially Interstate Highway 44 from St. Louis through Springfield, have encouraged suburbanization and commuting in many counties. Major metropolitan areas have stimulated growth as far as sixty to seventy miles from cities. These beyond-the-suburbs areas have followed patterns of growth and development typical of suburban sprawl.

Table 3.1. Population Change in the Missouri Ozarks and Missouri, 1900–1990

Year	Ozarks Population	Ozarks Change Net	Ozarks Change %	Missouri Change (%)
1900	903,658	–	–	–
1910	928,010	24,352	2.7	6.0
1920	884,777	(43,233)	(4.7)	3.4
1930	883,334	(1,441)	(0.2)	6.6
1940	945,495	62,161	7.0	4.3
1950	918,988	(26,507)	(2.8)	4.5
1960	986,184	67,196	(7.3)	9.2
1970	1,118,377	132,193	13.4	8.3
1980	1,356,398	238,021	21.3	5.1
1990	1,495,375	138,977	10.2	4.1

Sources: U.S. Bureau of the Census (1982); Missouri Office of Administration (1991).

Lower density of population, open space with few restrictions on use, lower land prices, improved infrastructure, employment and educational opportunities, less crime and other amenities have made these areas attractive to "refugees" from metropolitan areas.

The long out-migration of young people from most communities and in-migration of older people has produced a relatively old population in many parts of the Ozarks. In 1980, the median age of the Missouri Ozarks population was 33.9 years, compared with 30.8 years for the entire state. Thirty-eight counties of the Missouri Ozarks, however, had median ages above the state average and seven had median ages of 40.0 years or more (U.S. Bureau of the Census, 1983). These seven are a combination of two types of retirement counties. One type has had a long history of out-migration of the young people which has created a "residual" of older people. The second is the "created" retirement county situated predominantly around lakes, where large numbers of people have moved from urban areas to retire. The Lake of the Ozarks has attracted retirees from St. Louis and northern U.S. cities. The southern lakes area attracted people from the Southwest and the West as well as from the Midwest. In several areas of the Ozarks "returnees" have come home to retire.

In 1980, the proportion of population 65 years and over in the Ozarks was 23.6 percent, compared with 13.2 percent of the population of Missouri. Furthermore, forty counties of the Ozarks had a higher percentage of the population 65 years and over than the state average. In seven counties it was in excess of 20 percent (U.S. Bureau of the Census, 1983).

The Ozarks, finally, are very heterogeneous. Yet, some things do stand out: (1) population in many counties has increased; (2) average age is relatively old; (3) income levels by any of several measures are low for substantial numbers of residents; and (4) even in areas with higher median incomes, there are many who are in poverty. Of the region's fifty counties, the vast majority remain less developed. These counties are characterized by a predominantly rural population, lower income, lower educational attainment, more low-paying and low-skilled jobs, and higher poverty and unemployment rates. A long history of systematic exploitation of the human and natural resources in the Ozarks by both public and private sectors located in metropolitan centers has resulted in a residual which is poor in income, in marketable job skills, and in other resources.

In order to look beyond medians and averages for the region—to give the Ozarks a human face—we selected one county which is both poor and rural to examine in more detail. No one county can represent a region as heterogeneous as the Missouri Ozarks, but Douglas County illustrates the rural portion of the Ozarks where economic development has been very limited and consists mostly of exploitation of resources.

Douglas County: A Case Study of Uneven Development

Douglas County represents the "deep"[8] rural of the Missouri Ozarks. No major highways traverse its boundaries. The approximately 12,000 residents are a mixture of natives and in-migrants, both retirees and "back-to-the-landers." Most families have low to modest incomes. The county seat of Ava barely achieves urban status with 2,800 residents. It does have a Wal-Mart store, an indicator in the Midwest of a town's size and function, but only a small one and no other mass merchandisers. However, the citizens of Douglas County are not isolated. Many commute daily to places outside the county for employment, with some going as far as sixty miles to Springfield. Many travel similar distances to urban places to purchase goods and services.

Like the rest of the Ozarks, Douglas County has farming, services, and manufacturing as its largest sources of employment. The vast majority of the county's 1,200 farms are small (60 percent sold less than $10,000 worth of crops in 1987) and part-time. Most of the manufacturing jobs are low-skilled and low-paid. In 1989 transfer payments, of which the largest single source was social security, accounted for 45 percent of the total personal income in Douglas County (Hobbs, 1992).

People of Douglas County have attempted for several decades to adapt to chronic low income and limited resources through a large, informal economy in which many families produce a substantial portion of their food, where trading and sharing remain strong traditions, and where local mores encourage people to "make-do-or-do-without." Between 1979 and 1989 the growth of self-employed nonfarm proprietorships in Douglas County (75 percent) was more rapid than that in the state as a whole (64 percent). During this period total employment increased only 13 percent in Douglas County; the boarded-up stores in Ava and other small towns do not indicate growth in small retail businesses. We believe, therefore, that the informal economy is probably growing and that the increase in proprietorships is somehow related to that probable growth: an increasing number of people may be making a considerable part of their living through trade and barter. We turn to a description of the local knowledge which has produced an extensive informal economy for one Douglas County family.[9]

The Informal Economy

Economic statistics for Ozark households are less than complete.[10] Native Ozarkers hold a deep distrust of governments, in general, and of the federal government, in particular. In addition, most people and most households do not keep detailed and accurate records of even the cash parts of their economies. If they have a job where income is carefully recorded or if their farm income goes through official channels, then the cash portions of their economies are probably reported accurately. But it is our strong suspicion that very little, if any, of the marginal cash economic activities are reported. The following case study of one Douglas County household reveals the magnitude of this complex social (almost always informal) economy that is used to offset the lack of money.

Our observations of other households in this and other Ozarks communities suggest that the adaptive tactics this family uses are common. It is "local knowledge" shared and transmitted from person to person and from generation to generation.[11] Clearly, every family and every household is unique in the use of these tactics—at least in some ways—but at the same time, most Douglas low-income country families have much in common: gardens, meat production, food preservation, and trading and sharing of many resources are ubiquitous.

A Dairy Place

"When people hear 'dairy farmers' they think all we do is milk cows, shovel shit, and put up hay," Laura complained once when the term was used to introduce her. "Why not call us breeders of fine cattle, agronomists, entrepreneurs or something, because we do all that and a lot more. Milking is something we have to do every day, but it's only a part."

Don and Laura are native Ozarkers in their early fifties. They have lived on this dairy place for eighteen years. By Bureau of Census and USDA categorizations they are merely statistics: "Farmer, Dairy, annual gross sales of farm products $xxx.xx, size of farming operation xxx—the number of milking cows xx, the number of days of off-farm employment of the farm operator xxx, etc." The census would include the cash income as estimated and reported by Don and Laura, their ages, and other data. But neither agency would report about the numerous ways Don and Laura have found to do things without cash—their social or informal economy. Nor would anyone report on how their rich informal economy contributes to the quality of their lives.

The dairy place is a square one-half mile on each side—320 acres. It was once wooded and has been cleared into pastures and hayfields. The terrain slopes gently away in all directions from a cluster of four buildings at the center of the place. In the middle of a fescue lawn there is a modest one-story ranch house that, except perhaps for the large, hexagonal, attached greenhouse and the native stone facing, would fit in many middle-class urban neighborhoods. Nearby there is a thirty-by-forty-foot storage-work-machine shop and a similarly sized four-stall milk barn separated from the lawn and house by an unpaved drive, as well as several smaller buildings.

Two things confound attempts to categorize and quantify Don and Laura's economic activities; the first is the continuous nature of the work, and the second is the multiplicity of ways that they work to meet their needs. If it is possible for census takers and other statistics gatherers to precisely account for the hours of work, the amount of income, and the expenditures of, say, factory workers, teachers, or physicians, it is not possible to do so in Ozark open-country households.

A complex network of social economy exists. At first Don described things in the dairy operation simply. For example: "The whole secret to farming here is how much hay you can put up," he said, "and if you don't put it up on your place you have to buy it from somebody else, have it trucked in."

This statement would fit within most economic models. However, the situation is much more complex. The core enterprise of growing grass, raising cows, and milking produces opportunities for other, often informal, economic activities. As Don describes it:

> We'll raise all our calves, males and females alike. The girls become milk cows and the boys become uh . . . trading material. This year I've traded for wood [used for heating], I've got all my wood brought in from an outside source by trading calves. He brings wood and takes calves. Lot of times he brings wood and doesn't get a calf, 'cuz I get several trucks of wood before he gets a calf.

The business of trading and dealing is complicated and contingent. It depends on day to day situations and individual tastes and perceptions. Much machinery repair, the skilled labor needed for construction, and even some needed materials are in part or in their entirety traded or bartered. Sometimes there is a careful accounting and exchange that appears to follows the market model closely. Once a trading relationship is established, other opportunities present themselves and the social economy is extended. Don has an inclination to expand his deals, as he might expand a crop enterprise.

Laura works at her and Don's home-owned nursery-and-plant business in the nearby town. The town is about three miles away from the dairy place and is very small. It still has a post office but very few commercial enterprises. There is a bank branch office, a propane outlet, a beauty salon, a Masonic lodge, two automobile repair shops ("garages" in Ozark terms), and a couple of second-hand stores. Most of the buildings stand empty and have for years. The plant business is one of the few new businesses that suggests a possibility of growth.

Laura's parents (mother, aged sixty-nine, and father, aged seventy-three), her uncle in his late sixties, and Don's parents (mother, aged seventy-seven, and father, aged eighty-three), live in three two-bedroom mobile homes and a small, frame house on the site of the business. The mobile homes are modern, pleasant, and constantly being improved by new decks, additions, gardens, landscaping, and so forth. The parents and uncle have retirement income. They all keep quite busy, or as busy as they want, working on their places and in the plant business. Laura's father in particular works incessantly, growing a one-third acre garden of produce, plants, and shrubs to sell, and on various building projects around the place.

The business does not make a profit in the conventional sense of the word; Laura said, "We're making enough to purchase seeds, plants, materials [e.g., peat moss, vermiculite, fertilizer, for example], one of the greenhouses, and some of the mortgage payments on the place. But we're still paying out of pocket for most of the improvements made to the property. . . . We're still learning the business, growing things that people don't buy, trying things that don't work." Don and Laura own the property and are responsible for making payments. There is no formal arrangement with the parents and uncle, who own their trailers and contribute something like rent, but the contract is vague, verbal, contingent, and renegotiated frequently. Laura works there about five days a week, depending on the time of year and the demands of the dairy farm. A room in her parents' house serves as a storefront for the business and displays craft and decorative items that they make and sell.

Their farm and their plant place are combinations of what we social scientists would describe as both formal and informal economies. It is somewhat unclear to the researchers how much of this activity is reported in the official USDA and Bureau of Census statistics.

Types of Social Economic Activity

Most of the residents of the Ozarks open country do something other than farming for their principal formal income, but almost all share many of the same social economic activities as Don and Laura's.

The bank loans are paid by the milk checks. The loans are used to purchase property, buildings, and machinery. They buy feed, fuel, electricity, groceries, the occasional services of a dentist or mechanic, and so forth directly when they go to town. If this were the totality of their economic activities, we would be able to describe the dairy place and its importance to the economy, both local and nonlocal, from official statistics. But this represents only a small portion of the daily activities. We will use two types of income or wealth creation as examples: food production and capital creation. We collected information on several other types including production through salvage, through bricolage,[12] and the production of security and entertainment. And we hasten to add that these types do not exhaust the numerous innovative ways that Ozarkers have found to do things with minimal amounts of money.

Don and Laura produce vegetables, fruits, herbs, beef, pork, poultry and eggs, milk, rabbits, and more. These products are processed by canning, freezing, and drying and are used in several ways throughout the year. The primary use is to provide nourishment for the household. It is difficult to estimate what portion of the food that they consume Don and Laura produce. A guess is about two-thirds—no records are kept on the amount of garden products, milk, and meat consumed. Like most Americans, they eat for reasons and in ways other than those necessity dictates. They *could* be self-sufficient in food production, and they gain economic and psychological benefits from that possibility.

The food products are also used as gifts. Not formal gifts for Christmas or a birthday, though they would certainly be part of any celebration, but small, frequently given tokens of friendship. On another level the food items are traded and sold. They may be wages paid for labor or expertise, or goods exchanged for materials or tools. If we attempt to quantify the production by using market price, for example, we ignore much of the products' value. The value of orange-yolked, fresh eggs is different from the retail store price of factory eggs. The value of giving them is different from the value of selling them. And all of these things illustrate other aspects of the informal economy at work.

For many open-country residents the most expensive items on their places are the buildings and concomitant real estate improvements. Often, especially for small acreages, the value of buildings exceeds the value of the land. There are no building codes and inspectors and few expectations for conformity in style and appearance. Although a new brick colonial house would generally be admired, an old frame house or mobile home that has been practically and not aesthetically rehabilitated and expanded would also be accepted. Here, form follows function much more than in suburban and urban settings. The wealth that these buildings represent is poorly accounted for by official data.

Don and Laura's house gained a stone veneer and fireplace because a stonemason and the rocks were available. The couple were able to arrange a trade for his expertise and labor and provide much of the labor themselves. The mason was also willing to trade them a fireplace insert that he had salvaged from another job. Trading for labor meant that the job took longer—the mason's cash jobs received priority—but Don and Laura were willing to tolerate the inconvenience, trading time for money. This meant that they spent cash, the kind of expenses "you feel," as Don would say, only for masonry cement, sand, and the marginal cost of collecting rocks.

They added a large hexagonal greenhouse themselves, again spending time and saving money. The framing materials, roofing, and sliding glass doors that serve as glazing were purchased. The interior, plant beds, benches, stairs, terraces, and shelves, were made from salvaged materials. The floor is covered with small seashells that Don brought back from a trip to Louisiana. They are attractive and provide good drainage.

Recently, Don and Laura remodeled their bathroom. Don's father built some new cabinets for them and a friend installed them, as well as a shower and a urinal Don got for his birthday. The friend is a civilian maintenance worker at an air force base in California who chooses to spend his vacation at Don and Laura's. The work he does when visiting is not directly compensated and he views it as "a good time." The apparent irony of his leaving "vacationland" California to work for free on a Missouri farm illustrates the complexity and extent of the network of the prevailing local social economy.

Almost every outbuilding on the place has a story. For example, what is now a handsome thirty-foot-by-forty-foot shop in front of their house was half of a neighbor's forty-foot-by-sixty-foot shop. Don and a friend disassembled the building in large sections and, over a period of several days, hauled it over to his place on an old hay trailer. The two of them reassembled the building, tilting up the walls with Don's tractors and adding new metal to the roof trusses.

The wealth created by informal construction projects, where labor and materials are provided by the owner, neighbors, or acquaintances won't show up in official statistics. Typically, the work, production, and wealth created are considered marginal and unimportant. Yet, in this open-country Ozark setting, this type of construction may predominate. Even in urban and suburban settings the owner's contribution to housing maintenance and improvement is difficult to quantify. There are turnkey types of buildings constructed in Douglas County where everything is completed by workers hired for cash. Most commonly, these are done for the "outsiders," often the retirees who move from the city and assume that cash work is the way things are always done.

We must remind readers that these two examples of types of informal economy are only a few of the numerous ones that are being used by Don and Laura and the other Douglas County residents. We have tried to speculate on how much income or wealth is generated through the informal economy and have decided it is an impossible task. The tangled web of interactions is constantly changing from day to day and even from hour to hour.

Summary and Implications

The Ozarks continue to have large numbers of low-income households, primarily caused by the exploitation of people and natural resources by larger systems. Decades-old patterns of limited and mostly low-paid job opportunities continue in most parts of the region. Closely related to the substantial numbers of people in poverty is the adaptive use of the social informal economy as a part of the Ozarks subculture. The people developed and sustained the use of these survival tactics as a reaction to the lack of cash. At the same time, their success with these tactics has enabled larger numbers of low-income people who would otherwise have been forced to migrate to stay in the Ozarks.

The lives of Don and Laura are illustrative of some of the adaptive tactics used. These tactics are not unique to Don and Laura but are commonly found in the Ozarks culture. However, Don and Laura are more skilled than many families. These skills are an important form of empowerment which give Don and Laura and other people who possess them greater control over their lives.

In sum: (1) everyone in the Ozarks participates in the social informal economy; (2) there is a variable threshold of cash necessary for a satisfactory quality of life in the Ozarks. The level of the threshold will depend upon desires (ambition), stage of life cycle, current resources, health, etc. The amount of cash available in comparison to the necessary cash threshold will influence, in part, use of adaptive tactics of the informal economy; and (3) the more the formal or cash income, the less the participation in the social informal economy—people participated in the use of such tactics by necessity.

We have described only a small portion of the adaptive skills in one community of the Ozarks. Additional research is needed about the "local knowledge" in other communities and other regions concerning these adaptive tactics. To paraphrase Kloppenburg (1991), there is a need for reconstruction of regional economics, including economic development and starting with research on local knowledge. "What could characterize efforts to explore and define parameters of local knowledge is careful attention to both theorization and the direct observed contact . . ." with the everyday behavior of ordinary people (538).[13] Since the role of the federal government, including the amount of funds available to alleviate poverty in rural areas, is likely to be less than adequate during the next decade, local knowledge will continue to be important. Land grant colleges could make a substantial contribution through local knowledge research and dissemination of the results. By building upon existing knowledge and local systems, many rural low-income residents could greatly enhance the quality of their lives.

Research should also explore other regions as well as urban areas. Although Ozarks households may have some advantage in specific survival skills, i.e., producing food and shelter, many other survival skills are used by people living in other subcultures, including urban barrios. The Appalachian subculture includes a large number of such survival skills (Halperin, 1990). The Corn Belt culture may have a different mixture, as may other rural and urban subcultures.

We must as researchers, sociologists, and social scientists look beyond the statistics[14] to understand and appreciate the importance of local knowledge. Questionnaires and interviews will not be sufficient. Only in-depth participant observation will do. It is our experience that most people do not recognize and thus, cannot report, the full dimensions of their participation in the informal economy. Accurate records are not kept on many of its aspects. From the Ozarkers' perception: "it is none of the government's business what I do."

Both economic "booms" and "busts" are continuing in the Ozarks in the 1990s. The recreational and retirement areas and the metropolitan fringe areas have increasing numbers of middle-income households while many of the "deep" rural people are surviving at marginal levels. Many of the people in the old mining communities of the eastern Ozarks are today quietly desperate for food, clothing, and adequate shelter. Shoe and other factories continue to close. Unemployment in many communities is high. The need for adaptive strategies is high. Many Ozarks families are facing the choice of leaving the Ozarks to find an equally uncertain future elsewhere, grimly trying to survive in the Ozarks, or developing knowledge and skills to use more survival tactics.

We conclude by noting that adaptive skills can be learned from popular culture. These do not depend on success in educational institutions and the garnering of educational or career credentials. Programs can be developed to disseminate these skills of other people. The use of adaptive tactics will not eliminate poverty, but they can improve the quality of the lives of those in poverty.[15]

Notes

The term "Ozarks" has been used to describe a region of the United States from two perspectives—a geographic area and a region of unique cultural heritage (Bogue and Beale, 1961; Beale and Fuguitt, 1975). Slightly elevated above the surrounding terrain the rolling hills of the Ozarks lie in four states—Missouri, Arkansas, Oklahoma and Kansas—totaling approximately 55,000 square miles (Gerlach and Wedenoja, 1984).

1. The emphasis in this chapter is on the Missouri portion of the Ozarks because of the availability of data. The remainder of Missouri contains two major metropolitan areas, northern Missouri, which has traditional agriculture, and southeast Missouri, which includes the "bootheel" on the Mississippi River. Thus, the comparison between the Ozarks and the remainder of the state makes a comparison to a diversity of the midwestern United States. The Ozark subculture extends into northern Arkansas and eastern Oklahoma. The senior author, Campbell, has conducted several research projects over a thirty-year period in the Arkansas and Oklahoma portions of the region as well as numerous studies in the Missouri Ozarks.

2. The literature on underdevelopment and economic development is extensive. Chilcote (1984) and Arndt (1987) are examples of summaries of the literature. Chilcote covers the theories of development and underdevelopment whereas Arndt focuses on economic development.

The Ozarks have long been recognized as an area of underdevelopment. During the 1960s, Campbell and others (Bender, 1971) conducted research in the region on poverty. At the same time the Ozark Regional Commission was formed to address some of the problems evident in the region. This Commission funded a considerable amount of infrastructure projects which helped to provide better public services.

3. The recognition of the importance of indigenous knowledge in everyday behavior has increased in recent years. Geertz (1983) wrote extensively on the importance of local knowledge. He addressed art, common sense, and law as systems from local knowledge or culture. Most of the recent research on local knowledge has been directed towards technical information, especially in agriculture. McCorkle (1989) was one of the first social scientists to describe the importance of local knowledge in Third World farming systems. More recently, Kloppenburg (1991) has proposed a theory based upon the use of local knowledge, again primarily for technical information in agriculture. He notes that local knowledge is "the implication . . . that 'locality'—in the sense of inseparability from a particular *place* in the sense of embeddedness in a particular *labor process*—is the key distinguishing feature of this type of knowledge" (emphasis in the original) (537). Our use of "adaptation," "tactics" and "strategies" is an extension of the concept of local knowledge into another form of social behavior. We will describe forms of local knowledge used to reduce the impacts of or offset not having sufficient cash income to meet basic needs.

4. Rural areas in general and the Ozarks in particular have many characteristics similar to those of third world countries in terms of both politics and economics. The raw resources were taken to the outside for processing and utilization. The wage rates by the outside controlled industries have been kept low and the workers utilized unskilled or semi-skilled. The profits have gone to headquarters and investors located primarily in metropolitan areas. Recently, some exceptions to this pattern have developed especially in northwest Arkansas. Wal-Mart, Tyson foods (poultry) and Hunt trucking are all located in small towns in primarily rural areas.

5. The official poverty index used by the U.S. government since 1964 "is

based solely on money income and does not reflect the fact that many low-income persons receive noncash benefits such as food stamps, medicaid, and public housing" (U.S. Department of Commerce, 1990:423). In addition, the official definition no longer makes any distinction for farm families. A family of four with a low income will be included in the poverty category regardless of their place of residence or of noncash income of any type. It is conceivable that a family could have an adequate or even a good quality of life in terms of food, shelter, entertainment, etc. and still be in the official poverty category. Yet, it is very probable that many people who have incomes near the poverty level and who do not use adaptive tactics may be very "poor" and have insufficient food, clothing, and shelter. The term *poverty* has come to be used by the middle class as a designation for a category of low-income people. It has a number of negative connotations, such as inadequate food, clothing, and shelter. In the Ozarks, a more correct usage and term would be *low cash income.* Low cash income in the Ozarks may or may not indicate inadequate food, clothing, shelter, etc.

6. All data are from the 1980 and 1990 censuses unless otherwise indicated.

7. Voss and Fuguitt (1991) found that the net effect of in- and out-migration in chronic low-income counties was relatively small. They suggest that such migrations had little effect on net income levels. Voss and Fuguitt might have reached different conclusions if their study had been limited to the Ozarks where there are substantial age and income differences between the in- and out-migrants.

8. "Deep" is used here as a relative term. There is no place in the Ozarks of either Missouri or Arkansas where the urban world has not penetrated to a considerable extent. All of the mass media are available in Douglas County. The television programs watched are the same as those in the metropolitan areas. Many of the people, including many of the natives, have resided outside for significant periods. There are areas in the Ozarks with lower densities of population, slightly higher rates of poverty and greater geographical isolation, but attitudinal and behavioral differences will be small.

9. This family was selected as an exemplar of the Ozarks population's practices that include a mixture of both native culture and "outside" material culture. Primary descriptions of tactics as part of the local economy were collected from close to one hundred individuals. Case material is available from twenty families. We emphasize tactics and strategies that this family, like many others, uses to adapt to a lack of money.

10. This informal economy section is taken from a Ph.D. dissertation by John Spencer, one of the few studies of the informal economy in rural America. The description comes from intensive interviews and participant observation.

11. Two of the authors, Campbell and Spencer, have lived for extended periods of time in the same or similar settings and have both observed the transmission and been the recipients of such local knowledge. It is an essential portion of the local culture.

12. Some of the technical skills necessary have been much better described in various back-to-the-land literature than have the social skills. For example, Wood's *Your New Life in the Country* and *Mother Earth News* include a large amount of such information.

13. Kloppenburg's focus in this quotation was on agriculture. His sentence

actually ends with "farmers and agricultural workers." However, the thought is clearly applicable to many social situations.

14. There are important theoretical issues for both sociologists and other social scientists raised in this research. Spencer, in his dissertation, has used the "rhetoric of inquiry" perspective. However, the question of the interaction of macro- and microlevel theories and the integration of quantitative and qualitative approaches must be addressed by the discipline. Limitation of space does not permit such a discussion in this chapter. In future publications, we will utilize the theories of the following: Bourdieu (1984), Geertz (1983), Knorr-Cetina (1981), Latour (1984; 1988), and Nelson (1987).

15. We are not suggesting that major changes are not needed in the system. The macrolevel changes to provide more equity in the distribution of wealth and income are certainly needed. The massive changes necessary to achieve more equity are slow to occur, often taking decades. The tactics proposed herein are short-term and immediate. They can make a difference in a few months or years. We believe that such changes at both levels are needed and should be encouraged.

References

Amonker, Ravindra G., and James R. Pinkerton. 1991. "The Population Growth of the Missouri Ozarks in the 1980's: Change, Characteristics, Effects." *Governmental Newsletter* 14 (1, July). Columbia: University of Missouri.

Arndt, H. W. 1987. *Economic Development: The History of An Idea.* Chicago: University of Chicago Press.

Beale, Calvin L., and Glenn V. Fuguitt. 1975. "Population Trends of Non-metropolitan Cities and Villages in Subregions of the United States." *Center for Demography and Ecology Working Paper 75–30.* Madison: University of Wisconsin.

Bender, Lloyd D., Bernal L. Green, and Rex R. Campbell. 1971. "A Case Study: Trickle-down and Leakage in the War on Poverty." *Growth and Change* 2 (4):34–41.

Bogue, Donald J., and Calvin L. Beale. 1961. *Economic Areas of the United States.* New York: Free Press of Glencoe.

Bourdieu, Pierre. 1984. *Distinctions.* Cambridge, Mass.: Harvard University Press.

Chilcote, Ronald H. 1984. *Theories of Development and Underdevelopment.* Boulder, Colo.: Westview Press.

Costello, David F. 1975. *The Mountain World.* New York: Thomas L. Crowell Company.

Dailey, George H., and Rex R. Campbell. 1980. "The Ozark-Ouachita Uplands: Growth and Consequences." Pp. 45–69 in David Brown (ed.), *New Directions in Urban-Rural Migration.* New York: Academic Press.

Denny, Hugh (ed.). 1974a. *Ozark Foothills Regional Profile.* Columbia: University of Missouri, Extension Division.

Denny, Hugh (ed.). 1974b. *South Central Ozark Regional Profile.* Columbia: University of Missouri, Extension Division.

Geertz, Clifford. 1983. *Local Knowledge: Further Essays in Interpretive Anthropology.* New York: Basic Books.

Gerlach, Russel L. 1976. *Immigrants in the Ozarks: A Study of Ethnic Geography.* Columbia: University of Missouri Press.

Gerlach, Russel L., and William J. Wedenoja. 1984. *The Heritage of the Ozarks: A Study for Multicultural Curriculum.* Springfield: Southwest Missouri State University.

Halperin, Rhoda H. 1990. *The Livelihood of Kin: Making Ends Meet "The Kentucky Way."* Austin: University of Texas Press.

Harding, P., and R. Jenkins. 1989. *The Myth of the Hidden Economy.* Philadelphia: Milton Keynes.

Hite, James C. 1991. "Rural People, Resources, and Communities: An Assessment of the Capabilities of the Social Sciences in Agriculture." Pp. III–21–30 in Glenn Johnson and James Bonnen (eds.), *Social Science Agricultural Agendas and Strategies.* East Lansing: Michigan State University.

Hobbs, Daryl J. 1992. Personal conversation. Office of Social and Economic Data Analysis, University of Missouri, Columbia, May 31.

Hunt, Charles B. 1974. *Natural Regions of the United States and Canada.* San Francisco: W. H. Freeman.

Knorr-Cetina, K., and A. V. Cicourel, (eds.). 1981. *Advances in Social Theory and Methodology.* Boston: Routledge and Kegan Paul.

Kloppenburg, Jack, Jr. 1991. "Social Theory and the De/Reconstruction of Agricultural Science: Local Knowledge for an Alternative Agriculture." *Rural Sociology* 36 (4):519–48.

McCorkle, Constance M. 1989. "Towards a Knowledge of Local Knowledge and Its Importance for Agricultural RD&E." *Agriculture and Human Values* 6 (3):4–12.

Nelson, J., A. Megill, and D. McCloskey, (eds.). 1987. *The Rhetoric of the Human Sciences.* Madison: University of Wisconsin.

Rafferty, Milton D. 1980. *The Ozarks: Land and Life.* Norman: University of Oklahoma Press.

Roberts, B. R. Finnegan, and G. Duncan. 1985. *New Approaches to Economic Life.* Manchester, Eng.: Manchester University Press.

Rhodes, Richard, and the Editors of Time-Life Books. 1974. *The Ozarks.* American Wilderness Series. New York: Time-Life Books.

Sales and Marketing Management. "Nineteen Ninety-one Survey of Buying Power." *Sales and Marketing Management,* 19 August 1991.

Spencer, John C. 1992. "An Open-Country Social Economy," Ph.D. diss., University of Missouri.

Swanson, Louis E. 1991. "The Rural Development Dilemma." Pp. III–45–47 in Glenn Johnson and James Bonnen (eds.), *Social Science Agricultural Agendas and Strategies.* East Lansing: Michigan State University.

U.S. Bureau of the Census. 1982. Number of Inhabitants: Missouri. *1980 Census of Population,* Final Report PC(1)-A27. Washington, D.C.: Government Printing Office.

———. 1982. General Population Characteristics. *1980 Census of Population,* Final Report PC(1)-B27. Washington, D.C.: Government Printing Office.

———. 1983. General Social and Economic Characteristics. *1980 Census of Population,* Final Report PC(1)-C27. Washington, D.C.: Government Printing Office.

———. 1991. Electronic Data File—Missouri. *1990 Census of Population,* STF-1. Washington, D.C.: Government Printing Office.

————. 1990. *Statistical Abstract of the United States: 1990.* 110th ed. Washington, D.C.: Government Printing Office.

U.S. Department of Commerce. Bureau of Economic Analysis. 1989 computer data tape, Washington, D.C.

Voss, Paul R., Glenn V. Fuguitt. 1991. "The Impact of Migration on Southern Rural Areas of Chronic Depression." *Rural Sociology* 56 (4):660–79.

Wood, Gregory. 1987. *Your New Life in the Country: How to Plan and Manage It For Enjoyment and Profit.* Harrisburg, Pa.: Stackpole Books.

4 | Life in the Forgotten South: The Black Belt

William W. Falk, Clarence R. Talley, and Bruce H. Rankin, with the assistance of Kathleen Little

MOST RURAL AREAS in the United States have been romanticized: the rural Northeast with picturesque Vermont and the rugged coast of Maine with its commercial fishermen; the small-town Midwest with its spacious plains and independent farmers; the West with its expansive forests, towering mountains, and cowboy culture. But when one considers the South, the romanticized notions take a different turn.

More than anyone, Faulkner captured the tone of the rural South with its hardscrabble tenant farmers, sharecroppers, and others trying to eke out a living. The confrontation with nature was set in the context of a history of slavery. Although slavery was outlawed in the 1860s, in reality it did not end but merely changed its form. Chattel slavery no longer existed, but in its place one found the land tenancy system or the sharecropping system. Both cases involved a type of indentured status in which labor and commodities could be exchanged in only one marketplace through the large acreage and emporiums operated by white plantation managers. This system began immediately after the Civil War and continued well into the twentieth century. Today only vestiges remain.

Popular accounts of blacks in the rural South have highlighted the massive migrations to northern industrial cities (see Lemann, 1991). This occurred primarily in three periods: the period of the Civil War and Reconstruction, the period from World War I to World War II, and the postwar period (Fligstein, 1981; Johnson and Campbell, 1981). (Although it has received less attention, rural to urban migration within the South is also important.) The great waves of migration might suggest that so few blacks are left in the rural South that their social condition would no longer be important. This is not the case.

In a book about forgotten places, it seems especially appropriate to include the Black Belt area in the rural South. Almost no region of the country has been more excluded from developments in the nation. In this chapter, our aim is to remember these people and this region—the two sides of a "forgotten place": a people whose entire lives have been spent in a region known for its clannishness and its willingness to put race before all else, a region bypassed by modern industrial development.

We begin our chapter by describing what constitutes the Black Belt region and where it is located. We then compare the demographic, social, and economic characteristics of the Black Belt with other parts of the South in order to establish the unique contours of its population and quality of life. This analysis is complemented by a discussion and analysis of the industrial and occupational makeup of the Black Belt which affects life chances for its people. As a final step, we highlight those few counties in the region that have been more successful than others at educational and income attainment and try to establish the reasons for this success. We close the chapter by returning to our larger theme: The Black Belt is a forgotten place that must be brought back into the national conscience so that the particularly disadvantaged status of the region can be addressed. The social condition of the people and economic prospects of these rural southern counties hold important sociological lessons and strong implications for the formation of a rural development policy.

The Use of Region in Social Research

The sociological concept of region grew out of work done in the Sociology Department at the University of Chicago in the 1920s and 1930s. There, Robert Park and Ernest Burgess developed an approach that came to be called "human ecology," which posited that the lives of individuals were shaped not just by their sociocultural circumstances but also by their physical environments.

Nowhere was this view adopted with greater success than in North Carolina, where the idea of region was used to develop social, economic, geographic, and historical maps of the South. Howard Odum (1936), at the University of North Carolina, and Rupert Vance (1932), at Duke University, used this approach to conceptualize the ways in which regions stood apart from each other and to produce a massive amount of empirical evidence to document the validity of their claims. Working separately, they both concluded that the South was composed of several different regions. One region that they both identified is the "cotton counties," running east to west from North Carolina through South Carolina, Georgia, Alabama, Mississippi, and Louisiana, ending in east Texas. The demarcation line of these counties followed the Mississippi River northward and also included the eastern part of Arkansas and the western part of Tennessee. Billings (1988) refers to approximately this same group of counties as the Plantation South, which he distinguishes from the Piedmont South and the Appalachian South. His work is important for the present research because these regions, like the Black Belt, are characterized by historically unique social and economic traditions.

The more familiar association of region with geography is important sociologically because natural environments promote specific economic activities that, in turn, produce unique forms of social organization. Political economist Ann Markusen has provided a definition of region that we find particularly applicable to the Black Belt (see Rankin and Falk, 1991; Falk and Rankin, 1992): "[a] historically evolved, contiguous territorial society that possesses a physical environment, a socioeconomic, political, and cultural milieu, and a spatial structure distinct from other regions and major territorial units" Markusen, (1987:17).

The distinction between what others call "cotton counties" or alternatively "Plantation South" and what we refer to as the Black Belt is the prominence and importance of racial concentration in conjunction with other salient features, such as the historical importance of agriculture generally, not just cotton farming. W. E. B. DuBois (1899), working at Atlanta University, was perhaps the first to use the term Black Belt. In his famous essay, *The Negro in the Black Belt: Some Social Sketches*, DuBois captured the more expansive, sociological meaning of the term. For him, as for us, it was much more than just the color of the earth or a particular type of agriculture. Rather it was the historical legacy of slavery and the continued presence of large numbers of blacks whose entire histories were grounded in this truly unique American heritage. Nowhere else in the United States had there been slaves in such absolute numbers or in as large a proportion of the total population. Nowhere else was there a group of people who were "freed" but remained, quite literally, as peasants—freed from slavery, but indentured to the land by virtue of a system of contracts and economic arrangements supported by political might and physical violence.

Charles S. Johnson (1941) extended the conceptual work of DuBois by using census data and case studies to examine the effects of the political and economic arrangements in the Black Belt on the characters and personalities of young blacks growing up in that region. Where DuBois had confined his work on the Black Belt to Georgia counties, Johnson selected eight counties in five states for intensive case studies. Six of the counties were cotton counties and the other two contained diversified farming. The cotton counties also contained a diversity of type: two were Mississippi counties that were traditional plantation counties, one each in Alabama and Georgia were typical of plantation counties in decline, one was a mixed nonplantation county where black tenants and white landowners competed, and the last was a county that contained the large urban center of Memphis, Tennessee. Johnson found that among the county types, the residents of plantation counties, which are the heart of the Black Belt, suffered the most and none more than the area's black population.

Our definition of the Black Belt is based on—racial concentration: We have defined the "Black Belt" as counties drawn from the fourteen census-designated states of the South where 33 percent or more of the population is black. Some change did occur between 1970 and 1980 in Black Belt counties; this change is quite obvious for southwestern states and for parts of the southern Mississippi Delta. Changes also occurred in the shore areas of North and South Carolina. Overall, relatively few counties in the South changed their designation between 1970 and 1980. The number of rural Black Belt counties declined, whereas urban counties increased by about the same number.[1]

Much of the research analyzing industrialization and social change in the South has concentrated on differential patterns of industrialization (Cobb, 1984; Falk and Lyson, 1988), the consequences of industrialization for racial inequality (Elgie, 1980), or the effects of black population concentration on industrialization (Colclough, 1988; Till, 1986). Most of this work has been sensitive to areal variations within the South, but it has produced contradictory results. Colclough (1988) found that minority concentrations reduce manufacturing growth, whereas Till (1986) argues that the heavily minority Black Belt region has been successful at recruiting industry. We suspect that these contradictory results may be due, in large part, to the variations within Black Belt counties that are likely to be associated with differences in economic structure, rate of development, and kinds of jobs to be found.

The rural Black Belt is indeed a unique, disadvantaged area in the South. Data from the U.S. Census Bureau's *1988 County Statistics Files* (CO-STAT-3), the *1988 City and County Data Book*, and the 1990 Bureau of Economic Analysis data file show that selected demographic characteristics of rural Black Belt counties vary from those of rural white counties in ways that suggest that the residents are (as the President's National Advisory Commission on Rural Poverty put it [1967]) "people left behind." This conclusion is reinforced by statistics on earnings, poverty, and labor force participation. Industrial and occupational structures are related to both the demography and the persistent poverty of Black Belt counties. Conditions in the Black Belt

Map 4.1. Black Belt Counties in the South

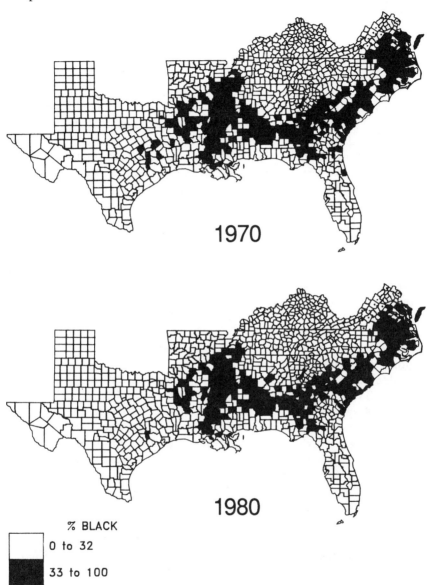

1970

1980

% BLACK

0 to 32

33 to 100

Source: Historical, Demographic, Economic, and Social Data: The U.S., 1790–1970
(Ann Arbor, Mich.: Inter-University Consortium of Political and Social Research, 1973).

illustrate both the consequences of official neglect and the need to break the cycle of decline and decay.

The Population Structure of the Black Belt

Our measures of the population structure are the percentage of the population under 18 years of age, the percentage of the population over 65 years of age, total population change, and the percentage of households headed by single women. Collectively, these measures help to provide a demographic profile of the Black Belt population *and* to indicate why poverty there is so prevalent, especially since a large proportion of the population is in some way dependent upon other people or programs for its well-being.

One important regional difference is that Black Belt counties have a larger proportion of their population under 18 than other counties (see Table 4.1). Rural Black Belt counties have the highest proportion of the population under 18, followed by the urban Black Belt counties, rural white counties, and urban white counties. In 1980 Black Belt rural counties had 2.5 percent more of their population under 18 than the regional average for rural counties, whereas Black Belt urban counties had 1.5 percent above the regional average (see Appendix). The trend over time is for decreasing proportions across the South, but regional patterns remain the same.

Black Belt counties had slightly lower proportions of their population over 65 in 1970 than white counties, but the growth in the population over 65 between 1970 and 1980 occurred mainly in Black Belt counties. This growth trend was most pronounced in Black Belt rural counties. In other words, the elderly population in the Black Belt is becoming more rural, whereas the elderly population is becoming more urban in white counties.

Our contention that Black Belt rural counties are less desirable places to live is supported by population change data. Rates of population growth in Black Belt counties were less than half of the regional growth rates in the period 1970–1980 and about a third of the regional rates in the period 1980–1985 (see Appendix). Regional growth rates for the South were higher among rural counties than urban counties in the 1970–1980 period; however, in the period 1980–1985 urban counties grew at a faster rate, despite the overall slowdown in regional growth rates. Growth rates in the rural Black Belt counties were lower than comparable rates for all other counties.

An important demographic factor that is highly correlated with

Table 4.1. Selected Demographic Measures for Black Belt and Other Counties, Means for 1970 and 1980 (percentages)

Variables	All Counties 1970	All Counties 1980	Rural Counties 1970	Rural Counties 1980	Urban Counties 1970	Urban Counties 1980
POPULATION < 18						
All counties	35.9	29.9	36.2**[a]	30.1**[a]	34.9**[a]	29.5**[a]
Black Belt	38.5**	31.8**	38.8**[b]	32.0**[b]	37.1**[c]	30.9**[c]
Other	35.1**	29.4**	35.2**[b]	29.5**[b]	34.6**[c]	29.2**[c]
POPULATION > 65						
All counties	11.2	12.8	11.6**[a]	13.3**[a]	10.1**[a]	11.5**[a]
Black Belt	10.8**	12.6	10.9**[b]	13.0*[b]	10.0	11.0
Other	11.3**	12.9	11.9**[b]	13.5*[b]	10.1	11.6
POPULATION CHANGE[d]						
All counties	20.2	6.0	20.6	5.2**[a]	19.1	7.9**[a]
Black Belt	10.0**	2.2**	10.5**[b]	2.0**[b]	6.2**[c]	3.0**[c]
Other	23.4**	7.0**	24.5**[b]	6.2**[b]	20.9**[c]	8.7**[c]
FEMALE-HEADED HOUSEHOLD						
All counties	10.9	13.0	10.8	12.6**[a]	11.1	13.8**[a]
Black Belt	14.7**	18.7**	14.4**[b]	18.1**[b]	16.5**[c]	21.2**[c]
Other	9.7**	11.4**	9.4**[b]	10.9**[b]	10.4**[c]	12.6**[c]
SAMPLE SIZE						
All counties	1,273	1,265	933	900	340	365
Black Belt	299	269	258	217	41	52
Other	974	996	675	683	299	313

Source: County and City Data Book (U.S.) Consolidated File: County Data, 1947–1977; County Statistics File 3: U.S.

Black Belt counties are defined as those with 33 percent or higher black population; those with less than 33 percent black population are "other." Rural counties are defined as those with less than 50.5 percent urban population; urban counties are defined as those with more than 50.5 percent urban population.

*p < 0.5
**p < 0.1 (one tail tests) BB/OTHER
[a]ttest RURAL/URBAN
[b]ttest BB RURAL/OTHER RURAL
[c]ttest BB URBAN/OTHER URBAN
[d]Figures under 1970 are for 1970–1980; those under 1980 are for 1980–1985.

poverty rates is the proportion of households headed by single women. Here urban and rural differences are relatively slight compared to the differences between Black Belt and white counties. The rates of households headed by women for Black Belt urban counties exceeded those of any category and reached a staggering 21 percent of all families. The increase from 1970 to 1980 in the proportion of households headed by women in Black Belt counties was more than double the increase in white counties. Despite the high absolute levels of households headed by single women in the Black Belt urban counties, the rate of increase in Black Belt rural counties was about the same as in Black Belt counties as a whole.

Some intraregional differences in demographic characteristics between Black Belt and white counties do exist. However, the major differences are those between the regional averages and the rural counties. The Black Belt counties have greater dependent populations—that is, more young people and those over 65 years of age—compared to regional averages. Local age structure is important because these segments of the population are the least productive and require the most social services. Furthermore, it is precisely these segments of the population that are growing the fastest, even though population growth as a whole is slowest in the Black Belt. The lower rates of population growth in the Black Belt reflect both the well-documented out-migration from the Black Belt (Fligstein, 1981; Marks, 1990) and the fact that the "Sun Belt boom" bypassed that region (Falk and Lyson, 1988).

The Social and Economic Status of the Black Belt

We argued above that the unique history of the Black Belt has meant that it has suffered the most from the pattern of uneven development in the South. The lagging economic conditions in the Black Belt are compounded by the "crisis in the rural South" (see Beaulieu, 1988). Although the rural South as a whole has not enjoyed much of the prosperity associated with the Sun Belt growth phenomenon, the rural Black Belt is doubly disadvantaged.

Education is one important indicator of economic conditions. The percentage of the adult population without a high school education indicates the extent to which people can take advantage of occupational opportunities as well as the extent to which industry may look favorably on relocating to a particular area. The proportion of adults with less than twelve years of education in all southern counties was 65 percent in 1970 and 50 percent in 1980 (see Appendix). The comparable figures for Black Belt rural counties were 71 percent in 1970 and 57 percent in 1980; for rural white counties, the figures were 68 percent and 53 percent, respectively. Urban counties had lower proportions of adults with less than twelve years of education, but again, Black Belt urban counties had lower levels of adult education than white urban counties. Moreover, the overall gap between the county regions had

Table 4.2. Socioeconomic Characteristics of Black Belt and Other Counties, Means for 1970 and 1980

Variables	All Counties		Rural Counties		Urban Counties	
	1970	1980	1970	1980	1970	1980
% < 12 YRS EDUCATION						
All counties	65.4	50.4	69.1**a	53.8**a	55.3**a	41.9**a
Black Belt	69.7**	54.8**	71.1**b	56.9**b	61.1**c	46.0**c
Other	64.0**	49.2**	68.3**b	52.8**b	54.5**c	41.2**c
MEDIAN FAMILY INCOME ($)						
All counties	6,435	15,403	5,977**a	14,538**a	7,694**a	17,535**a
Black Belt	5,707**	13,871**	5,542**b	13,467**b	6,744**c	15,558**c
Other	6,659**	15,816**	6,143**b	14,878**b	7,824**c	17,863**c
PER CAPITA INCOME ($)						
All counties	2,102	5,601	1,948**a	5,277**a	2,521**a	6,401**a
Black Belt	1,798**	4,875**	1,730**b	4,687**b	2,229**c	5,662**c
Other	2,194**	5,798**	2,032**b	5,465**b	2,561**c	6,523**c
% FAMILIES IN POVERTY						
All counties	23.6	15.8	25.9**a	17.1**a	17.4**a	12.8**a
Black Belt	31.2**	21.2**	32.3**b	21.9**b	24.7**c	18.2**c
Other	21.3**	14.4**	23.4**b	15.5**b	16.5**c	11.9**c
% UNEMPLOYMENT						
All counties	4.3	7.2	4.4**a	7.7**a	4.1**a	6.3**a
Black Belt	4.8**	7.9**	4.7**b	8.0*b	5.0**c	7.8**c
Other	4.1**	7.1**	4.2**b	7.5*b	3.9**c	6.0**c
SAMPLE SIZE						
All counties	1,273	1,265	933	900	340	365
Black Belt	299	269	258	217	41	52
Other	974	996	675	683	299	313

Source: County and City Data Book (U.S.) Consolidated File: County Data, 1947–1977; County Statistics File 3: U.S.

Black Belt counties are defined as those with 33 percent or higher black population; those with less than 33 percent black population are "other." Rural counties are defined as those with less than 50.5 percent urban population; urban counties are defined as those with more than 50.5 percent urban population.

*p < 0.5
**p < 0.1 (one tail tests) BB/OTHER
attest RURAL/URBAN
bttest BB RURAL/OTHER RURAL
cttest BB URBAN/OTHER URBAN

increased; Black Belt rates of adults with less than twelve years of education were 6 percent higher than other counties in 1970 and 11 percent higher in 1980.

The low educational level in rural Black Belt counties has attracted or encouraged industries that require the least amount of education in the work force (Dunbar, 1990). Thus, low levels of educational attainment and limited occupational opportunities are mutually reinforcing. A poorly educated labor force attracts low-wage industry, which, in turn, might both reduce the incentives for acquiring education and encourage well-educated residents to migrate.

Median family income for both 1970 and 1980 was significantly lower in the Black Belt than in other counties. In 1970, the median family income for residents of Black Belt counties was 86 percent that of white counties. Ten years later the median family income for residents in Black Belt counties was still only 87 percent that of white counties. This income gap persisted across the decade despite the fact that growth in the median family income was higher in Black Belt counties than in white counties—143 percent in the former, 137 percent in the latter. This pattern held for both rural and urban counties, although among rural counties the income gap was slightly less. Median family income in rural counties was lower than in urban counties for both years; Black Belt rural counties have consistently lower levels than rural white counties.

Another measure is per capita income. This measure also includes income from all sources, but it is not based on the statistical median, thus it provides an alternate picture of the distribution of income in a county. This is particularly important in counties with large dependency ratios (e.g., large proportions of the county population under 14 years of age and over 65 years of age) or with a small pool of employed persons, both things we know to be exaggerated in the Black Belt. Per capita income was significantly lower in Black Belt counties for all periods. Among rural counties, average per capita income in the Black Belt was 85 percent of the per capita income of white counties for 1970 and 1980 and 89 percent for 1984. Although urban counties as a whole had higher per capita incomes, the ratios of urban Black Belt per capita incomes to white per capita incomes were similar to the rural ratios for each year. The trend in per capita incomes between 1980 and 1984 suggests that the Black Belt county incomes are improving relative to white counties. However, rural Black Belt counties rank the lowest of all counties in per capita income (for more on this, see Rankin and Falk, 1991; Falk and Rankin, 1992).

To get a more accurate picture of the distributional characteristics of regional economic inequality we also look at the percentage of families in poverty. For both years and across all three county breakdowns the Black Belt had the largest proportion of families in poverty. In 1970 nearly one-third (31 percent) of all families in Black Belt counties were in poverty, and by 1980 one out of five (21 percent) families were poor.[2] This compares to a poverty rate for white Southern counties of 21 percent in 1970 and 14 percent in 1980. Although poverty rates have decreased across all counties, regional disparities have increased. Rural Black Belt poverty was 38 percent greater than rural white counties in 1970 and 41 percent greater in 1980. For urban counties, Black Belt poverty was 50 percent higher than in white counties in 1970 and 52 percent higher in 1980.

Poverty rates are largely a function of the supply and demand of employment in a local labor market. In the South, unemployment rates in the civilian labor force increased in all county categories from 1970 to 1985, in most cases more than doubling. Unemployment rates in Black Belt counties increased from 4.8 percent in 1970 to 10.3 percent in 1985; the figures for white counties were 4.1 and 8.5 percent for the same years. The comparison between rural and urban counties shows that rural Black Belt counties fared worst, followed by rural white, urban Black Belt, and white urban counties. Although regional differentials in unemployment rates declined during the 1970s (the difference between unemployment rates in the Black Belt and other counties dropped from 16 to 13 percent), by 1985 they had risen to levels even higher than those of 1970: Black Belt unemployment was 21 percent greater than the rate in other southern counties.

In summary, the Black Belt suffers from lower levels of education, lower income levels, more people in poverty, and greater unemployment than the rest of the South. Moreover, while there has been improvement in absolute terms on some of the measures (e.g., income, family poverty), in relative terms the economic gap between the Black Belt and the rest of the South has grown. One demographic factor which may reduce Black Belt family incomes, due to the well-known gender gap in earnings, is the greater incidence of households headed by single women in the Black Belt. In short, the unevenness that has characterized much of southern development may in fact be accelerating, leaving much of the Black Belt behind (see Falk and Lyson, 1988).

The Industrial Structure of the Black Belt

In the 1970s and 1980s, significant change occurred in the structure of employment in the Black Belt. (Our analysis of the composition of regional employment by industrial sector and occupation uses 1970 census categories. Since census data are used, statistics refer to employment composition by county of residence and not by county of employment.) The percentage of employment in the primary sector (i.e., agriculture, forestry, fishing, and mining) increased for all county types between 1970 and 1985, and for each period we find statistically significant differences between Black Belt counties and white counties (see Table 4.3). White urban counties have a greater percentage of their work force employed in the primary sector than either white rural counties or Black Belt rural counties. At first glance, we may be surprised at these findings, given the history of the Black Belt as the old plantation South. But several factors have contributed to a decline in the Black Belt agricultural labor force over time—the breakdown of tenancy and sharecropper systems, mechanization, and more recently, a farm crisis that has affected black farmers disproportionately. The number of black farm operators declined almost 94 percent between 1900 and 1978, whereas the number of white farm operators declined about 56 percent (U.S. Commission on Civil Rights, 1978).

Almost a quarter of all residents of the South worked in the manufacturing sector in 1970; the portion had decreased slightly by 1985. Throughout that period the level of employment in manufacturing in Black Belt counties was higher than the average for the South as a whole and had in fact grown during that period. Manufacturing employment was concentrated in the rural counties and was highest in the rural Black Belt counties; indeed, more rural Black Belt residents are employed in manufacturing than in any other single major industrial category. Does this mean that the Black Belt has enjoyed the fruits of the Sun Belt boom? Some writers have argued that the new manufacturing in the Black Belt is like the old—concentrated in the nondurable sector, where wages and skill requirements are low (Falk and Lyson, 1988). These peripheral industries, whose routine and labor-intensive production of goods is at the end of its product cycle (Thompson, 1965), are unlikely to contribute much to Black Belt development. Although our statistics do not break out nondurable manufacturing, we may find indirect evidence in regional occupational structures, which we discuss in the next section.

Service-sector employment, including finance, insurance, real estate, and the category of other services, increased from the third largest category of industrial employment in 1970 to the second largest, behind manufacturing employment, in 1980 and the first by 1985—a pattern that is consistent with national trends. Throughout the period finance, insurance, and real estate were about one-fourth of regional service employment. The Black Belt had less employment in the finance, insurance, and real estate sectors, which provide more skilled high-paying jobs and more in the sector of "other services," which offers less desirable employment (see Falk and Lyson, 1988)." Urban counties of all types have more service-sector workers than rural counties, although these differences were not significant after 1970. But we do find a significant difference between rural Black Belt and rural white counties.

Government-sector employment was consistently among the top three sectoral categories. Consistent with national trends, government employment declined for all counties in the South. Within the region the Black Belt had higher levels of government employment for 1980 and 1985 than the rural white counties, supporting the notion that local governments in areas with restricted labor markets become the employer of last resort and account for a larger proportion of the total active labor force. Furthermore, these areas are likely to have a greater demand on social services, thus requiring more workers in that sector.

The Occupational Structure of the Black Belt

Local occupational structures are a critical factor in the economic success of individuals and regions. If the Black Belt is a truly disadvantaged region, it should have fewer better-paying, highly skilled jobs and more low-wage, low-skill jobs. That is the basic pattern we found (see Table 4.4). In 1970 and 1980, the Black Belt had fewer high-level white-collar jobs (i.e., executive, administrative, and managerial) than white counties, especially in rural counties; Black Belt and white urban counties (with their more diverse economies) were more similar. With respect to sales workers, a diverse category that ranges from corporate sales representatives to store clerks, again the Black Belt had slightly smaller proportions of such workers than white counties did for both 1970 and 1980, especially among rural counties in the latter year.

The percentage of employment in farming, forestry, and fishing reveals statistically significant differences for rural and urban counties for both 1970 and 1980 but not for Black Belt counties. It is also evident that employment in service occupations, with the exception of private household services, favored rural white counties. As we might expect, private household service employment was concentrated in both urban and rural Black Belt counties for both time periods. However, the difference between Black Belt and white counties was statistically significant only for 1970. There are significant regional differences in rural employment in "other service" occupations (i.e., comprising mainly janitors, waiters, cooks, nursing aides, and hairdressers). Black Belt counties had fewer of these less-skilled service jobs than white counties in 1970, but the reverse was true in 1980.

The three categories of blue-collar workers (i.e., precision produc-

Table 4.3. Industrial Composition of Black Belt and Other Counties, Means for 1970, 1980, and 1985 (percentages)

Variables	All Counties			Rural Counties			Urban Counties		
	1970	1980	1985	1970	1980	1985	1970	1980	1985
AGRICULTURE									
All counties	3.5	4.5	4.4	3.4	4.2**[a]	4.0**[a]	4.1	5.3*[a]	5.4**[a]
Black Belt	2.1**	2.4**	2.6**	2.2**[b]	2.7**[b]	2.9**[b]	1.4**[c]	1.5**[c]	1.7**[c]
Other	4.0**	5.0**	4.8**	3.8**[b]	4.6**[b]	4.4**[b]	4.4**[c]	6.0**[c]	6.0**[c]
CONSTRUCTION									
All counties	5.7	6.5	6.5	5.7	6.4	6.5	5.9	6.7	6.7
Black Belt	4.3**	5.9	5.7**	4.2**[b]	5.8	5.7*[b]	5.3	6.5	5.7
Other	6.2**	6.6	6.8**	6.2**[b]	6.6	6.7*[b]	6.0	6.7	6.8
MANUFACTURING									
All counties	23.7	22.7	21.2	25.8**[a]	24.9**[a]	23.6**[a]	17.6**[a]	16.8**[a]	14.7**[a]
Black Belt	26.0**	25.9**	24.6**	26.9	27.5**[b]	26.3**[b]	19.4	19.2	17.5
Other	23.1**	21.9**	20.3**	25.3	24.1**[b]	22.7**[b]	17.4	16.3	14.3
TRANSPORTATION, COMMUNICATIONS, & PUBLIC UTILITIES									
All counties	4.1	4.2	4.3	3.8**[a]	3.9**[a]	4.1**[a]	5.2**[a]	5.1**[a]	4.7**[a]
Black Belt	3.4**	3.5**	3.7**	3.1**[b]	3.2**[b]	3.4**[b]	5.1	5.0	4.9
Other	4.4**	4.4**	4.4**	4.0**[b]	4.1**[b]	4.3**[b]	5.3	5.1	4.7
WHOLESALE & RETAIL TRADE									
All counties	19.3	19.4	19.7	18.7**[a]	18.8**[a]	19.0**[a]	21.0**[a]	21.2**[a]	21.8**[a]
Black Belt	17.6**	18.5**	18.8**	17.2**[b]	18.1**[b]	18.3	20.2	20.3	21.0
Other	19.8**	19.7**	20.0**	19.3**[b]	19.0**[b]	19.2	21.1	21.4	21.9
FINANCE, INSURANCE, & REAL ESTATE									
All counties	3.3	4.4	4.9	3.0**[a]	4.0**[a]	4.5**[a]	4.1**[a]	5.3**[a]	5.9**[a]
Black Belt	2.6**	3.6**	4.0**	2.4**[b]	3.2**[b]	3.6**[b]	4.2	5.2	5.7
Other	3.5**	4.6**	5.2**	3.2**[b]	4.3**[b]	4.8**[b]	4.1	5.3	6.0

	(1)	(2)	(3)	(4)	(5)	(6)	(7)	(8)	(9)
OTHER SERVICES									
All counties	18.5	17.2	19.1	18.2*a	16.7**a	18.4**a	19.2*a	18.7***a	20.9***a
Black Belt	21.6**	17.5	18.7	21.5**b	17.0	18.0	22.3**c	19.5	21.5
Other	17.5**	17.2	19.2	17.0**b	16.6	18.5	18.7***c	18.6	20.7
GOVERNMENT									
All counties	21.9	21.1	19.9	21.5	21.1	19.9	22.8	21.0	19.9
Black Belt	22.4	22.6**	21.9**	22.5	22.6**b	21.9**b	22.2	22.8	22.0
Other	21.7	20.7**	19.4**	21.2	20.7**b	19.4**b	22.9	20.6	19.6
SAMPLE SIZE									
All counties	1,234	1,234	1,234	926	905	905	308	329	329
Black Belt	289	261	261	251	212	212	38	49	49
Other	945	973	973	675	693	675	270	280	280

Source: U.S. Bureau of Labor Statistics, *Bureau of Economic Analysis Data File, 1990* (Washington, D.C.: Government Printing Office, 1990.

Black Belt counties are defined as those with 33 percent or higher black population; those with less than 33 percent black population are "other." Rural counties are defined as those with less than 50.5 percent urban population; urban counties are defined as those with more than 50.5 percent urban population.

*p < 0.5
**p < 0.1 (one tail tests) BB/OTHER
[a]ttest RURAL/URBAN
[b]ttest BB RURAL/OTHER RURAL
[c]ttest BB URBAN/OTHER URBAN

Table 4.4. Occupational Composition of Black Belt and Other Counties, Means for 1970 and 1980 (percentages)

	All Counties		Rural Counties		Urban Counties	
Variables	1970	1980	1970	1980	1970	1980
EXECUTIVE & MANAGERIAL						
All counties	7.6	7.3	7.1**a	6.6**a	8.8**a	9.0**a
Black Belt	7.1**	6.8**	6.9**b	6.4**b	8.5	8.7
Other	8.0**	7.5**	7.2**b	6.7**b	8.9	9.1
PROFESSIONAL & TECHNICAL						
All counties	10.2	11.4	9.1**a	10.4**a	13.3**a	13.9**a
Black Belt	9.6**	11.2	9.1	10.5	13.0	14.1
Other	10.4**	11.5	9.1	10.4	13.3	13.8
SALES						
All counties	5.3	8.4	4.6**a	7.7**a	7.0**a	10.1**a
Black Belt	4.8**	7.7**	4.5	7.1**b	6.8	9.8
Other	5.4**	8.6**	4.7	7.8**b	7.0	10.2
CLERICAL						
All counties	11.4	12.5	10.1**a	11.6**a	15.3**a	15.0*a
Black Belt	10.4**	11.9**	9.6**b	11.2**b	14.8	15.0
Other	11.8**	12.7**	10.2**b	11.7**b	15.3	15.0
FARMING, FORESTRY, & FISHING						
All counties	9.6	7.4	11.1**a	8.5**a	5.5**a	4.6**a
Black Belt	10.6	7.7	11.5	8.7	5.1	3.8
Other	9.3	7.3	10.9	8.5	5.6	4.7
PRIVATE HOUSEHOLD SERVICES						
All counties	3.0	1.0	3.1*a	1.0	2.8*a	1.0
Black Belt	5.1**	1.7**	5.1**b	1.8**b	4.9**c	1.5**c
Other	2.4**	.8**	2.3**b	.8**b	1.4**c	.9**c
OTHER SERVICES						
All counties	9.7	11.3	9.2**a	10.9**a	11.2**a	12.2**a
Black Belt	9.1**	11.7**	8.8**b	11.4**b	11.3	12.9
Other	9.9**	11.1**	9.4**b	10.7**b	11.1	12.1
PRECISION PRODUCTION, MACHINE OPERATORS, & CRAFT						
All counties	32.3	28.4	34.1**a	30.3**a	27.3**a	23.7**a
Black Belt	30.9**	28.3	31.6**b	29.4*b	26.1	23.5
Other	32.7**	28.5	35.1**b	30.6*b	27.4	23.7
TRANSPORTATION						
All counties	4.6	6.3	4.8**a	6.7**a	4.0**a	5.4**a
Black Belt	4.8**	6.2	4.9	6.4*b	4.1	5.1
Other	4.5**	6.4	4.7	6.8*b	4.0	5.4
LABORERS						
All counties	6.3	6.0	6.8**a	6.3**a	5.0**a	5.2**a
Black Belt	7.6**	6.9**	8.0**b	7.2**b	5.5	5.6
Other	5.9**	5.7**	6.4**b	6.0**b	5.0	5.1
SAMPLE SIZE						
All counties	1,263	1,265	924	900	339	365
Black Belt	299	269	257	217	42	52
Other	964	996	667	683	297	313

(Table 4.4. continued)

Source: Summary Tape File-4, U.S. Census, 1970; Summary Tape File-4, U.S. Census, 1980.

The 1980 Census Bureau occupational classification system differs from that of 1970, mainly in that several major categories were subdivided to create new ones. We recombined several 1980 categories to conform as closely as possible to the 1970 categories. Combining "professional speciality" and "technical and related support" occupations approximates the 1970 "professional, technical, and kindred" occupations; combining "protective service" and "other services" (not private household) occupations approximates the 1970 "service" occupations; and combining "precision production, craft, and repair" and "machine operators, assemblers, and inspectors" occupations approximates the 1970 "precision production, machine, and craft" occupations.

Black Belt counties are defined as those with 33 percent or higher black population; those with less than 33 percent black population are "other." Rural counties are defined as those with less than 50.5 percent urban population; urban counties are defined as those with more than 50.5 percent urban population.

*$p < 0.5$
**$p < 0.1$ (one tail tests) BB/OTHER
[a]ttest RURAL/URBAN
[b]ttest BB RURAL/OTHER RURAL
[c]ttest BB URBAN/OTHER URBAN

tion, machine operators, and craft; transport workers; and laborers) reveal two different trends. First, there were the statistically significant differences between rural and white counties. Second, the Black Belt had fewer skilled blue-collar jobs (i.e., precision production, machine operators, and craftsmen) than white counties. The difference was especially great between white and black among rural counties, although by 1980, the differences were small. Consistent with other research, a much larger proportion of the rural labor force was employed in blue-collar occupations, although there were substantial declines between 1970 and 1980 (Lyson, 1988).

The breakdown of data on rural and urban counties again shows the urban advantage. Urban areas have more labor market opportunities than rural areas. They have more white-collar and other service jobs and fewer blue-collar workers than rural counties. When they are compared with the Black Belt and white counties a more complicated pattern emerges. The picture is one of similarities between urban Black Belt and white counties, but dissimilarities between rural Black Belt and white counties. The 1980 data shows that Black Belt counties had more of the semiskilled jobs (i.e., machine operators, assemblers, and inspectors) and fewer of the skilled jobs (i.e., precision production and craft). The Black Belt also had more lower-paying, less-skilled occupations, for example, in service/private household jobs, transport operators, and laborers. The differences in occupational employment were due mainly to differences between the rural Black Belt and white counties. Again, rural Black Belt counties fared the worst of all southern counties and are characterized by an occupational structure that is tilted toward less desirable jobs.

"Successful" Black Belt Counties

Even within the Black Belt there is intraregional variation. "Success stories" within the Black Belt approached the level of development found in the white, urban South. What characteristics set them apart? We identified as successful forty-three counties that had either education completion rates (for high school or college) or median incomes of greater than one standard deviation above the mean or poverty rates of one standard deviation below the mean for all Black Belt counties. Out of these counties nearly half (eighteen) were adjacent to large metropolitan areas.[3] Another eight (all education outliers [having above average levels of education]) had institutions of higher education within their boundaries. One education outlier county is also the site of a military base (Fort Stewart near Savannah, Georgia). One higher-income county was in a resort area (Camden County on the coast of Georgia). In the rest of the outlier counties we could not definitely identify the causes of success.

As the above suggests, the characteristics of Black Belt successes are varied and unlikely to help in formulating a single plan to improve conditions throughout the Black Belt. Metropolitan proximity has advantages for a variety of reasons (e.g., better jobs, education, social services), but counties have no control over this factor. Likewise, it will not be possible to establish universities, military bases, or resort areas in most Black Belt counties. Thus, our "stars" provide little insight into what an appropriate policy for economic development in the Black Belt would look like.

Summary and Conclusions

Although the world economy has changed drastically in the past decade, and the United States has moved from being the world's largest creditor to its largest debtor, rare is the person (or country) who thinks of the United States as "less developed." By most measures, ours is an advanced capitalist economy with the kinds of technology and social relations found in such places. But, what is less known about the

United States is that as advanced as the economy and its accompanying socioeconomic characteristics may be in some places, it may be quite underdeveloped in other places.

Rural areas in general are poor when compared to urban areas (Singelmann and Deseran, 1992). This is true for the South, but more important, urban-rural disparities there have overshadowed the high levels of regional inequality. It is these very qualities that led Hoppe (1985) to refer to much of the rural South as "persistently poor." The evidence of this uneven development in the American South is the continuing gap between the Black Belt and white counties. Those living in the Black Belt are more likely to have less education and lower incomes and to suffer from poverty and unemployment. Moreover, the economic gap between the Black Belt and white counties does not appear to be closing; indeed, differences in median and per capita incomes, poverty, and unemployment rates are increasing.

Black Belt workers are concentrated in more peripheral industries in the manufacturing and service sector. Occupationally, this area employs fewer higher-level white-collar and skilled blue-collar workers and more lower-level white-collar and semiskilled and unskilled workers. These structural characteristics help explain demographic patterns in the South. The slow population growth and the small relative size of the working-age population in the Black Belt indicates that this is a region much less attractive to live in or to move to than other parts of the South. We cannot overemphasize that, because of the crosscutting inequalities of residence and region, the *rural* Black Belt is doubly disadvantaged. It is no wonder this place is best known for its long history of out-migration in search of better opportunities. Furthermore, among the few educationally and economically "successful" Black Belt counties that we identified, most have qualities that are not readily transferable to other parts of the region.

But ties to the land and to place are hard to break. Recent journalistic accounts of the Black Belt (see Dunbar, 1990; Lemann, 1990) demonstrate this, even for black residents who have lived their lives under trying circumstances. "The land of cotton" may have been a place of terrible oppression for black workers, but it was also the place where their families were born, reared, and died; this was the place where generations of black folk had their "roots" in the United States. For those who have stayed behind, these personal reasons may be compounded by the very social and economic conditions we have discussed. Those with lower levels of "human capital" (e.g., education, experience, skills) and fewer resources necessary to relocate are less likely either to migrate or to benefit substantially from doing so.

Ultimately, the question must be asked: Should population policy be determined by the market, while the government stands aside and allows certain areas to decline slowly, and the best and brightest migrate out, leaving behind the less fortunate? We believe that a consideration of the South's history of not-so-benign neglect of this area warrants the answer no. But even if the answer is yes, there must be some consideration of the needs of those unable or unwilling to migrate.

Rural areas in general—and we would stipulate the Black Belt in particular—need special attention from the federal government if they are to have any chance for economic success in the future. Local governments and states cannot compete across jurisdictional boundaries without running the risk of promising more than they can reasonably deliver when recruiting new industries. Incentives offered today, such as free land and tax abatements, have costs that will be born by generations to come. What may be needed is an "affirmative action" program for rural America (Falk and Lyson, 1991). Just as some school districts were found to have perpetuated dual and discriminatory educational schemes, so, too, is this true for the policies aimed at developing urban and rural areas. The federal government tried to develop an urban policy, but no such attempt was made for rural America. This means that places like the Black Belt remain "forgotten," unlikely to get much attention in any programmatic way.

To halt the continual erosion of the area's population and economy some mix of public and private initiatives is necessary. Investment in public education is vital. Investment in public health must ensure that *all* local residents have reasonable access to health care. Investment in decaying infrastructure must enable these areas to compete for jobs and industries. Investment in business must develop creative ways to encourage and finance local entrepreneurial activity and to help diversify rural economies. Finally, as in nearly all highly industrialized countries around the world, investment is needed in programs to encourage population dispersion, not concentration. At heart, this last prescription is an economic one predicated on the notion that population distribution is a national rather than a local problem, and it must be addressed as such. Otherwise, population dynamics get reduced to one more aspect of the marketplace to be played out with their own human ebb and flow and with little attempt at planning. We believe that this battle to develop the Black Belt and other rural areas must be fought on multiple fronts. To invest in education, for example, without improving the quality of jobs, would only increase out-migration.

Unfortunately the current period does not bode well for improving conditions in the Black Belt. The prospects for extensive government intervention are not good, given both the shrinking pool of public resources at all levels of government and the lack of political will at the federal level. At a time when state and local governments are least able to deal with them, national problems are being redefined as state and local ones. Thus, help is unlikely to come from the federal government, and state and local governments will be limited by tight budgets. This means that, in the short term, public initiatives may not be enough to induce the cooperation of private interests, who will look elsewhere to invest. The relative attractiveness of investing in the Black Belt is also affected by the new international mobility of capital. Industry that once came to such areas for the low-wage and non-unionized work force has subsequently moved on to Third World locations that even the Black Belt can't compete with (Portes and Walton, 1981).

No part of the United States has been more forgotten or overlooked than the Black Belt. It is a region like no other—here African Americans first were enslaved, were later freed, and remain in large numbers to this day; here political oppression was a way of life for blacks, a historical fact of life that is still slow to change; where poverty in nearly all aspects of life is still normal for many people. Lacking substantial public and private efforts to improve Black Belt conditions, the region seems destined slowly to stagnate and decline. If this happens, it will be a tragedy for which we will all bear responsibility.

Notes

1. Since the data sources did not identify urban and rural counties, we defined counties that had less than 50 percent urban population as rural and 50 percent or more as urban.
2. "Poor" here is based on the census definition.
3. The following counties fit our criteria of significant outliers among Black Belt counties. Their outlier type (I = income, E = education) and assumed advantage (e.g., metropolitan proximity or university location) is also indicated.

County	Type	"Advantage"
Jefferson, Ala.	E,I	Birmingham
Macon, Ala.	E	Tuskegee Institute
Montgomery, Ala.	E,I	Montgomery
Bibbs, Ga.	I	Macon
Bulloch, Ga.	E	Georgia State College
Camden, Ga.	I	Coastal resort (?)
Chatham, Ga.	E,I	Savannah

County	Type	"Advantage"
Dougherty, Ga.	E	Albany State College
Fulton, Ga.	E,I	Atlanta
Liberty, Ga.	E	Fort Stewart Army Base
Richmond, Ga.	E	Augusta
Caddo, La.	E	Shreveport
Lincoln, La.	E	Grambling State University, Louisiana Tech University
Natchitoches, La.	E	Northwest State University of Louisiana
Orleans, La.	E	New Orleans
St. James, La.	I	Baton Rouge, New Orleans
St. John Bpt, La.	I	"
W. Baton Rouge, La.	I	"
Claiborne, Miss.	E	Alcorn State University
Hinds, Miss.	E,I	Jackson
Madison, Miss.	E	Jackson
Oktibbeha, Miss.	E	Mississippi State University
Durham, N.C.	E,I	Durham
Pitt, N.C.	E	East Carolina University
Charleston, S.C.	E	Charleston
Richland, S.C.	E	Columbia
Shelby, Tenn.	E,I	Memphis
King William, Va.	I	Washington, D.C.

References

Beaulieu, Lionel J. (ed). 1988. *The Rural South in Crisis: Challenges for the Future.* Boulder, Colo.: Westview Press.

Billings, Dwight. 1988. "The Rural South in Crisis: A Historical Perspective." Pp. 13–29 in Lionel J. Beaulieu (ed.), *The Rural South in Crisis: Challenges for the Future.* Boulder, Colo.: Westview Press.

Bureau of Labor Statistics. 1990. *Bureau of Economic Analysis Data File, 1990.* Washington, D.C.: Government Printing Office.

Choate, Pat, and Susan Walter. 1984. *America in Ruins: The Decaying Infrastructure.* Washington, D.C.: TRW, Inc.

Cobb, J. 1984. *Industrialization and Southern Society, 1877–1984.* Lexington: University of Kentucky Press.

Colclough, Glenna. 1988. "Uneven Development and Racial Composition in the Deep South." *Rural Sociology* 53(1):73–86.

Dunbar, Anthony P. 1990. *Delta Time: A Journey through Mississippi.* New York: Pantheon Books.

DuBois, W. E. B. 1899. "The Negro in the Black Belt: Some Social Sketches." *U.S. Department of Labor Bulletin,* no. 22 (May).

Elgie, Robert A. 1980. "Industrialization and Racial Inequality within the American South." *Social Science Quarterly* 61(3 and 4):459–72.

Falk, William W., and Thomas A. Lyson. 1988. *High Tech, Low Tech, No Tech: Recent Industrial and Occupational Change in the South.* Albany: State University of New York Press.

Falk, William W., and Bruce Rankin. 1992. "The Cost of Being Black in the Black Belt." *Social Problems* 39:299–313.

Fligstein, Neil. 1981. *Going North: Migration of Blacks and Whites from the South, 1900–1950.* New York: Academic Press.

Hoppe, Robert A. 1985. "Economic Structure and Change in Persistently Low-Income Nonmetro Counties." Economic Research Service, Report no. 50, Washington, D.C.: U.S. Department of Agriculture.

Johnson, Charles Spurgeon. 1941. *Growing Up in the Black Belt: Negro Youth in the Rural South.* New York: Schocken Books.

Johnson, Daniel M., and Rex R. Campbell. 1981. *Black Migration in America: A Social Demographic History.* Durham, N.C.: Duke University Press.

Lemann, Nicholas. 1991. *The Promised Land: The Great Black Migration and How It Changed America.* New York: Random House.

Lyson, Thomas A. 1989. *Two Sides to the Sunbelt: The Growing Divergence between the Rural and Urban South.* New York: Praeger.

Marks, Carole. 1989. *Farewell, We're Good and Gone: The Great Black Migration.* Bloomington: Indiana University Press.

Markusen, Ann R. 1987. *Regions: The Economics and Politics of Territory.* London: Rowman and Littlefield.

Odum, Howard W. 1936. *Southern Regions of the United States.* Chapel Hill: University of North Carolina Press.

Portes, Alejandro, and John Walton. 1981. *Labor, Class, and the International System.* New York: Academic Press.

President's National Advisory Commission on Rural Poverty. 1967. *The People Left Behind.* Washington, D.C.: Government Printing Office.

Rankin, Bruce H., and William W. Falk. 1991. "Race, Region, and Earnings: Blacks and Whites in the South." *Rural Sociology* 56(2):224–37.

Singelmann, Joachim, and Forrest Deseran. 1992. *Inequality in Labor Market Areas.* Boulder, Colo.: Westview Press.

Thompson, Walter R. 1965. *A Preface to Urban Economics.* Baltimore: Johns Hopkins University Press.

Till, Thomas E. 1986. "The Share of Southeastern Black Counties in the Southern Rural Renaissance." *Growth and Change* 17:44–55.

U.S. Commission on Civil Rights (USCCR). 1982. *The Decline of Black Farming in America.* Washington, D.C.: Government Printing Office.

U.S. Department of Commerce. Bureau of the Census. 1988. *County and City Data Book (U.S.) Consolidated File: County Data, 1947–1977.* Washington, D.C.: Government Printing Office.

———. 1988. *County Statistics File 3: U.S.* Washington, D.C.: Government Printing Office.

Vance, Rupert B. 1932. *Human Geography in the South.* Chapel Hill: University of North Carolina Press.

5 | The Mississippi Delta: Change or Continued Trouble

Stanley Hyland and Michael Timberlake

My mother told me before I left the door
Lord, my mother told me before I left the door
You gonna have trouble, son, everywhere you go.
Well you talk about trouble, I've had it all my days . . .
Seems like trouble gonna carry me to the grave.

Lord, I wonder what's the matter; there's something going on wrong . . .
—Trouble: I've Had It All My Days, *as sung by Mississippi John Hurt*

THE PUBLIC IMAGE of the Mississippi Delta region of the southern United States is akin to that of a typical Third World country—one of many people experiencing serious personal troubles, living in a historically troubled area with persistently high rates of poverty, slow economic growth, poor standards of health, and political and cultural backwardness (Farney, 1989). As usual, reality is more complex than popular perception.

The Delta is full of contradictions. For example, the Lower Mississippi Delta culture is rich and influential. Roots of blues, jazz, and rock 'n' roll music are found in the Delta.[1] Yet to many of the region's citizens this music remains, in some respects, less accessible than to people in most other parts of the country. Similarly, some of the nation's most widely acclaimed writers—William Faulkner, Eudora Welty, William Wright, Maya Angelou, Anne Moody, Peter Taylor, Shelby Foote—are from the region yet the region has historically been home to a higher percentage of functionally illiterate people than any other comparably large region in the United States. Like the rest of the South it is also regarded as being politically and socially separate, resistant to progressive social change affecting the rest of the country, and therefore rather untypical of "real" America. At the same time, the high rate of southern participation in the armed services and the patriotic fervor that seems embedded in southern fundamentalism create an image of ultra-Americanism. Finally, the Delta seems remote and unconnected with mainstream American economic life, but in fact the conditions that characterize the region have been etched in large part by very real and specific cultural, political, and economic relationships with the rest of the country and the world.

The Delta is to the United States as poor countries of the Third World are to the industrialized countries of Western Europe, North America, and Japan. In either case we have the poor compared to the affluent. We therefore find it heuristically useful to borrow some of the concepts used in the new international political economy scholarship on macrolevel social change (see Evans and Stephens, 1988). Implicit in our discussion are four themes borrowed from this broad perspective. First, the Mississippi Delta region is viewed as an "underdeveloped" region, and "underdevelopment" is understood as a product of systemic factors as well as historically contingent factors, both of which must be seen in terms of the global system of competitive capitalism in which the region is embedded. The region is an integral geographic part of this system, but in the language of "world-system theory" (see Chase-Dunn, 1989), it is integrated as a "periphery" within the "core." Second, a great deal of attention must be paid to the social groupings whose identities, actions, and relations have been formed within a rigid system of race, ethnic, class, and gender stratification. For example, the role of race and class relations in determining access to educational and political resources in the region has been fundamental. Third, the role of the state at all levels must be understood in relation to stratification and the logic of (peripheral) capitalism. Finally, the importance of culture and ideology to social, economic, and political relations in the Delta cannot be ignored.[2] In this chapter we try to make sense of these contradictions.

Underdevelopment: A Historical Overview

Inhabited as long ago as 10,000 B.C. by hunting and gathering Native Americans, the Lower Mississippi Delta region was continuously occupied through European contact (Morse and Morse, 1983). Beginning approximately 1000 A.D. the region saw the domestication of plants, intensive agriculture, and the development of the most complex cultural system in North America (Dye and Cox, 1990). DeSoto's expedition through this region in 1541 introduced smallpox, measles, and warfare and subsequently caused displacement and migration (Dye, 1989).[3] Since the beginning of European and African settlement, the history of the Lower Mississippi Delta has been shaped by its role as an agricultural producer and supplier of surplus population to other regions of the country. Although subject to frequent flooding, the low-lying valley is home to exceptionally fertile soil (Clay et al., 1989). The major population centers, built on the bluff hills above the floodplain, developed to export the natural resources and agricultural products out of the region to commercial and manufacturing centers in the North and abroad. These bluff cities include Memphis, Vicksburg, Natchez, and Baton Rouge. New Orleans, at the mouth of the Mississippi with a population of 1.3 million, is the largest city in the region, but it exists principally as a world port city with an identity quite separate from that of the agricultural world of the Delta.

Except for the bluff hills, the Lower Mississippi Delta Valley is a series of five major backswamps or basins (St. Francis, Black River, Yazoo, Tensas, and Atchafalaya).[4] Since over 80 percent of the valley is estimated to be wetlands and swamps (Smith, 1990), considerable human effort has long been directed at channeling the Mississippi River and its tributaries and draining the swamps. As soon as flood control projects appeared in the late 1800s, human agricultural settlements spread. Similarly, populations of the bluff cities quadrupled in size within a decade of draining their bayous and building sanitation systems (in the 1890s and 1900s) in efforts to control diseases such as yellow fever (Brownell and Goldfield, 1977). As Dunbar (1990) points out, Mississippi land owners have depended since this time on the federal government's help in designing and implementing these and other flood control and water channeling projects in the region.[5]

The political geography of the region did not follow its natural ecology. The westwardly expanding state of Kentucky, Tennessee, and most of Mississippi used the Mississippi River as their western boundary, with Arkansas and most of Louisiana lying across the river. It is the areas relatively near the river in these states that comprise the heart of the "Delta" region. Despite the firm belief held by most of us with ties to Memphis that the Delta begins in the lobby of the Peabody Hotel, other definitions expand the region northward to include the "Bootheel" counties in Missouri, and some encompass the southernmost counties of Illinois as well. Whereas Memphis became recognized as the cultural and commercial hub of this region, the Delta as a whole suffered neglect as a result of its political fragmentation into seven federal states, in none of which Delta residents constituted a majority. Ever since President Lincoln's strategy to conquer the South by controlling the Mississippi River, federal agencies have continued to artificially divide the region, often imposing contradictory policies on either side of the Mississippi River (Lower Mississippi Delta Development Commission [LMDDC], 1990). By default, the effective ruling units increasingly became the large agricultural plantations or county governments (Pearsall, 1966; Cobb, 1984).

In the absence of adequate rail and highway systems interlinking various parts of the Delta, the plantations and county governments became isolated political and extended-family units. Seen as irrelevant to—even at odds with—the needs of an agricultural work force, local educational systems remained underdeveloped, receiving little public revenue (Dyer, 1989). The wealthy typically sent their sons (and occasionally their daughters) outside the region for whatever higher education they received. The legacy of slavery further accentuated educational backwardness. At the turn of the century, music and trade along the Mississippi River were the only unifying factors in this growing but isolated rural region.

The tradition of relatively strong and exclusive local government in the region can be seen as a concomitant of the process of class formation under peripheral capitalism. As in underdeveloped, dependent, agricultural countries in the Third World, a political and economic elite emerged in the South whose interests were vested in maximizing the profitability of export agriculture. In the Delta, this has overwhelmingly meant cotton, which has historically been exported out of the region for all but the most basic processing. Of course the wealth and power of the planter class relied for many decades on the reproduction of a large, economically weak, and politically compliant class of agricultural workers. Although the brutal system of chattel slavery was put to end with the Civil War, an almost equally effective, though somewhat more subtle, system of oppression quickly evolved to assure that "compliance" was maintained. Had freed slaves really been given their "forty acres and a mule," it is possible that by combining subsistence agriculture with market production and wage labor they could have escaped their subsequent fate. However, the Jim Crow South provided a potent system for keeping African Americans politically and economically oppressed and socially separate (see Woodward, 1971). Coupled with effective elite opposition to industrial development in the Delta, this system assured the planters that there would be continued access to cheap labor for chopping cotton in the spring and harvesting in the fall.

Migration provided one of the few outlets available to this surplus population. With mechanization of farming and the depletion of the hardwood forests in the 1920s and 1930s, thousands of poor sharecroppers and tenant farmers were forced off the agricultural land in the Lower Delta. Although some ended up in the region's bluff cities, many more continued northward to cities such as St. Louis, Chicago, and Kansas City (see Lemann, 1991). In spite of the extreme poverty in the Delta, the federal response to southern poverty in the 1920s and 1930s focused principally on the Appalachian region through the creation of the Tennessee Valley Authority. Because of political indifference and the independence of plantation owners, the Lower Mississippi Delta remained largely ignored and undeveloped. This underdevelopment continues to be reproduced, and its effects are reflected in the dismal conditions now faced by many of the region's citizens.

Current Conditions

The Demographics of Underdevelopment

The Lower Mississippi Delta Development Commission (LMDDC) recently compiled data on economic and social conditions for the Delta (1989a, 1989b, 1990).[6] Although its definition of the Delta includes many counties we consider outside the region,[7] particularly counties in the eastern hills of the Ozarks in Missouri and Arkansas as well as in the hills of southern Illinois that are different in terms of geography and history and tend to be better off in terms of average standards of living— these figures illustrate the extent to which the region is disadvantaged. Since at least 1970 per capita income has been 20 to 25 percent lower in the Delta than in the nation as a whole. In 1988 per capita income in the Delta was $10,192 compared to $13,577 in the United States. Average income figures for the region mask exceptionally low levels in many counties in the heart of the Delta. In 1986, the poorest twenty-five counties in the region had average incomes of between $6,287 (Lee, Arkansas) and $7,449 (Caliborne, Mississippi).

Of course low income translates into high rates of poverty. In the Delta, the 1980 individual poverty rate was 21 percent and 16 percent of all families in the Delta were living in poverty. This compares with a national family poverty rate of less than 10 percent. Even other historically poor regions of the country are less impoverished than the Delta. For example, the Appalachian Regional Commission's target counties had a family poverty rate of 13.7 percent in 1980. African Americans and women are particularly disadvantaged in the Delta. The poverty rate for Delta blacks in 1980 was nearly 42 percent, compared to 30 percent nationwide, and the rate of poverty for households headed by females is 42 percent in the Delta compared to 30 percent in the United States. We know also that the poverty rate among black children across the entire South is appallingly high. In 1986 57 percent of African American children in the rural South were living in poverty, and among those living in single-parent households, 78 percent were in poverty (O'Hare, 1988). Because it is the poorest area of the South, we can be certain that these figures do not exaggerate the extent of child poverty in the Delta.

Poverty in the region is linked to the high rates of unemployment characteristic of Delta counties. The 1988 unemployment rate in the region (8.87 percent) was 61 percent higher than the U.S. rate (5.5 percent), and in Mississippi and Louisiana unemployment was more than double the national rate. In fact in several Mississippi counties more than one in five workers were unemployed in the first quarter of 1989. Even when workers have jobs, they and their families are not guaranteed escape from poverty. As in rural regions everywhere, wages tend to be lower than in metropolitan areas, and therefore, the poor are more likely to be working. O'Hare points out that "62 percent of poor rural adults . . . held a job at least part of the year" in 1986. Moreover, "In 1986, 72 percent of the children of young rural families in poverty lived in families where at least one adult was working, compared to only 59 percent of the poor children in urban areas" (1988:11).

In addition to the Delta Commission statistics, a 1985 U.S. Department of Agriculture (USDA) report (Bender et al., 1985) identified a series of rural counties that have persistent poverty (tracked since 1950). Twenty-seven percent (57 of 214 counties) of the nonmetropolitan Delta counties have been labeled "persistent poverty counties." This represents 24 percent of the nonmetropolitan persistently poor counties in the U.S. According to the USDA report these persistent poverty counties tend to have low income levels that have persisted for decades and disproportionate numbers of people with disadvantages affecting their participation in the productive labor force. Subsistence in these counties appears to be closely tied to federal transfer payments.

Many local business leaders in the Delta point to the need to improve education levels in the region to attract industries that pay relatively high wages (Timberlake et al., 1989). Whether or not this implied human-capital approach to economic development would help, it is clear that educational standards in the Delta are far below the national average. The average county high school dropout rate in 1980 for the region was 26 percent, compared to 21 percent for the United States, and the average percentage of adult populations of Delta counties with high school education was 56 percent, in comparison to a U.S. average of 65 percent. Yet in the poorest Delta counties and parishes the situation is worse. It is common for counties to have dropout rates in excess of 30 percent and high school graduation rates of less than 50 percent in Mississippi and Louisiana. In fact, Mississippi's Delta counties average a 28 percent dropout rate and a 53 percent high school graduation rate.

Overall funding for public schools is substantially less in the Delta than elsewhere in the country, largely because the contributions of local districts to education costs are so low. In Mississippi's Delta counties, the average per pupil public education expenditure was only $1,784 in 1982 compared to $2,700 in the United States. Low levels of local financing for public education explain much of this difference. On average across all counties in the country, 9.3 percent of educational expenditures come from the federal government and 43 percent from local government, with state governments supplying the rest. In Mississippi 24 percent of the public education budget is federally supported, with local communities supplying only 19 percent (see Figure 5.1). This lack of local support for public education must be understood not only in terms of the poverty and subsequent weak tax base of Delta counties, but also in terms of race relations. Rural areas in the Delta experienced the same response to school desegregation that urban school districts faced across the country—white flight. In the case of many Delta communities private, predominantly white "academies" sprang up in even the smallest counties. At the same time support for public education expenditures declined among whites. As Dunbar (1990:178) points out, "What school desegregation in the 1960s and 1970s meant throughout virtually all of the Delta was that the white children were pulled out of the public system and enrolled in hastily organized private academies. The public schools became virtually all black overnight. That picture has changed gradually in some communities, but not much at all in others."

Not surprisingly, residents of the Delta region are also disadvantaged in terms of health and housing. One standard measure of adequate health care is the infant mortality rate, which reflects not only access to health care, but also nutrition (via mothers' prenatal nutrition). Measured in terms of deaths of children under one year old per 1000 live births in 1984, the overall infant mortality rate in the United States was 10.7. Although the U.S. rate is high in comparison to other industrialized countries (e.g., France, Spain, the United Kingdom, Japan, Australia, and Canada all had rates between 6 and 10 per 1000), it is worse in the Delta with a rate of 12.7 per 1000. Once again, however, in the heart of the historic Delta the rates are much higher. Fifteen counties and parishes in Mississippi, Louisiana, and the "Bootheel" of Missouri had infant mortality rates averaging over 20 per 1000 for

Figure 5.1. Per Pupil Spending for Education

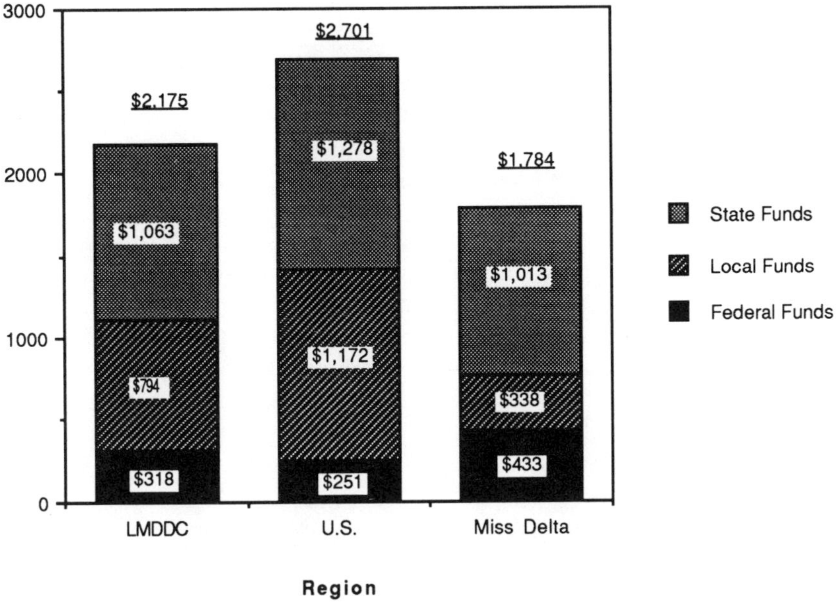

1980–84. Low birth weight is a major contributing factor to the high rates. Babies weighing less than 5.5 pounds are about forty times more likely to die than others, and in Mississippi the low weight rate is higher than anywhere else in the country (*Los Angeles Times*, 1990). The LMDDC points out that these rates are higher than those found in French Guiana, Chile, and Malaysia for the same time period (LMDDC, 1989a:XXIX). The high rate of pregnancy among unmarried teens is usually mentioned in connection with the high rate of infant mortality found in the Delta (e.g., *Los Angeles Times*, 1990).

The availability of health care practitioners is also severely restricted in the Delta. On average, there are only 5.2 physicians and registered nurses per 1000 Delta residents. In comparison the U.S. rate is 8.5. Away from the metropolitan areas, access is even more limited, with an average of fewer than 3.5 practitioners per 1000 people. In 1989, three clinics were forced to close in one Mississippi county in the Delta because there was no money for seven of the fifteen nurse positions in the county health department (*Los Angeles Times*, 1990; see also Hawkins and Hyland, 1990). In 1990 Lake County, Tennessee, with a population of about 7500, had only one physician who divided her time between clinics in the two incorporated towns in the county—

Tiptonville and Ripley. She testified at LMDDC hearings that "should an emergency such as cardiac arrest (or) multiple trauma occur, the chances of survival in Lake County are approximately zero" (quoted in LMDDC, 1989a:13). In a separate interview she told us that most of the health care needs coming to her attention are directly or indirectly attributable to the high level of poverty in the county: illness related to poor nutrition and unsanitary living conditions, and work-related injuries common in the kinds of low-wage jobs that are most readily available.

Lack of access to transportation exacerbates many of the problems faced by the Delta's poor, including access to health care. As in most rural areas in the country, public transportation is nonexistent. Significant numbers of the rural poor live many miles from the nearest doctor or clinic. In Coahoma County, Mississippi, for example, poor residents of Jonestown must travel twelve miles to Clarksdale to obtain health care or even to purchase groceries. The many that do not have cars must rely on the good will of neighbors or the entrepreurial spirit of those who are slightly better-off. The going rate for a round-trip ride to Clarksdale from Jonestown is $10. For a single mother on welfare receiving $140 per month in Aid-to-Families-with-Dependent-Children (AFDC) payments the decision to use this informal service is carefully weighed—and infrequently made. Dr. Donald Ellis, a Clarksdale obstetrician concerned about the frequency with which his poor patients miss appointments, found that four out of five miss because they lacked transportation (*Los Angeles Times,* 1990).

Poor housing conditions also characterize life in the Delta. About one-third of all housing units were rated substandard in the 1980 Census of Housing and Population. The rate for the country as a whole is also shamefully high at about 17 percent, but that is only about half the rate in the Delta. Moreover, the LMDDC estimates that "the real figure for substandard housing is much higher [than 33 percent], given that dilapidated structures and overcrowding were not factored into this percentage" (1989:19). It is common to find families living in seriously dilapidated structures in which some rooms are unheated, broken windows are covered with plastic, and rain is kept at bay by a quilt of makeshift materials, obviously added incrementally until the entire roof is virtually covered with everything but conventional roofing material.

The dismal conditions in which so many of the Delta's people live are part of its heritage as a historically underdeveloped, internal periphery. For most of its history, agriculture has been the most important economic sector. Just two or three crops dominate (cotton, soy beans, and rice), and they are, for the most part, exported out of the region after having gone through only the most basic processing (e.g., ginning). The rural economic sector is not integrated to urban markets, although half of all Delta residents are rural. Urban markets in the region rely on finished goods imported from outside the region, whereas unrefined products are exported out of the region. This vertical division of labor, with the Delta as exporter of unfinished goods and importer of processed goods, is another way in which the Delta is like a dependent Third World country. The Delta region has little venture capital, almost no centers of industrial or financial management and control, and a small tax base, largely because its links to export agriculture, poverty, and low levels of human capital have been institutionalized in the region's class structure, its pattern of race relations, its political system, and its culture. This institutionalization of dependency has emerged in the context of a geographic division of labor that subordinates the region to financial and management centers elsewhere in the country and, increasingly, elsewhere in the world (e.g., Tokyo).

The Ideology of Underdevelopment

The legacy of the region's long history of structural dependency, with planter and elite political dominance, has shaped the culture of the Delta and the character of its people. The Mississippi Special Task Force for Economic Development Planning described this condition as "The Legacies of Dependency." "For generations, Mississippi has been a paternalistic society—timber companies, railroads, plantation owners, ·plant owners, the government—handed out the 'goodies' in the form of jobs, land, money . . . This legacy—and the fear of change that accompanies it—is insidious and persistent. It dominates our thinking about economic development" (1989:9).

Closely intertwined in this legacy of dependency is a complex set of regional beliefs that have been described by some scholars as ruralism (Goldfield, 1981; Biles, 1986) and others as fractionalism, fatalism, and individualism or personalism (e.g., Cash, 1941; Ciaramitaro et al., 1988). Ciaramitaro and her colleagues, in their study of a rural Delta county, note that fractionalism is a dominant feature of the organizational structure and interpersonal interaction patterns in the Delta. It occurs in several forms: between long-term (generational) residents and outsiders (e.g., northerners), between the residents of different towns, between specific interest groups including kin, but mostly between African Americans and European Americans. Acceptance is usually based on appeals to genealogy, ethnicity, and geographic identification.

Fatalism is also a dominant characteristic of interpersonal relations. Partially conditioned by historical religious beliefs, many perceive their own destiny as controlled by forces larger than themselves. The trust that residents put in government or a benign boss to take care of them often leads to a lack of risk taking and a lack of personal and institutional accountability in the educational and business worlds (e.g., "What difference does it make since it will all turn out the same?"). Of course this fatalism may be as much an accurate assessment of risk as it is a product of a unique regional culture. (See Duncan and Tickamyer [1988] and Tomaskovic-Devey [1987] for discussions of the role of culture-of-poverty theories in research on rural poverty.)

Likewise, a strong sense of individualism or personalism permeates not only social relations but also the individual's perception of institutions. Rather than demand greater accountability from their public and private institutions, residents of the Delta have come to expect great leaders to be personally accountable for their clients' security. The members of political machines in the cities as well as in the small towns continue to reinforce the perception that they will personally provide for the individual's needs if it is within their power. The resulting failure to produce change is then attributed to fractionalism or fatalism, and the legacy of dependency is continued.

Federal and State Initiatives

Solving the problem of underdevelopment and poverty in the Delta has been seen as involving issues of economic growth and social welfare expenditures. The success of federal initiatives in the Delta has always been limited by local elite resistance and shaped by the historic nature of class and race or ethnic relations. Much of the scholarship on the implementation of New Deal programs in the region is limited to urban areas or generalizes to the South as whole. Nevertheless, it is suggestive of how these programs have been received in the rural Delta. Smith indicates that the "new public assistance network" that emerged during the New Deal paved the way for a small change of attitudes in the region away from exclusive reliance on the whims of local-elite generosity. The major impact, though, was to establish an organizational infrastructure of permanent social welfare institutions and a "permanent relationship between the federal government and municipalities" (Smith, 1988:164). Of course this was true across the nation. What seems to be different in the Delta was that New Deal programs were almost always made to fit closely to the existing system of patronage and racial separatism.

New Deal projects rarely helped black Delta communities more than superficially except when whites would also benefit, as in the case of public health measures. For example, the National Recovery Administration (NRA) not only allowed differentials between the North and the South in prescribed wage rates, but also endorsed through a variety of ploys the Southern employers' practice of paying blacks less than whites (Smith, 1988:56–57). In addition, among the few southern black workers employed in NRA-regulated industries, many feared that equalization would cost them their jobs. Flynt reports that "some complained that NRA really stood for 'Negro Removal Act' or 'Negro Rarely Allowed'" (1984:85). Moreover, when southern blacks, whose expectations had been raised by the labor union and civil rights rhetoric of the New Deal, mobilized to resist economic and political inequities, they were often dealt with harshly. For example, in Memphis an NAACP and Urban League effort to persuade blacks to register in the Democratic party was, after initial success, crushed by "Boss" Crump.

> Turning to the stick and eschewing the carrot, he included in his strategy the withholding of municipal and federal funds from public works projects in Negro residential areas. Even the historic Beale Street section, a nationally renowned center for black clubs and the blues, was allowed to fall into shameful disrepair. Physical intimidation was a tactic as well . . . [I]ncidents of police brutality in Memphis increased dramatically in 1937 and 1938. (Smith, 1988:257)

Other historians are even less cautious in dismissing the impact of New Deal programs on fostering social change in the South. For example, Goldfield notes that they may have altered the "physical landscape" of the South, "but the social and economic framework of Southern society remained intact" (1987:4).

Cobb (1984; 1990), however, does not quite so easily discount the impact of the New Deal. His research on the Delta counties in Mississippi, the "Yazoo–Mississippi Delta," indicates that the conservative planters in the region were able to control the implementation of New Deal programs to their own benefit (1990). They were able to do this, on the one hand, by situating themselves or their representatives on the county-level boards that determined who would benefit from work programs, income subsidies, and food supplements. On the other hand Roosevelt's need for their political support within the Democratic party assured them autonomy from Washington (see also Sitkoff, 1984).

> Planters found that locally administered relief programs could be turned on and off like faucets to produce a stream of alternative employment in periods of slack demand for farm labor, only to dry up when hands were needed to plant, chop . . . , or pick cotton. Black newspapers reported that Works Progress Administration (WPA) projects in the Delta were suspended regularly in order to provide harvest labor for planters. (Cobb, 1990:914)

At the same time, the New Deal's Agricultural Adjustment Administration (AAA) provided subsidies to planters as inducement to limit cotton production and thus contributed to the creation of a surplus labor force in the region (Cobb, 1990:915). Carefully controlled by the interests of the planter class, New Deal programs did not significantly alter the oppressive social and economic conditions faced by the Delta's black population.

Cobb also maintains that subsequent federal programs aimed ostensibly at permanently changing the lives of the poor have also been manipulated by elites to reinforce, rather than change, the vastly unequal nature of social, political, and economic relations in the Delta. He indicates, for example, lack of support from the Kennedy administration to enforce voting rights in the region and diluted implementation of the War on Poverty measures under Johnson's administration. Full implementation in the Delta was rare even in response to forceful, organized grass-roots efforts such as the Freedom Vote organized by the Student Nonviolent Coordinating Committee in 1963 (Cobb, 1990: 922). In the meantime farm subsidy programs continued to enrich the planters.

One of the major thrusts of the New Deal in the South was the Tennessee Valley Authority (TVA). Some sixty-six of the counties it serves are located in the Mississippi Delta. Since its inception TVA has brought electric lines into the Delta counties and provided low utility rates to the customer. Apart from the low rates, TVA presence in the Delta and particularly in the minority counties remained obscure until the past decade. Responding to political pressures, TVA conducted a minority counties study in 1985 and attempted to design a targeted economic development program. Despite this effort, minority participation in their energy conservation programs in the Delta remained low. In 1989 TVA's record of procuring Delta products and hiring of minority and Delta companies was publicly questioned by Tennessee Congressman Harold Ford. Leaders from the Delta area noted that less than one percent of TVA's procurements came from this region. Memphis Light, Gas, and Water, the largest utility company in the TVA region, attempted to find another electric supplier because of this historic neglect. Presently, perhaps in an effort to compensate for this history of neglect, TVA has initiated a multimillion-dollar minority economic development program.

The New Deal also contributed to a reorientation in the South, in general, away from agriculture and toward industrialization-led economic development strategies, according to Cobb (1982; 1984). The New Deal was one element of a four-pronged attack on the primacy of agriculture in the South, the other three being the boll weevil, the Depression, and World War II (Cobb, 1984:150).[8] However, the nature of southern industrial development strategies did not challenge southern social structure. As Cobb put it, "plantation-style industrial development persisted even as traditional plantation agriculture was fading away" (1984:150). There are two sorts of evidence that support this claim. One is that most state and local efforts to attract industries were very careful to recruit those that would be most compatible with southern social structure. Mississippi's Balance Agriculture with Industry subsidy program (BAWI) operated much more aggressively in counties outside of Mississippi's Delta, and when it did help attract industry to the Delta it sought assurances that, except for the dirtiest, most arduous, and poorest-paid jobs, only whites would be hired (Cobb, 1982:115–17). Cobb notes that planters were well represented on the BAWI. Until very recently black women were even less likely to find employment in manufacturing. Thus was maintained the "caste system" whereby "a ready supply of agricultural and domestic labor" was made available to the planters and to the small town "rich" in the Delta (Cobb, 1982). Underscoring Cobb's observations is scholarship showing that in areas of the South less heavily populated by blacks, planters have been more likely to support industrialization, even through direct investments. Billings (1982) shows that Piedmont planters have long invested in manufacturing, and he suggests that the absence of this kind of support in the Deep South and the Delta is attributable, in part, to the higher concentrations of blacks there. More recent work indicates that racially aversive patterns of industrial growth continue in the South. Aggregate census data from the 1970s indicate that across southern counties, racial composition continues to explain patterns of wage distribution, capital investments, and new industry starts (see Colclough, 1988).[9]

Cobb argues that these economic development strategies served to keep the South, particularly the Delta, underdeveloped. Practices in place from the 1930s through the 1960s created barriers to attracting higher-wage industries. One barrier is that with low per capita income built so firmly into the present economy, industries serving larger consumer markets find little reason to locate in the region (Cobb, 1982: 121). Another barrier is that infrastructural changes that would attract industry were less likely to be made in predominantly black areas of the South than elsewhere. For example, recent interviews with local boosters of industrial development in several Delta communities almost uniformly listed the absence of four-lane, limited access highways or adequate rail transportation as major impediments to industrial growth. The historical record of federal and state government initiatives in the Delta thus reveals actions to promote development that were severely constrained by the local social, economic, and political structures. Even the ostensibly progressive programs of the New Deal and the Great Society were often tailored in the Delta to meet the needs of local elites. Protecting their interests has meant that the region's peripheral economic relationship with the rest of the country has been preserved, and rigid race/ethnic and class stratification has been reinforced. True development will require actions of a much different sort than those that have been carried out through most of the region's history.

Recent Initiatives in the Lower Mississippi Delta

The picture of the Delta that we have painted so far is not bright. It is one of a poor rural region where the structures that have given rise to underdevelopment have survived the New Deal, the post–World War II industrial boom, the War on Poverty, and Reagan's supply side economic development strategies. In 1988, prompted by the growing awareness of federal neglect of this region, U.S. Senator Dale Bumpers of Arkansas teamed with then-freshman Congressman Mike Espy of Mississippi and powerful Congressman Jamie Whitten of Mississippi to create a new approach to the region's poverty. They created a federal commission (the LMDDC) to produce a comprehensive strategic plan for the economic development of the Delta region for the year 2000.

Departing from legislation establishing previous federal commissions, the 1988 legislation mandated strong state participation and public hearings. After eighteen months the final report, the *Delta Initiatives*, presented sixty-eight major goals in the areas of education, health care, housing, community development, natural resources, agriculture, infrastructure, environment, and private enterprise. Each ten-year goal was accompanied by a series of recommendations targeted to a combination of "stakeholders," notably federal, state, and local governments, the private sector, nonprofit organizations (e.g., churches, schools, and community-based groups) and the individual. In addition to the ten-year goals and recommendations, the Commission noted that twelve central themes permeated all the public testimony and discussion at the state and local level (LMDDC, 1990:12):

1. Develop leadership.
2. Change attitudes regarding tradition and image.
3. Improve education at all levels.
4. Build institutional know-how and capacity.
5. Achieve comprehensive approaches to solving problems.
6. Improve abilities to function in a multicultural society; face race and class problems and bridge the gap.
7. Build on and protect existing resources.
8. Streamline institutional processes.
9. Increase capital for development.
10. Create and penetrate markets.
11. Improve physical infrastructure.
12. Build technical competence.

The Commission's themes reinforce our position that economic development in the Delta cannot be conceptualized simply in terms of new factories. Instead, planning and implementation for the Delta must recognize the region's complex history of race and class relations, lack of capital (marginality to the core), lack of rural and urban integration of markets, political marginality and paternalistic political traditions, and educational deficiencies.

In light of the Commission's final report (LMDDC, 1990), several immediate actions were taken. At the congressional level, a Delta Caucus was formed to discuss existing legislation as it affects the entire region. Several rural demonstration programs for housing have been targeted to the Lower Mississippi Delta. The Caucus also worked to secure federal commitments to build three federal prisons in the region (Forrest City, Arkansas; Yazoo City, Mississippi; and Pollock,

Louisiana) as well as to expand a federal infant mortality program (i.e., the $171 million Healthy Start initiative of the U.S. Department of Health and Welfare) to include rural Delta areas.

At the regional level the seven participating states agreed to form a nonprofit organization, the Lower Mississippi Delta Development Center to facilitate action on the recommendations and report accomplishments. Because of state financial crises only three of the seven states have been able to contribute to the newly formed Delta Center (Duffy, 1991). The lack of state funding has jeopardized Congressman Espy's attempt to secure matching federal funds. Apart from the Delta Center, the governors of Mississippi, Arkansas, and Louisiana have entered into a historic interstate compact. Similar agreements between state departments of transportation, economic development, and tourism have been established as well (McLendon and Lynch, 1990).

At the regional, institutional, nonprofit level, two initiatives are noteworthy. First, over fifty institutions of higher education participated in a Delta Summit on their future role in economic development (see Lower Mississippi Delta Commission, 1989a). At an October 8, 1991, meeting at Arkansas State University, the Delta university presidents proposed a Lower Mississippi Higher Education Association for the purpose of joining the resources and expertise of its members to improve the economic climate and quality of life in the region. Second, more than 150 representatives of the region's major religious denominations assembled to discuss and formulate strategies for involvement of churches in solving the economic problems of the region over the next ten years. Their report (Purdy, 1990) outlined a series of new initiatives for collaborative action in job training, literacy, housing construction, and health care. Other notable church-based initiatives include the Rural Interfaith Association in west Tennessee and Louisiana CrossLines. CrossLines is indicative of the growing emphasis on building the capacity of local churches to develop outreach programs consistent with the needs and goals of indigenous communities and agencies.

A major regional initiative in the private sector is the Mid-South Common Market. Initiated by the Memphis Chamber of Commerce in 1988, the Mid-South Market serves a 105-county, six-state area. In addition to presenting a regional marketing plan to the outside community, the Common Market provides technical assistance to its members and works to form a unified economic growth agenda for the region.

At the state level Delta governors have all embarked upon major educational reform. The Delta Commission's interim report (LMDCC,

1989b) notes, "Great strides have been made since the early 1980s, including implementing increased curriculum requirements, higher teacher salaries, and innovative teaching methods; expanding preschool and kindergarten instruction; and cutting out unnecessary administrative costs, especially in Arkansas and Mississippi." Increasingly non-profit organizations, such as the Mississippi Delta Council and the newly formed Arkansas Delta Council, have expanded their economic development efforts to include educational reform and literacy programs.

At the grass roots level there is increasing evidence of community-based initiatives in economic development throughout the Delta. The LMDDC requested, through public testimony and written submission, documentation of economic development programs at the community level that could serve as models throughout the Delta. Hundreds of such programs were submitted. Some efforts have been directed toward local leadership initiatives in rural economic development. Both the National Governors Association and President Bush's Rural Development Task Force have emphasized the critical need for fundamental civic skills training. Within the Delta, the Mississippi Association for Community Education (MACE)/Charles Bannerman Institute program, TVA's South L-I-N-K 2000, and the Henry J. Kaiser Family Foundation Health Initiatives have all implemented major local leadership-building programs throughout the rural Delta.

The MACE program was originally established as an outgrowth of the Delta Foundation, Inc., a rural nonprofit community-development corporation set up by Charles Bannerman in 1969. This early effort in minority community economic development has continually sought to combine government aid with private contributions to generate jobs that the private sector could not or would not provide (see *Wall Street Journal*, 1984). During its history, the Delta Foundation and MACE have created over 1000 jobs and set up and operated eleven businesses.

Model early childhood education and literacy programs are now found in many rural areas throughout the Delta. Nationally recognized programs include the Home Instruction Program for Preschool Youngsters in Arkansas, the Keenan Family Literacy Project in Mississippi, the Parent and Child Education program in Kentucky, and Parents as Partners in Louisiana.

Similarly, model adult literacy and job training programs are springing up in the rural Delta. The President of Plumley Rubber Company testified before the Delta Commission that he initiated an on-the-job computer literacy program for his employees; this was so successful that it was transferred to the public schools in west Tennessee. Entergy

Services Corporation, the major utility holding company in the Delta, has initiated a traveling literacy van and a Summer Institute for High School Counselors program to provide current information about businesses, professions, and educational opportunities in the Delta states.

One noteworthy grass-roots initiative that is working toward progressive economic development is the Arkansas Land and Farm Development Corporation (ALFDC) that was established in September 1980 by African-American farmer, Calvin King. The primary purpose of the organization is to stop and reverse the decline in land ownership among blacks and the decline, in general, in the number of small farmers in seventeen counties in the Delta section of eastern Arkansas.[10] In an interview King noted that "the future is not bright for the regional farm population. Unemployment in this seventeen-county region is about 12 percent, compared with the state average of 7.9 percent" (unpublished testimony at LMDDC hearings, Little Rock, Arkansas, September 1989). To address this problem, the organization began providing legal and community economic development assistance through a fivefold approach: advocacy, training, membership development, emergency support, and program development. In the area of advocacy ALFDC has helped establish a $10 million national minority set-aside program for land purchases. Training efforts have focused on conversion techniques to nontraditional crops. Intensified membership drives over the past two years have increased membership to over 1300. ALFDC emergency support efforts have been targeted to livestock replacement and upgrading. They have worked with the Heifer Project International in this effort. Program development efforts involve operating an East Arkansas Land Trust.

In the future, King's efforts and those of the ALFDC will expand to include a rice processing facility and jobs in a fiberglass tank manufacturing operation that serves the growing catfish industry. Keeping agricultural products in the region for further processing is seen as one viable way to increase employment opportunities and reverse dependency on external forces. Calvin King's leadership over the past ten years was recognized by the MacArthur Foundation in July 1990 when it named King one of thirty-six recipients of $240,000 fellowships.

There are several examples of seemingly progressive industrial leadership in the region that may offer useful models for the Delta. One is Delta Wire, a manufacturer of wire used in automobile, truck, and aircraft tires operating in Clarksdale, Mississippi, since 1978. The Delta Council, a regional chamber of commerce once dominated by conservative planters, cooperated with local officials in bringing the company into the area. Local industrial bonds were used to help finance the firm's operation. Whereas many industrialists in the area see the high unemployment rate as a function of high poverty, low education, and low aspirations, Delta Wire owner and president George Walker sees it as an opportunity (personal interview). There is a ready supply of labor in the area, and the low level of skills would only be a problem if "you didn't train the folks." Delta Wire takes advantage of state-supported job training available through Mississippi State University. The university developed several training modules, including manuals and video presentations that are used to train Delta Wire employees to perform production tasks in the plant's capital-intensive work environment. Attesting to the success of the job training and the quality of the work force, the company has received awards for quality from many of the largest tire manufacturers that it supplies.

Walker describes the background of the firm's work force, which numbers 102 (65 percent are African American), as "primarily agricultural" and almost entirely local in origin. The training is done "constantly." Mississippi State updates the training materials every two years, and Delta Wire was the first company in the state to participate in Mississippi's Skills Enhancement program. According to Walker, the constant training Delta Wire employees go through compensates for the low levels of educational attainment in the local work force and the poor public education system in the area. As a result of the success his company has had in producing a high-quality product at competitive prices, Walker feels that "anything you can do anywhere else in the world, you can do in the Delta if you do it right." This is in sharp contrast to many other industry managers in the region who typically lament that the only kinds of industry appropriate to the Delta are those using low-skill, low-wage labor. Clearly "doing it right" means recognizing the human-capital limitations and improving them by making use of state-supported training programs.

By taking advantage of initial community and state subsidies Delta Wire's owners were able to build the plant in this relatively underdeveloped area. By pursuing an aggressive skills-development program, also partly subsidized by the state, the company has been able to compensate for the low levels of human capital that are a legacy of the region's underfunded public education system. Finally, an innovative wage system and excellent health care benefits provide the company's workers with a significantly higher standard of living than most Delta working-class residents (12 percent of whom are unemployed) are able to attain.[11]

Prospects for the Future

The contradictory nature of the rural Mississippi Delta region is evident in what its residents envision for the future as well as in its historical transformation. On the one hand, our examples of apparently successful locally based efforts at economic development indicate that a brighter future is possible. On the other hand, these efforts are too rare and involve relatively few of the region's citizens. The lives of many of the Delta's poorest citizens continue to reflect hopelessness and despair. The high levels of poverty, unemployment, and teenage pregnancy are comparable to conditions in inner cities. Many of the region's citizens share a perception of the future in which "making it" involves surviving on the wages of irregular, underpaid work, meager AFDC payments, food stamps, and the help of kin (see Dill and Williams, 1992). These expectations are based upon what are probably accurate readings of the structure of opportunities for impoverished, poorly educated, unskilled African Americans in the region. Given the current capitalistic global economy, they will require significant structural changes for the successes to outweigh the reasons for despair.

First, steps need to be taken to help overcome the peripheral economic relationship of the Delta to the rest of the country. One beginning would be to improve local access to capital through a regional development bank, along the lines suggested in the LMDDC's report (1990). Of course, guidelines would have to be carefully followed to assure that such a bank would promote true development, rather than merely reinforce underdevelopment. However, by carefully promoting and selecting projects to fund, the bank could serve as an important catalyst in developing a more diverse industrial base involving more skilled-labor inputs and producing more finished goods. Delta Wire, for example, shows that such industries are possible even now. Expanding the market base of the region is also necessary to overcome peripheralization, and the increasing vitality of the Mid-South Common Market is promising in this respect. Its activities and goals should be closely coordinated with those of the development bank.

Second, efforts must be made to overcome the divisive nature of existing class, race/ethnic, and gender relations in the region.[12] Institutions such as the development bank and school systems must directly incorporate the interests of *all* of the region's "stakeholders." Without acting on the basis of grass-roots consensus, such institutions will be unlikely to pursue goals that reflect the interests of the region's many poor, and in any case they will lack the legitimacy to operate effectively. This leads to the third area of concern, the "state."

The political history of the region is characterized by the hegemony of local patriarchal elites over local and state government. There are vestiges of this dominance which still serve as obstacles to overcoming the region's peripheralization. Even when local government has been wrested from this elite (e.g., by organized efforts of the African-American community), the extreme poverty of the locales usually limits its effectiveness. Thus, due to either resistance by a narrow planter-elite or their own lack of resources, local governments in the region have been able neither to educate their citizens properly nor to pursue economic development effectively.

It is difficult to envision any solution to providing greater educational resources other than greater support from the federal government. Delta communities are usually either too poor or its affluent, private-school-educated citizens too indifferent to support more spending on public education. Perhaps the most promising avenue for change would be the development of broad-based regional organizations operating across the Delta states. Such organizations could coordinate development efforts and promote educational reforms through the various state governments and the federal government. Yet there are many ways in which the distribution of educational resources in the Delta seems guided by forces similar to those operating in metropolitan areas all over the country. Many of the same local, state, and federal policies that allow the existence of large differences between central cities and affluent suburban areas in the distribution of educational resources also allow the rural Delta to remain relatively disadvantaged. At base are federal policies that, by reinforcing the autonomy of subnational political jurisdictions, allow race/ethnicity, class, and regional wealth (or lack thereof) to determine access to educational resources (i.e., "human capital").

We indicated early in the chapter that another factor opening to keep the region underdeveloped was an ideology and culture of underdevelopment. Paternalism, fatalism, and fractionalism have been identified as undergirding social interaction and community organizational structures in the rural Delta. We believe that these ideological orientations are to a large extent cultural responses to peripheralization and dependency. Therefore, attacking the region's underdevelopment along the three fronts of peripheral economies, divisive social relations, and the "state" should help to weaken significantly the attraction of these dispositions. However, the ideology of underdevelopment can be addressed directly, as many of the local initiatives mentioned above have done. Adult literacy programs give those who have been denied basic education new confidence. A sense of political strength is instilled among disadvantaged groups as grass-roots political movements achieve success, such as those that have propelled African Americans into local and state political offices in many Delta communities. Job-training programs encourage feelings of competence, and financial support for locally based business enterprises is also support for an ideology of economic efficacy. In conjunction with fundamental structural reform, such individually targeted strategies can go a long way toward transforming both the ideology and the reality of underdevelopment in the Delta. To do this will help to move the region out of the periphery and into the mainstream of the U.S. political economy. At the same time, this should help to change a future of individual "trouble," which many Delta citizens expect, to a future freer of hunger and sickness, where work is available and where the hard work that the region's poor have always been willing to perform will finally begin to pay off.

Notes

1. In the Mississippi Delta today, one can find "Charley Patton's grave, Robert Nighthawk's bedroom, the Robert Johnson memorial, and Ike Turner's birth place" (O'Neal, 1991:39), not to mention the ruins of the shack in which Muddy Waters was born, around the Stovall Plantation.

2. See Feagin, 1989, for a similar list of guiding assumptions in his analysis of the political economy of Houston.

3. A few impressive monuments to these ancient mound builders have so far survived the cotton-planting "land levelers" who now populate the region (Dunbar, 1990:9).

4. As Dunbar (1990) points out, the area now referred to as the Mississippi Delta is not the true geographic delta of the Mississippi River. The true delta is at the mouth of the river near New Orleans.

5. Moreover, "this [government involvement in flood control] illustrates once again an overriding fact of life in the Delta: there is very little that is not touched by the federal government" (Dunbar, 1990:136).

6. Much of the statistical work of these reports was conducted at Mississippi State University (e.g., Reinschmiedt and Green, 1989).

7. According to longstanding convention, the Mississippi Delta begins in Memphis, a good 150 miles south of the northernmost counties of the LMDDC definition.

8. It is to World War II that Goldfield (1987) attributes this reorientation. Cobb's work, though, makes it clear that aggressive state-led industrialization efforts were well under way prior to the war (see Cobb, 1982; 1984).

9. African Americans and whites overwhelmingly dominate the region in terms of demographic statistics, politics, image, and ideological discourse. However, many other ethnic or racial groups have populated the region and

contribute to it in important ways. For example, within Mississippi American Indians, Chinese, and Lebanese are present in significant numbers, and, of course, in Louisiana Cajuns are very significant.

10. According to a 1989 Arkansas Agricultural Experiment Station report, the number of farms in Arkansas declined by about 10,000 over the ten previous years.

11. Walker and many other local Delta industry heads were interviewed by Timberlake in connection with a Ford Foundation/Aspen Institute–funded project with Bonnie Thornton Dill (principal investigator) and Bruce Williams. (See Timberlake et al., 1988).

12. Along these lines, Dunbar points out that land-owning whites in the Delta have "more choices" than blacks. They can leave, or at least they can watch their sons and daughters "drift off." "Or they might decide to turn it around, get the economy moving again, build up those schools, and cast their lot with the black majority in a land too pretty to part with" (1990:239).

References

Bender, Lloyd, Bernal Green, Thomas F. Hady, John A. Kuehn, Marlys K. Nelson, Leon B. Perkinson, and Peggy Ross. 1985. *The Diverse Social and Economic Structure of Nonmetropolitan America.* Rural Development Research Report no. 49. Washington, D.C.: Agriculture and Rural Economics Division. Economic Research Service, U.S. Department of Agriculture.

Biles, Roger. 1986. *Memphis in the Great Depression.* Knoxville: University of Tennessee Press.

Billings, Dwight. 1982. "Class Origins of the 'New South': Planter Resistance and Industry in North Carolina." Pp. 552–85 in Michael Buraway and Theda Skocpol (eds.), *Marxist Inquiries. American Journal of Sociology* 88 supplement.

Brownell, Blaine, and David Goldfield, (eds.). 1977. *The City in Southern History: The Growth of Urban Civilization in the South.* Port Washington, N.Y.: Kennikat Press.

Cash, Wilbur J. 1941. *The Mind of the South.* New York: Alfred A. Knopf.

Chase-Dunn, Christopher. 1989. *Global Formation: Structures of the World-Economy.* Cambridge, Mass.: Basil Blackwell.

Ciaramitaro, Bridget, Stanley Hyland, James Kovarik, and Michael Timberlake. 1988. "The Development of Underdevelopment in the Mid-South: Big Farmers and the Persistence of Rural Poverty." *Humanity and Society* 12(4):347–65.

Clay, James, Paul Escott, Douglas Orr, and Alfred Stuart, 1989. *Land of the South.* Birmingham, Ala.: Oxmoor House.

Cobb, James C. 1982. *The Selling of the South 1936–1980.* Baton Rouge: Louisiana State University Press.

———. 1984. *Industrialization and Southern Society 1877–1984.* Lexington: University Press of Kentucky.

———. 1990. "'Somebody Done Nailed Us on the Cross': Federal Farm and Welfare Policy and the Civil Rights Movement in the Mississippi Delta." *Journal of American History* 76:912–36.

Colclough, Glenna. 1988. "Uneven Development and Racial Composition in the Deep South: 1970–1980." *Rural Sociology* 53(1):73–86.

Dill, Bonnie Thronton, and Bruce Williams. 1992. "Race, Gender, and Poverty in the Rural South: African American Single Mothers." Pp. 97–109 in Cynthia M. Duncan (ed.), *Rural Poverty in America.* New York: Auburn House.

Duffy, Joan. 1991. "Center to Help Delta Sinks into Poverty." *Memphis Commercial Appeal*, 30 July: 1, 10.

Dunbar, Tony. 1990. *Delta Time: A Journey through Mississippi.* New York: Pantheon Books.

Duncan, Cynthia, and Ann R. Tickamyer. 1988. "Poverty Research and Policy for Rural America." *American Sociologist* 19:244–59.

Dye, David. 1989. "Death March of Hernando de Soto." *Archaeology* 42 (May/June): 26–31.

Dye, David, and Cheryl Cox, (eds.). 1990. *Towns and Temples along the Mississippi.* Tuscaloosa: University of Alabama Press.

Dyer, Thomas G. 1989. "Education." Pp. 233–310 in Charles Wilson and William Ferris (eds.), *Encyclopedia of Southern Culture.* Chapel Hill: University of North Carolina Press.

Evans, Peter, and John Stephens. 1988. "Development and the World Economy." Pp. 739–73 in Neil Smelser (ed.), *Handbook of Sociology.* Newbury Park, Calif.: SAGE.

Farney, Dennis. 1989. "River of Despair: Along the Rich Banks of the Mississippi Live the Poorest of U.S. Poor." *Wall Street Journal* 13 October: 1, A16.

Flynt, Wayne. 1984. "The New Deal and Southern Labor." Pp. 63–95 in James C. Cobb and Michael V. Namorato (eds.), *The New Deal and the South.* Jackson: University Press of Mississippi.

Goldfield, David R. 1981. "The Urban South: A Regional Framework." *American Historical Review* 86:1009–34.

———. 1987. *Promised Land: The South since 1945.* Arlington Heights, Ill.: Harlan Davidson.

Hawkins, Wilbur F., and Stanley E. Hyland. 1990. "Rural Health Care Issues in the Lower Mississippi Delta: An Agenda for the Year 2000." *Journal of Health and Social Policy* 2(1):79–94.

Lemann, Nicolas. 1991. *The Promised Land: The Great Black Migration and How It Changed America.* New York: Alfred A. Knopf.

Los Angeles Times. 1990. "Babies Are Born to Die in the Delta." 30 September, 1.

Lower Mississippi Delta Commission. 1989a. *Proceedings of Lower Mississippi Delta Higher Education Conference.* Memphis, Tenn.: September.

———. 1989b. *Body of the Nation: Interim Report to Congress.* Memphis, Tenn.: 16 October.

———. 1990. *The Final Report: Delta Initiatives—Realizing the Dream . . . Fulfilling the Potential.* Memphis, Tenn.

McLendon, Teresa, and Lynch, James R. 1990. "Interstate Cooperation, Regionalism, and Economic Development in the Delta." Report for the Lower Mississippi Delta Development Commission, Memphis, Tenn.

Mississippi. Mississippi Special Task Force for Economic Development Planning. 1989. *Seizing the Future.* Jackson: State of Mississippi.

Morse, Dan, and Phyllis Morse. 1983. *Archaeology of the Central Mississippi Valley*. New York: Academic Press.

O'Hare, William P. 1988. *The Rise of Poverty in Rural America*. Washington, D.C.: Population Reference Bureau.

O'Neal, Jim. 1991. "A Mississippi Delta Travelers' Guide." *Living Blues*, no. 11 (November/December): 39–42.

Pearsall, Marion. 1966. "Cultures of the American South." *Anthropological Quarterly* 39:128–41.

Purdy, Paul. 1990. "Role of the Church in Economic Development: Survey of Churches in the Lower Mississippi Delta Region." Report for the Lower Mississippi Delta Development Commission. Memphis, Tenn.

Reinschmiedt, Lynn, and Bernal Green. 1989. "Socioeconomic Conditions: The Mississippi Delta." MAFES Bulletin 965. Mississippi State University. Division of Agriculture, Forestry, and Veterinary Medicine. Department of Information Services. December.

Sitkoff, Harvard. 1984. "The Impact of the New Deal on Black Southerners." Pp. 117–34 in James C. Cobb and Michael V. Namorato (eds.), *The New Deal and the South*. Jackson: University Press of Mississippi.

Smith, Douglas L. 1988. *The New Deal in the Urban South*. Baton Rouge: Louisiana State University Press.

Smith, John W. 1990. "Wetlands and Economic Development: Conflict or Compatibility." Research report for the Lower Mississippi Delta Development Commission. Memphis, Tenn.

Timberlake, Michael, Bonnie Thornton Dill, Bruce Williams, and Darryl Tukufu. 1991. "Race and Economic Development in the Lower Mississippi Delta." Center for Research on Women, Memphis State University. Working paper.

Tomaskovic-Devey, Donald. 1987. "Labor Markets, Industrial Structure, and Poverty: A Theoretical Discussion and Empirical Example." *Rural Sociology* 52(1):56–74.

Woodward, C. Vann. 1971. *Origins of the New South, 1877–1913*. Baton Rouge: Louisiana State University Press.

6 | Industrial Development and Persistent Poverty in the Lower Rio Grande Valley

Rogelio Saenz and Marie Ballejos

IN THE SOUTHERNMOST TIP of Texas, far from the limelight of national and state debates concerning the poor, lies a region known as the Lower Rio Grande Valley (or simply "the Valley"). The three counties (Cameron, Hidalgo, and Willacy) composing the Valley contained more than 661,000 people in 1990. Approximately 250 miles of sparse brush land separates the area from any major northern neighbor.

The two salient factors about the Valley's population are ethnicity and poverty. The people of the Valley are predominantly Hispanic, and of Mexican origin in particular. According to the 1990 census, approximately 84 percent of the region's population was Hispanic. Because of the geographic setting and its historical relationship with Mexico, it is not surprising that there is a symbiotic relationship between the Valley and the area immediately across the border in Mexico. Here the culture, politics, socioeconomics, and demography of each setting collide and merge to create forms distinct from those found in other parts of each country. Many Valley Hispanics are fluent in both Spanish and English, and many continue to have family ties across the border. Such ties and the ongoing arrival of Mexican immigrants, legal and illegal, serve to intensify the symbiotic relationship between the two border areas. Unfortunately, the Valley is affected not only by changes in the economic situations in Texas and the United States but also by changes in Mexican economic conditions. Since 1982, with the devaluation of the peso, economic conditions in Mexico have had adverse effects.

The Valley has historically been among the socioeconomically most disadvantaged regions of the United States. For example, in 1986 the McAllen-Edinburg-Mission and Brownsville-Harlingen metropolitan statistical areas (MSAs), the Valley's two MSAs, were ranked at or near the bottom in per capita income and employment rates among the nation's 281 MSAs (Population Reference Bureau, 1987). In addition, in 1990 the three Valley counties had some of the highest annual average unemployment rates among Texas' 254 counties (Hidalgo, 19.1 percent; Willacy, 15.2 percent; Cameron, 11.7 percent) (Texas Employment

Commission, 1990). The Hispanic segment of the population has been associated with this disadvantaged position; in fact, the terms "poor" and "Hispanic" are relatively synonymous in the Valley. To illustrate, while Hispanics accounted for 80 percent of the total population in 1980, they made up 93 percent of the population living in poverty. Valley residents have been called the "poorest of Americans" (Maril, 1989).

For many of the Hispanic poor in the Valley, poverty is a way of life. Indeed, many of the area's poor exist in a vicious cycle of poverty involving such factors as inadequate housing, poor health care, inferior education, high unemployment, unskilled dead-end jobs, and low wages. These problems are particularly acute in the *colonias* (unincorporated shantytowns) throughout the Valley, where health and socioeconomic problems are comparable to those in developing countries.

Ironically, in the last couple of decades the Valley has experienced tremendous, unprecedented industrialization and growth in population. In particular, the Valley's industrial makeup has been shifting rapidly from an agricultural to a more diverse industrial manufacturing economy. Such growth to a large extent has been tied to the growth of assembly plants (*maquiladoras*) on the Mexican side of the border. Still, local Hispanic residents continue to find themselves among the ranks of the poor.

The Historical Context of
Mexican-Anglo Relations

The contemporary socioeconomic conditions of Hispanics in the Valley can best be understood through the use of the internal colonialism perspective focusing on the historical experiences of Mexicanos or Chicanos in the United States. We use the terms Hispanic, Mexican, Mexicano, Mexican American, and Chicano interchangeably, reflecting both the dominance of people of Mexican origin among Hispanics in the Valley and the diversity of ethnic identity. In order to understand the subordinate socioeconomic position of Hispanics in the Valley, we need to grasp the historical conditions that established the subordinate position of Chicanos. Chicanos are the only U.S. ethnic group whose initial entry occurred through colonialism in the guise of manifest destiny. In fact, the signing of the Treaty of Guadalupe Hidalgo in 1848, at the conclusion of the Mexican-American War, marked the creation of Mexican Americans. Mexicans living on land that Mexico was forced to turn over to the United States were given

one year to decide whether they would remain on their land and become U.S. citizens or return to Mexico and retain their Mexican citizenship. People electing to become U.S. citizens would be entitled to
all rights of citizenship. The vast majority took this route. Essentially,
these new Americans were Mexicans living in the United States, since
they were "Mexican by birth, language, and culture; United States citizens by the might of arms" (Alvarez, 1973:924).

The new Americans quickly encountered structural barriers that
blocked their participation in American society. Forces were set in motion that were destined to make Mexicans a conquered, powerless, and
alienated ethnic minority. Perhaps the greatest vehicle for the subordination of the group was the transformation of the southwestern
small-scale ranch economy to a large-scale capitalist farm economy
(Barrera, 1979; Mirande, 1985; Montejano, 1987). This change was facilitated by the massive wave of Anglo newcomers arriving in the Southwest after the end of the Mexican-American War and by the massive
turnover of land from Mexican to Anglo hands through legal and extra-
legal means. In the capitalist farming system, Chicanos were largely
relegated to the most menial, low-paying jobs, particularly in agriculture, mining, and the railroad, where they occupied the subordinate
position in a dual-wage economy (Barrera, 1979). Relations between the
Mexican and Anglo populations after the Mexican-American War were
hostile. To a large extent, the pattern was one of Anglos using violence
to control and subordinate Mexicans and the latter retaliating.

Although large-scale economic transformations were to occur
early in many parts of the Southwest, these changes would be slower in
the Valley. This delay resulted from its isolation and its relatively high
proportion of Mexicans. However, the introduction of the railroad con-
necting Brownsville with Corpus Christi in 1904 quickly ushered in
the rise of the farm economy and the fall of the ranch economy (Montejano, 1987). The railroad succeeded in opening profitable markets for
the area's agricultural products, and these developments served as mag-
nets for Anglo migration. Many ranches were divided into small farms
and sold for exorbitant prices (Montejano, 1987). Land became a priced
commodity. Mexicans with limited resources were hardly able to compete effectively for the available land.

In a matter of two decades, the number of farms grew significantly
whereas the average size of farms declined noticeably (Montejano,
1987). At the same time, the number of cattle dropped substantially. In
the Valley's new economic order, the predominant positions were held
by Anglo business merchants and lawyers (Montejano, 1987). The capi-

tal and legal expertise of these newcomers represented the downfall of the old ranch economic system and the transfer of land to Anglo hands.

Valley Mexicans quickly found themselves as landless proletarians. Paul Taylor (1934) observed that South Texas consisted of Anglo farmers and Mexican laborers. Ethnic tensions were heightened by the blunt form of discrimination the Mexicans experienced at the hands of the Anglo newcomers. The relationship between Mexicans and Anglos in the old ranch system in the Valley could be characterized as "paternalistic accommodation"; that between the Anglo newcomers and Mexicans in the Valley was far from civil (Montejano, 1987). Tensions became so severe that some segments of the Mexican community revolted against their treatment. Indeed, large-scale violence was to take place between 1915 and 1917. The Texas Rangers were quickly brought to the Valley to quell the revolts, resulting in the deaths of anywhere from 500 to 5,000 Mexicans but only 62 Anglo civilians and 64 soldiers (Webb, 1935). Montejano (1987) observes that the Texas Rangers were brought in to make farms safe for the Anglo newcomers.

Whereas education has traditionally been viewed as a vehicle for upward mobility, this option created few opportunities for Mexicans in Texas in the early part of the twentieth century (see San Miguel, 1984). Economic necessity kept many Mexican children out of the classroom. Furthermore, educational segregation prevented Mexican children from pursuing the same education as their Anglo counterparts. The Texas Constitution of 1876 declared that "there must be separate schools for white and colored children." Local educational officials of schools with a considerable number of Mexican students interpreted "colored" broadly and established separate Mexican schools as early as 1896 (San Miguel, 1984). By 1942–1943, at least 122 school districts in Texas maintained separate Mexican schools.

This historical context for the early relationships between Anglos and Mexicans and the subsequent subordination of the latter can help in understanding the contemporary situation, which may be described as internal colonialism.

The Internal Colonialism Model

The historical conditions involving Chicanos in the Valley can be placed within the internal colonialism framework developed by Robert Blauner (1972). The model draws on the experiences of developing countries throughout the world that have been conquered and colonized at one time or another by European powers and extends them to situations involving a conquered minority group less powerful than a conqueror majority group within a particular country. The internal colonialism model has been used to explain the conditions of groups (i.e., African Americans, Chicanos, native Americans, and Puerto Ricans) that have been incorporated into the United States through means other than voluntary migration. Several analysts have applied the model to Chicanos (Acuna, 1988; Almaguer, 1971; Barrera et al., 1972; Maril, 1989; Mirande, 1985; Moore, 1970). Blauner (1972:84) has outlined four basic components of the internal colonialism:

1. Colonialization begins with a forced, involuntary entry.
2. The colonizing power carries out a policy that constrains, transforms, or destroys indigenous values, orientations, and ways of life.
3. The lives of the subordinate group are administered by representatives of the dominant group.
4. Racism is a principle of social domination by which a group seen as inferior or different in alleged biological characteristics is exploited, controlled, and oppressed socially and psychically by a superordinate group.

Each of these components of internal colonialism is applicable in varying degrees to Chicanos in the Valley.

For example, Mexicans living in the Valley when the land was transferred to the United States following the end of the Mexican-American War found themselves as a conquered people, for their only choices were to surrender their land or to remain on their land and become U.S. citizens. In addition, Chicanos in the Valley and in the United States in general have been able to hold onto their culture despite forces set in motion by the majority group to suppress this culture. As late as the 1960s, Chicanos in the Valley were punished for speaking Spanish in school. Furthermore, persons holding positions of authority (e.g., elected officials, school boards, police chiefs, teachers, school principals) in the area have long tended to be primarily Anglos, although this has been changing in recent years. McAllen, the Valley's second largest city, has never had a Chicano mayor. However, Barrera et al. (1972) argue that the racial component of the internal colonialism model only applies to Chicanos to a certain extent, for cultural factors have been at least as important as biological ones as a basis for discrimination.

Chicanos have confronted institutional and personal barriers to upward mobility in the Valley. In fact, Maril (1989), working within the internal colonialism model, suggests that the Valley represents a colony for the rest of Texas and the United States. The Valley has been an ideal source of cheap labor, fruits, and vegetables. Given the high levels of poverty and unemployment and low level of unionization in the Valley, American capitalists have been more than eager to move their operations to the border region, with many continuing southward in search of even cheaper labor in Mexico. In fact, one can logically argue that the presence of an abundant supply of cheap labor in the Valley has been at least partly responsible for the dramatic industrial growth in the region over the last couple of decades. Still, as if it were a traditional colonial economy, fruits and vegetables are frequently shipped out of the region to be processed elsewhere, only to be brought back and sold to Valley consumers at higher prices (Maril, 1989).

Recent Demographic and Socioeconomic Changes in the Valley

Between 1970 and 1990 the population of Texas experienced rapid growth, with the population increasing by close to 52 percent. During the same time, however, population of the Valley nearly doubled. Yet, the growth was largely that of the Hispanic population. For example, the Valley Hispanic population increased by 111.3 percent between 1970 and 1990 compared to an increase of 42.1 percent in the non-Hispanic population (since Anglos account for almost all of the non-Hispanic population, we will refer to the residual category as Anglo).

The uneven population growth patterns of Hispanics and Anglos was due mostly to the different age structures of these groups. The Valley Hispanic population is young, with a median age of 21.4 in 1980 (see table 6.1). In contrast, Valley Anglos had a median age of nearly 43. Two demographic factors, fertility and immigration, have also favored the greater growth of the Hispanic population in the region. For instance, Hispanic women between the ages of 35 and 44 had an average of 4.4 children in 1980 compared to their Anglo peers, who had an average of 2.6 children. Furthermore, 5.3 percent of Valley Hispanics' 1980 population had moved there from abroad during the 1975–1980 period compared to only 1.6 percent among the Anglo population. The growth in the Anglo population has occurred largely through internal migration. Over one-fifth of the Anglo population in 1970 and 1980 had lived elsewhere in the United States five years earlier; this was true of less than 8 percent of the Hispanic population during the same periods. The internal flow of Anglos to the Valley included a significant number of elderly people (known as "snowbirds") who come annually to the Valley during the winter months. The presence of this subpopulation is clearly reflected in the older age structure of the Anglo population.

The data also demonstrate the deep roots of Hispanics in the region. Of the 1980 Hispanic population in the Valley, seven of ten were born in Texas. In contrast, less than half (46.2 percent) of Anglos were born within the state. The birthplaces of those that were not native Texans differed by ethnicity; the majority of Hispanics were foreign-born and the majority of Anglos were born elsewhere in the United States.

Socioeconomic statistics from the 1970 and 1980 censuses reveal the subordinate position of Valley Hispanics. The patterns observed suggest that socioeconomically Valley Hispanics fare significantly worse in comparison to their Valley Anglo counterparts and to all Hispanics in Texas. The most basic sign of the low socioeconomic standing of Valley Hispanics is educational attainment. In 1980, only 29 percent of Valley Hispanics 25 and older held a high-school diploma compared to 73 percent of Valley Anglos and 33 percent of Texas Hispanics (see table 6.1). One sign of hope, however, is that the ratio of Valley Anglos to Hispanics who are high-school graduates declined from 3.4 to 1 in 1970 to 2.5 to 1 in 1980.

In contrast, the subordinate position of Valley Hispanics on the occupational structure remained fairly constant between 1970 and 1980. In both years there were proportionately three times as many Anglo as Hispanic managers and professionals in the Valley, but Hispanics held a two-to-one advantage in the service and farm occupations. Although Valley Hispanics were fairly comparable to their Hispanic counterparts in the state in their proportional representation in managerial and professional and service jobs, they had twice as high a proportion working in farming occupations.

Valley Hispanics experienced significant industrial shifts from agriculture to manufacturing during the 1970s. In particular, the percentage of Hispanic workers employed in the agriculture sector dropped by approximately 50 percent between 1970 and 1980, while the percentage working in manufacturing rose by slightly more than 50 percent during the same period. Valley Anglos and Texas Hispanics shifted their activities in the agricultural and manufacturing sectors in the same direction, but the magnitude of changes was not anywhere near that of Valley Hispanics. At the same time, however, the wholesale and

Table 6.1. Summary Statistics for Selected Groups, 1970 and 1980

	1970			1980		
	Valley Hispanics	Valley Anglos	Texas Hispanics	Valley Hispanics	Valley Anglos	Texas Hispanics
Total population[a]	262,572	74,901	2,059,671	406,037	104,414	2,982,583
Median age	18.6	41.3	19.3	21.4	42.8	22.1
% foreign-born	—	—	—	23.3	3.8	19.1
% Texas-born	—	—	—	70.4	46.2	73.8
% internal migrants in last 5 years	7.7	26.2	15.6	7.9	29.4	18.8
% immigrants in last 5 years	5.0	1.2	4.0	5.3	1.6	5.9
Average no. of children ever born, women 35–44[b]	5.2	3.3	4.6	4.1	2.6	3.7
% high school graduates	18.2	61.9	24.7	29.0	73.2	32.9
% unemployed	7.4	3.3	5.4	9.7	3.6	6.4
% professional occupations	7.0	21.0	7.6	12.7	35.4	10.7
% service occupations	11.1	6.3	13.8	14.8	7.6	16.1
% farm occupations	16.3	8.2	6.5	9.3	5.2	4.2
% agricultural industry	18.9	9.7	7.7	9.9	6.5	4.3
% manufacturing industry	9.7	6.5	17.4	15.0	8.1	19.2
% wholesale/retail industry	28.1	23.1	23.4	25.0	23.0	22.2
Median family income						
Current dollars	3,960	8,454	5,897	10,692	19,394	13,483
1989 constant dollars	12,666	27,018	18,846	16,090	29,186	20,290
% families in poverty	52.0	13.6	31.4	35.4	7.7	24.7

[a] According to the 1990 census, there were 554,904 Valley Hispanics, 106,466 Valley Anglos (with 4,205 being black, American Indian, Asian, or "other"), and 4,339,905 Texas Hispanics.
[b] The 1970 average is for "ever-married" women, whereas the 1980 average is for all women.

retail industry has provided employment for a large segment of the Valley population. One-fourth of Valley Hispanics were working in the wholesale and retail industry in 1980, as were more than one-fifth of Anglos.

These significant industrial changes occurred at the same time that the unemployment rate of Valley Hispanics rose from 7.4 percent in 1970 to 9.7 percent in 1980. Although the unemployment rates of Valley Anglos and Texas Hispanics also rose during the period, the increase was less dramatic, especially for Valley Anglos. In 1980, Hispanics had an unemployment rate 2.7 times higher than that of Anglos.

In purely monetary terms, Valley Hispanics have also consistently found themselves in an unfavorable position. In 1979, the median income of Valley Hispanic families was only $10,692 compared to $19,394 among Valley Anglo families and $13,483 among Texas Hispanic families. Moreover, Hispanic families earned approximately fifty-five cents for every one dollar earned by Anglo families in the area in 1979. Yet, measured in 1989 constant dollars, the median income of Hispanic families in the Valley rose at a brisk pace (27.0 percent) during the 1970s, while the median incomes of Valley Anglo (8.0 percent) and Texas Hispanic families (7.7 percent) grew significantly slower. As a result, the relative position of Hispanic families in comparison to Valley Anglo families improved between 1970 (forty-seven cents earned by a Hispanic family for every one dollar for an Anglo family) and 1980 (fifty-five cents versus one dollar). Valley Hispanic families made similar levels of improvements vis-à-vis Texas Hispanic families during the same period (1970: sixty-seven cents earned by Valley Hispanic families for every one dollar earned by Texas Hispanic families; 1980: seventy-nine cents versus one dollar).

However, the starkest sign of socioeconomic well-being, percentage of families with incomes below the poverty level, presents a less favorable portrait of Valley Hispanics. Approximately 35 percent of Hispanic families were living in poverty in 1979 compared to close to 8 percent of Valley Anglo families and close to 25 percent of Texas Hispanic families. In fact, in the Valley the ratio of Hispanic families to Anglo families with incomes below the poverty level rose during the 1970s. In 1969 there were proportionately 3.8 Hispanic families in poverty in the area for each Anglo family in similar economic conditions, but this ratio increased to 4.6 to 1 in 1979.

Although data for the post-1980 period are scarce, data are available from the 1985 Special Texas Census conducted by the Texas Department of Human Services (see Saenz and Murdock, 1988) to assess the socioeconomic situations of Valley Hispanics during the 1980s.

The economic situation in the 1980s resembled a roller coaster in Texas, where the decade commenced with the economic boom that began in the late 1970s. The oil bust and farm crisis of the early 1980s, however, quickly turned the state economy sour. Yet, the economic problems in the Valley were further intensified by the peso devaluation which began in 1982 and a hard freeze in 1983 that practically decimated the citrus industry. Minority workers, equipped with low levels of human capital, are particularly vulnerable to downturns in the economy, for they tend to be positioned at the end of the ethnic queue of jobs (Jensen and Tienda, 1989; Saenz and Thomas, 1990). They are most likely to be among the last workers hired and among those first fired during difficult economic times.

Research has demonstrated that in Texas as a whole, minorities, particularly Hispanics, were disproportionately affected by the economic problems of the early 1980s (Saenz and Murdock, 1988). However, such problems appear to have been even more severe for Valley Hispanics. Data from the 1985 Texas Department of Human Services survey show that about 16 percent of Valley Hispanics were unemployed in 1985, compared to only 5 percent of Valley Anglo and 7 percent of Texas Hispanics. Of particular significance is the fact that the unemployment rate for Valley Hispanics increased from 7.4 percent in 1970 to 9.7 percent in 1980 to 15.7 percent in 1985. In addition, the median income of Valley Hispanic families declined the most significantly between 1979 and 1985. Measured in 1989 constant dollars, the median income of Hispanic families declined 19.1 percent from $16,091 in 1980 to $13,014 in 1985, compared to a decline of 5.2 percent among Valley Anglo families and 4.1 percent among Texas Hispanic families. Proportionately, Valley Hispanic families lost relative ground to their Valley Anglo and Texas Hispanic counterparts between 1979 and 1985. For example, whereas Hispanic families earned fifty-five cents for every dollar earned by Anglo families in 1979, this ratio dropped to fifty-one cents per one dollar in 1985; the ratio also dropped relative to Texas Hispanic families (seventy-nine cents per one dollar in 1979 versus seventy-two cents per one dollar in 1985). These recent trends suggest that the income gains that Valley Hispanic families had made in the 1970s were almost wiped out in the early 1980s.

Who Leaves and Who Arrives in the Valley?

The Valley experienced significant net in-migration during the last half of the 1970s. Data from the 1980 census (U.S. Bureau of the Census, 1984) show that the Valley had a net in-migration of 9,099 Hispanics and 5,455 Anglos in the 1975–1980 period. Data from the 1980 Public Use Microdata Sample (PUMS), a 2.5 percent sample of the entire population, are available to determine the points of destination of Valley Hispanic out-migrants and points of origin of Valley Hispanic in-migrants. In this part of the analysis, the Valley refers only to Cameron and Hidalgo counties since Willacy County was included in a different county group in the PUMS. Because adults are more likely to be involved in migration decisions, we limit this part of the analysis to persons eighteen and older.

Of the Hispanics moving to the Valley between 1975 and 1980, the majority (37.1 percent) were living abroad in 1975, while 34.4 percent were living elsewhere in Texas at that time. About 27 percent of Hispanic in-migrants were living in a southwestern (9.9 percent), midwestern (9.3 percent), or southern (7.9 percent) state in 1975, with California, Florida, and Illinois being the most frequent states of origin.

Among Hispanics leaving between 1975 and 1980, close to 74 percent made their home elsewhere in Texas in 1980, whereas about one-fourth were generally found in the Southwest (11.9 percent), South (8.2 percent), and Midwest (4.4 percent). The most frequent states of origin were also the most popular states of destination: California, Florida, and Illinois.

The 1980 PUMS data also allow us to examine the demographic and socioeconomic characteristics of Hispanic in-migrants (entered the Valley between 1975 and 1980), out-migrants (left the Valley between 1975 and 1980), and nonmigrants (lived in the Valley in both 1975 and 1980). Such an analysis allows us to assess the extent to which there has been a brain-drain out-migration among Valley Hispanics. The three migrant and nonmigrant groups differ substantially along demographic lines (see table 6.2). For example, Hispanics leaving between 1975 and 1980 tended to be the youngest group, with an average age of 28.3. By contrast, Hispanics living in the Valley in 1975 and 1980 tended to be older (average age, 40.4). Among the three migrant and nonmigrant groups, Hispanic out-migrants were the most likely to have been native-born [born either in Texas (69.2 percent) or the United States (76.1 percent)]. The highest proportion of the Hispanic in-migrants arriving between 1975 and 1980 were born in Mexico (43.7 percent). More than nine of ten (93.1 percent) Hispanic out-migrants were of Mexican origin; the recent arrival of Central Americans is reflected in the fact that about 15 percent of Hispanic in-migrants were not of Mexican origin.

Significant socioeconomic differences exist among the three mi-

Table 6.2. Demographic and Socioeconomic Characteristics of Valley Hispanic Out-migrants, In-migrants, and Non-migrants 18 and Older, 1975–1980

	Out-migrants	In-migrants	Nonmigrants
Median age	28.3	34.1	40.4
% born in Texas	69.2	46.4	63.7
% born in U.S.	76.1	53.0	66.8
% born in Mexico	20.1	43.7	29.8
% of Mexican origin	93.1	85.4	87.3
% speaking English well or			
very well	84.3	62.3	67.1
% high school graduates	56.0	40.4	33.7
% occupational distribution in 1980			
Managerial and professional	11.6	13.4	9.6
Technical, sales, and administration	35.7	26.9	26.0
Service	10.1	12.6	16.6
Farm	10.1	7.6	8.3
Precision production, crafts	9.3	10.9	13.3
Operators, laborers, fabricators	23.2	28.6	26.2
Average weeks worked in 1979	31.9	27.4	24.0
Average hours usually worked			
in 1979	30.7	25.7	23.3
Average total personal income			
in 1979 ($)	6,778	5,399	5,313
Average hourly wage in 1979 ($)	6.69	4.55	5.10
% in poverty in 1979	21.8	42.6	33.1
N	151	159	996

grant and nonmigrant groups (see table 6.2). In particular, Hispanic out-migrants tended to have the most socioeconomic resources. For example, 56 percent of Hispanic out-migrants held a high school diploma and approximately 84 percent spoke English "well" or "very well." The Hispanic out-migrants also had the highest average number of weeks worked (31.9), hours usually worked per week (30.7), total income from all sources ($6,778), and wages ($6.69 per hour) in 1979. Hispanic out-migrants also had the lowest poverty rate in 1979, with 21.8 percent living in families with incomes below the poverty level. Yet, Hispanic out-migrants are not a homogeneous group, as exemplified by the occupational distribution data—among the three groups, Hispanic out-migrants had the highest percentage of members employed in technical, sales, and administrative occupations (35.7 percent) and farming occupations (10.1 percent).

In certain respects, the Hispanic in-migrants held socioeconomic advantages over the Hispanic nonmigrants. For example, two-fifths of Hispanic in-migrants were high-school graduates, compared to one-third of the nonmigrants, and 13.4 percent of in-migrants were employed in managerial and professional occupations, compared to 9.6 percent of nonmigrants. The in-migrants also held slight advantages over the nonmigrants in weeks worked, hours usually worked, and total income from all sources in 1979. In contrast, however, Hispanic nonmigrants possessed higher levels of English proficiency (67.1 percent spoke English "well" or "very well" versus 62.3 percent of in-migrants), earned higher wages ($5.10 per hour compared to $4.55 per hour), and had lower poverty rates (33.1 percent versus 42.6 percent) than their counterparts who had moved to the Valley between 1975 and 1980.

It is clear, then, that Hispanics leaving the Valley tend to have the most favorable socioeconomic attributes. This represents the loss of valuable human capital. Indeed, Valley communities may not receive returns on their investments in educating the out-migrants. This is a brain-drain problem that has been experienced by areas (e.g., rural areas and developing countries) with limited employment opportunities that have been unable to retain their better-educated residents [Miller (1982) has also made this observation in his Brownsville survey]. Furthermore, the Valley lost valuable human capital in the net exchange between in-migrants and out-migrants. For the Valley to retain its younger, better-educated Hispanics, more favorable employment opportunities will need to be created in the immediate future. Failure to do so will result in the loss of valuable productive residents.

Colonias: Colonies within the Colony

The socioeconomic problems observed in the Valley are perhaps most acute in the colonias that dot the region's landscape. The colonias are essentially rural unincorporated subdivisions characterized by substandard housing, inadequate plumbing and sewage disposal systems, and inadequate access to clean water (Salinas et al., 1988). Colonias grew in the Valley in the early 1950s as poor families pursued the American dream of owning a house (Colonias Task Force, 1989). In response to such demand, developers subdivided land into lots which were sold without adequate water, sewage, or drainage. Once the land was sold, developers failed to provide such basic necessities and the residents did not have the financial resources to make improvements. There were 435 colonias, containing 71,478 people, in the Valley in 1987 (see Colonias Task Force, 1989).

Data from a Texas Department of Human Services survey conducted in 1988 (see Salinas et al., 1988) can provide a profile of the population inhabiting the colonias. Colonia residents are almost exclusively Hispanics: only 1.2 percent are Anglo. The population is relatively young, having an average age of 18.5. Contrary to popular belief, the majority (two-thirds) of Valley colonia residents were born in the United States. Like their counterparts in the Valley, colonia residents are plagued by low levels of education. For example, three out of every four family heads did not finish high school, with 39 percent never setting foot in school. With this low level of educational attainment, only 53 percent of colonia residents were employed at the time of the survey. Among those who were employed, agricultural field work was the most common occupation. Such seasonal jobs do not offer stable employment. Close to half (48 percent) of colonia workers earned $3.35 an hour (the minimum wage at the time) or less in 1988. The average household income in 1987 was only $6,784.

Data from the survey also illustrate the substandard housing and environmental conditions of colonia residents. Although 87 percent of colonia residents own their homes, many of these houses are essentially shacks constructed from shabby materials. Many do not possess adequate heating and cooling systems. One-fifth of the households lack any source of treated water. Furthermore, 30 percent of colonia homes have outhouses or cesspools rather than adequate sewage disposal systems. Consequently, raw sewage seeps into existing water supplies, contaminating them and subjecting residents to disease. These water sources are what many colonia inhabitants must use to bathe, cook, and drink. Under such conditions, Valley colonias are places where Third World diseases (e.g., tuberculosis and hepatitis) still survive. To exacerbate the problem, health insurance is a luxury that close to three-fourths of the residents do not enjoy.

These are the harsh conditions that colonia residents must endure on a daily basis. Colonia residents are essentially the poorest of the poor.

Federal Policies

A number of social programs stemming from President Johnson's War on Poverty made their way into the Valley in the late 1960s; the Comprehensive Employment and Training Act (CETA) enacted in 1973 and related programs stemming from the Manpower Development Training Act are particularly relevant. These programs provided employment for many poor. In part, the introduction of these programs in the late 1960s and 1970s improved the socioeconomic standing of Valley Hispanics in the 1970s. The data in table 6.1 clearly demonstrate that the percentage of Hispanic families living in poverty declined significantly, from 52.0 percent in 1970 to 35.4 percent in 1980. During the same period, the median income of Hispanic families in the Valley rose at a very healthy pace.

Still, it is clear that while federal social programs have been help-ful in providing economic relief to the region, they have fallen short of solving the socioeconomic problems of the area. For example, the unemployment rate of Valley Hispanics actually increased at the time that these social programs were in full force. Because of the Valley's large growth and its young population structure, jobs provided by such federal social programs tended not to keep pace with the numbers needing employment. At the same time, both the nature and the tenure of the jobs were far from ideal in providing continuous employ-ment, since most of the jobs available were low-skill, low-wage jobs offering few opportunities for advancement. In fact, the jobs provided only sporadic, temporary employment. In the end, workers going through such programs failed to obtain skills necessary to compete effectively for more stable employment. Instead, they had merely pro-vided cheap temporary labor for Valley employers.

The significant cuts in funding for federal social programs begin-ning with the Reagan administration nonetheless have largely taken away this safety net. In 1982, the Job Training Partnership Act (JTPA) replaced CETA. Unlike its predecessor, however, JTPA generally does not create new jobs because of its emphasis on local, private-sector initiatives (Lyson, 1989). In addition, Lyson notes that JTPA currently receives approximately 40 percent as much funding as did CETA dur-ing 1979, its peak year. JTPA appears to be inadequate to solve the problems of the area.

Maquiladoras

For the most part, business leaders and economic development specialists have chosen industrialization as the solution to the Valley's socioeconomic problems. Newspapers regularly highlight efforts being made by local development groups to attract industry into the area, with one of the key incentives for businesses being the large supply of cheap labor. Industrialization has been taking place at a very rapid pace over the last couple of decades, and much of this growth has been tied to the growth of maquiladoras (assembly plants) along the Texas-Mexican border. The introduction of maquiladoras to Mexico came about through the initiation of the Border Industrialization Program (BIP) in 1965, following the termination of the Bracero Program in 1964, when approximately 200,000 former braceros were "stranded" in the border region, further exacerbating the region's unemployment problem (Pena, 1980). The Mexican government created BIP under such conditions.

BIP basically sought to encourage foreign firms, particularly those from the United States, to establish assembly shops along Mexico's northern border. These assembly shops are called "maquiladoras," a Spanish term whose original meaning referred to "the portion of flour retained by a miller as payment for grinding someone else's grain" (House, 1982:216). The Mexican and U.S. tariff codes essentially allow U.S. firms to ship raw materials into Mexico duty-free, to use these to produce goods in the maquiladoras, and to import the assembled product into the United States. Thus, duties are only paid on the value added to the product in Mexico, which essentially consists of wages paid to maquiladora workers.

The tariff schedule, however, stipulates that the goods must be finished in the United States. Because of this stipulation, a number of maquiladoras have a "twin plant" on the U.S. side of the border. The plants on the Mexican side are involved in labor-intensive operations, whereas those on the U.S. side are generally used as distribution plants. Not surprisingly, the overwhelming majority of workers are employed in the Mexican plants. Fernandez (1977) noted that Transitron, for example, an electronic manufacturer, had 75 employees in Laredo, Texas, and 1,500 in Nuevo Laredo (Mexico). The cheaper labor in Mexico accounts for the unequal distribution. Indeed, the official Mexican minimum wage including benefits averages seventy-five cents an hour, or $6 a day (Texas Department of Commerce, n.d.). Thus, to a large extent, the concept of the "twin plant" has not been realized (Patrick, 1989).

Despite such unequal employment distributions, U.S. border communities have aggressively sought to attract maquiladoras because it has been contended that such operations stimulate local economies. For instance, a significant amount of the wages of Mexican maquiladora employees is spent in the U.S. border region (see Konig, 1979). The argument has also been made that businesses along the U.S. border serve as suppliers of goods and services to the assembly plants. Patrick and Arriola (1987) note that of the $130 million payroll of the Matamoros, Reynosa, and Nuevo Laredo maquiladoras in 1987, about 30 percent was spent in South Texas border communities. In addition, they estimate that during the same year, approximately 10,000 support jobs in transportation, warehousing, and business services were created in South Texas border cities. According to such arguments, benefits from the growth of maquiladoras eventually "trickle down" to the Valley poor (Maril, 1989).

The growth in the number of maquiladoras and employees in such plants in Mexico has been impressive. For example, in 1987 there were 1,005 maquiladoras employing approximately 308,000 workers in Mexico, compared to 443 and 78,000, respectively, in 1977 (Wilkie and Ochoa, 1988). Maquiladora activity has blossomed in the two Mexican cities (Matamoros and Reynosa) bordering the Valley. For example, as of September 1990, there were ninety-four maquiladoras employing 23,475 workers in Matamoros and Reynosa (Perez Cornejo, personal communication). The number of maquiladora plants has increased by six times over the twenty-year period from 1970 to 1990, while the number of workers has increased nearly twenty-three times. In recent years, Japanese, Korean, Taiwanese, and European firms have joined U.S. firms in Mexican border areas.

Other Local Development Efforts

In contrast to the more long-term development efforts being carried out by business leaders and economic development specialists, over the last couple of decades a number of organizations have attempted to address the more immediate needs of the Valley poor. Among these, Maril (1989) has hailed Valley Interfaith, an Industrial Areas Foundation grass-roots organization comprised of various community groups, as the most prominent. Catholic parishes have served as the glue holding together the diverse community groups. Valley Interfaith has enjoyed large success in organizing the poor to demand better public services and jobs (Acuna, 1988). One of the initial feats of Valley Interfaith was to pressure the Environmental Protection Agency successfully to forbid the burning of toxic waste on ships in the Gulf of Mexico (Acuna, 1988). More recent successes of Valley Interfaith have included lobbying the State of Texas for funding in the development of the colonias, indigent health care, and financial assistance to farmworkers affected by the freeze of 1983 (Maril, 1989). Valley Interfaith has also been successful in recent years in leading efforts to incorporate colonias into nearby cities to hook colonia residences to city water, the Las Milpas colonia near Pharr being an example.

Other organizations have also taken up the cause of the colonia poor by organizing grass-roots development efforts.[1] The College of Architecture at Texas A&M, as part of a Valley colonia project, was able to secure funding from the Texas legislature to build one community center (demonstration project) in Hidalgo County and one in Cameron County. Because the colonias are isolated, these community centers will help bring needed social services to the colonias. The design of these centers along with the development of particular programs and services to be housed within the centers have derived directly from local colonia residents. Self-help development efforts have also surfaced in the colonias. The Hidalgo County Extension Agency obtained a grant from the Levi Strauss Company to provide training in sewing to thirty-one colonia women, who each train in turn fifteen other colonia residents. The grant provided teaching materials, kits, and equipment. The next phase of the project involves linking the trainees up with the Small Business Administration to develop home-based sewing businesses.

Another organization that deserves mention because of its efforts to help the Valley poor is the Texas Rural Legal Aid (TRLA). TRLA has provided essential legal services to the poor, who have traditionally been locked out of the legal arena because of their lack of financial resources. TRLA has also devoted much energy to issues affecting farmworkers.

Another legal organization that has made significant contributions to Hispanic Valley residents is the Mexican American Legal and Educational Fund (MALDEF). MALDEF has been instrumental in taking up the causes of Hispanic education. Recent court cases have successfully challenged unequal funding of school districts around the state and the underrepresentation of graduate programs in the Texas border area. Such efforts in the political arena are crucial to the struggle to improve the lives of Hispanics.

Conclusions

Using the internal colonialism theoretical perspective, we suggest that the historical relationships placing Chicanos at the bottom of the Valley's socioeconomic structure and Anglos at the top of the structure help explain the contemporary socioeconomic problems of Hispanics. Valley Hispanics have encountered numerous obstacles solidified in the institutional structure of the region that have impeded their climb up the socioeconomic ladder. They continue to receive inferior education, which severely limits their possibilities for upward mobility. In addition, even though demographic changes have been changing the political situation, Hispanics continue to be relatively underrepresented politically in particular areas of the region. Furthermore, because of the presence of high levels of poverty and unemployment and of limited levels of human capital and unionization, the Valley has been quite attractive to American capitalists interested in cutting their labor costs. The Valley, with its large reserve army of the unemployed, can be viewed as a labor colony for U.S. capitalists.

Although the Valley's persistent socioeconomic problems resemble those experienced by numerous rural communities in the United States, to a certain extent, because of the ethnic and historical situations, the region's problems also resemble those of many developing countries. For example, both developing countries and the Valley share colonial histories; both have also experienced significant levels of brain-drain out-migration; both tend to have shantytowns containing their poorest inhabitants; both have dependent relationships with capitalist powers, as exemplified by the presence of multinational corporations in many developing countries and the influence of the maquiladora industry in the Valley. Both developing countries and the Valley have also been experiencing high levels of population growth, due to significant levels of natural increase. In fact, in both settings, employment growth has been unable to keep up with population growth.

Given this situation, then, we must understand that policies designed to alleviate problems in rural America may not necessarily be applicable in the Valley. Indeed, the Valley can only be considered "rural" because of its geographic isolation and its historical dependence on the agriculture sector. In many other respects, the Valley tends to be more metropolitan, particularly with regard to population size. Indeed, population projections suggest that by 2025 the Valley could contain a population of 1.7 million (Saenz and Murdock, 1990).

Since the turnaround decade of the 1970s, many rural communities in the United States have experienced trouble attracting industries. This has not been the case for the Valley, however. In fact, the region has experienced large-scale, unprecedented growth in population and industrialization over the last couple of decades. Despite such growth, socioeconomic problems continue to persist. To a certain extent, this mismatch has occurred because most of the jobs being imported have been low-wage, dead-end jobs in the service and industrial sectors. Given the combined presence of high unemployment rates, low levels of unionization, and the presence of low-wage, undocumented labor, Valley workers have been in an unfavorable position to negotiate with their employers for better wages. Furthermore, the addition of such jobs partially explains the brain-drain migration of Hispanics. Better-educated Hispanics possessing higher levels of human capital tend to find limited employment opportunities in the

Valley. The departure of this portion of the population represents a tremendous loss of human capital, for these are the individuals that are best equipped to occupy the more prestigious positions in the occupational, social, and political structures. The out-migration of this selective population also represents the loss of valuable revenue for the area. Thus, Valley leaders must create employment opportunities for this segment of the population. Failure to do so will result in further loss of productive workers.

Leaders should also examine carefully their policies designed to attract industry in the form of maquiladoras. Although maquiladoras have been credited for stimulating local economies, one must question the extent to which benefits have trickled down to rank-and-file Hispanics. Our guess is that, whereas particular businesses in the Valley have benefited from the presence of maquiladoras, the ameliorative socioeconomic impact on the poor in the region has been minimal. In fact, Patrick (1989) estimated that of the $1.3 billion that maquiladoras located in the Mexican border area across from the Valley spent on component parts and materials, less than 2 percent involved Valley companies. It is also important to assess the stability of employment opportunities in the maquiladoras. Indeed, as U.S. labor unions and rural areas in the South (Lyson, 1989) can testify, U.S. capitalists are constantly on the lookout for cheaper labor. Thus, corporations having maquiladoras along the border are not married to the region, and the presence of cheaper labor elsewhere could quickly dissolve the existing relationship. It is no secret that, immediately before the devaluation of the peso, many U.S. corporations were planning to move their operations to places such as Hong Kong and Haiti, where they could find workers willing to work for cheaper wages (Miller, 1982). Ironically, it was the peso devaluation of 1982 that saved many jobs on the Mexican border and that stimulated much growth in the maquiladora industry (Fernandez, 1989). It appears that the free-trade agreement between the United States, Mexico, and Canada is inevitable. Although the agreement may provide certain benefits to the U.S. and Mexican border regions, it could also draw jobs away from the border region into the interior of Mexico, where wages are lower.

Because of the low levels of education and high rates of unemployment among Hispanics in the Valley, educational programs and policies to increase the educational attainment of Hispanics are needed. Jobs being imported into the Valley tend to be low-wage, low-skill jobs because of the area's relative shortage of workers who can adequately fill better-paying, high-skill jobs. A solid educational infrastructure is thus needed to educate and train workers for jobs that offer opportunities for upward mobility. Investment in such an educational infrastructure is essential for breaking the Valley's long-standing cycle involving poor educational opportunities, low-paying jobs, and the exploitation of labor.

Finally, we call on the U.S. government to revert to its policies of the 1960s and 1970s, which attempted to provide the poor with much-needed training and skills. Both the Reagan and Bush administrations have emphasized foreign policy, much to the neglect of domestic social policies. When domestic policies have been addressed, they have ignored the poor. If this country has the economic resources to bail out the savings-and-loan institutions, it certainly has the means to create programs and policies designed to better the lives of its poorest inhabitants. Because of the changing demographics, failure to address the concerns of the poor and minorities today will ultimately come back to haunt the country in the near future, as these individuals, ill-equipped to participate in an increasingly technological work force, will be called on to bear the brunt of generating revenues to support an increasingly elderly population.

Notes

1. This paragraph was developed from a personal interview with Ida Acuna Patrick (1992), Hidalgo County extension agent.

References

Acuna, Rodolfo. 1988. *Occupied America: The Chicano's Struggle toward Liberation*. 3d ed. New York: Harper and Row.
Almaguer, Tomas. 1971. "Toward the Study of Chicano Colonialism." *Aztlan* 2 (1):7–21.
Alvarez, Rodolfo. 1973. "The Psycho-historical and Socioeconomic Development of the Chicano Community." *Social Science Quarterly* 53 (4):520–42.
Barrera, Mario. 1979. *Race and Class in the Southwest: A Theory of Racial Inequality*. Notre Dame, Ind.: University of Notre Dame Press.
Barrera, Mario, Carlos Munoz, and Charles Ornelas. 1972. "The Barrio as an Internal Colony." Pp. 465–98 in H. Hahn (ed.), *People and Politics in Urban Society*. Beverly Hills, Calif.: Sage.
Blauner, Robert. 1972. *Racial Oppression in America*. New York: Harper and Row.
Colonias Task Force. 1989. *Colonias Task Force Report*. Austin: Texas Department of Human Services.
Fernandez, Raul A. 1977. *the United States–Mexico Border: A Political-Economic Profile*. Notre Dame, Ind.: University of Notre Dame Press.
———. 1989. *The Mexican-American Border Region: Issues and Trends*. Notre Dame, Ind.: University of Notre Dame Press.

House, John W. 1982. *Frontier on the Rio Grande: A Political Geography of Development and Social Deprivation.* New York: Oxford University Press.

Jensen, Leif, and Marta Tienda. 1989. "Nonmetropolitan Minority Families in the United States: Trends in Racial and Ethnic Economic Stratification, 1959–1986." *Rural Sociology* 54 (4):509–32.

Konig, W. 1979. "Efectos de la Actividad Maquiladora Frontizera en la Sociedad Mexicana." Paper presented at the National Symposium on Border Studies. Monterrey, Nuevo Leon (Mexico).

Lyson, Thomas A. 1989. *Two Sides to the Sunbelt: The Growing Divergence between the Rural and Urban South.* New York: Praeger.

Maril, Robert Lee. 1989. *Poorest of Americans: The Mexican Americans of the Lower Rio Grande Valley of Texas.* Notre Dame, Ind.: University of Notre Dame Press.

Miller, Michael V. 1982. *Economic Growth and Change along the U.S.-Mexican Border.* Austin: Bureau of Business Research, University of Texas at Austin.

Mirande, Alfredo. 1985. *The Chicano Experience: An Alternative Perspective.* Notre Dame, Ind.: University of Notre Dame Press.

Montejano, David. 1987. *Anglos and Mexicans in the Making of Texas, 1836–1986.* Austin: University of Texas Press.

Moore, Joan. 1970. "Colonialism: The Case of the Mexican Americans." *Social Problems* 17 (Spr.):463–72.

Patrick, Ida Acuna. 1992. Personal communication, 14 May.

Patrick, J. Michael. 1989. "Maquiladoras and South Texas Border Economic Development." *Journal of Borderland Studies* 4 (1):89–98.

Patrick, J. Michael, and Roland S. Arriola. 1987. "The Economic Impact of Maquiladoras on Border Development: A Rio Grande Valley Case Study—Some Preliminary Findings." Paper presented at the annual meeting of the Western Social Science Association, El Paso.

Pena, Devon Gerardo. 1980. "Las Maquiladoras: Mexican Women and Class Struggle in the Border Industries." *Aztlan* 11:159–229.

Perez Cornejo, Jose A. 1991. Personal communication (American Chamber of Commerce in Mexico, Mexico D.F.).

Population Reference Bureau. 1987. *Metro U.S.A. Data Sheet.* Washington, D.C.: Population Reference Bureau.

Saenz, Rogelio, and Steve H. Murdock. 1988. *Socioeconomic Changes among Anglos, Blacks, and Hispanics in Texas, 1980–1985.* Departmental Technical Report 88-5. College Station: Texas Agricultural Experiment Station, Texas A&M University.

———. 1990. *Population Changes among Racial/Ethnic Groups in Texas, 1970–2025.* Departmental Technical Report 90-3. College Station: Texas Agricultural Experiment Station, Texas A&M University.

Saenz, Rogelio, and John K. Thomas. 1990. "Minority Poverty in Nonmetropolitan Texas." Paper presented at the annual meeting of the Rural Sociological Society, Norfolk, Va.

Salinas, Exiquio, Michelle Bensenberg, and Jan Amazeen. 1988. *The Colonia Factbook: A Survey of Living Conditions in Rural Areas of South and West Texas Border Counties.* Austin: Texas Department of Human Services.

San Miguel, Guadalupe. 1984. "The Origins, Development, and Consequences of the Educational Segregation of Mexicans in the Southwest." Pp. 195–208 in E. E. Garcia, F. A. Lomeli, and I. D. Ortiz (eds.), *Chicano Studies: A Multidisciplinary Approach*. New York: Teachers College Press.

Taylor, Paul S. 1934. *An American-Mexican Frontier: Nueces County, Texas*. Chapel Hill: University of North Carolina Press.

Texas Department of Commerce. N.d. *Competitive Manufacturing: An American Alternative, A Guide to the Texas Border Region*. Austin: Texas Department of Commerce.

Texas Employment Commission. *Estimates of Labor Force and Unemployment for Counties, 1990*. Austin: Texas Employment Commission.

U.S. Bureau of the Census. 1984. *Gross Migration for Counties: 1975 to 1980*. Supplementary Report PC80-S1-17. Washington, DC: Government Printing Office.

Webb, Walter Prescott. 1935. *The Texas Rangers: A Century of Frontier Defence*. Boston: Houghton Mifflin.

Wilkie, James W., and Enrique Ochoa, eds. 1988. *Statistical Abstract of Latin America*. Vol. 26. Los Angeles: Latin American Center Publications, University of California at Los Angeles.

7 | The Forgotten of Northern New England

A. E. Luloff and Mark Nord

He chose to be rich by making his wants few.
—*Ralph Waldo Emerson, on his friend Henry David Thoreau*

MAINE, NEW HAMPSHIRE, and Vermont, the three northern New England states, present ironic anomalies both in landscape and in population. The landscape combines breathtaking natural beauty, which attracts and holds those who fall under its spell, with generally poor, infertile, and rocky soils that stubbornly resist agricultural development. Natives include former president George Bush, a disproportionate share of the nation's millionaires, scions of wealthy early settlers and land and sea barons—the politically powerful and connected. Yet as recently as 1981 this region was described as one of the poorest places in the nation, with two of its states among the three poorest (Garreau, 1981).[1] The people of northern New England, both rich and poor, share some basic attributes, including a fiercely independent character, a defiance toward the plight of making a living in this difficult and often unforgiving environment, and a belief that this region is really the only civilized place in North America. These common beliefs despite life-space differences contribute to the diversity of human chances characteristic of the region (cf. Garreau, 1981).

Among the area's natural resources are miles of spectacular ocean views and beaches, scenic vistas, Rockwellian landscapes, and numerous swamps and bays, all balanced by some of the highest mountains in the eastern United States. Offshore are the rich fisheries of Georges Banks. The area boasts many lakes and rivers, which serve the fertile valleys, maintaining the region's limited agriculture, and providing some of the nation's best white-water recreation. Dominating the region is the vast forest cover that accounts for three-quarters of its 52,128-square-mile area. A sizable proportion of this land is in the Green and White Mountain national forests, in Vermont and New Hampshire respectively, which together make up more than 12 percent of the region's total land area. New Hampshire and Vermont rank first and third among states east of the Mississippi in proportion of total land that is federally owned.

These resources, which provided the means of sustenance for early settlement, continue to play a vital, though changed, part in the region's economy. Part of the story behind the forgotten of northern New England can be traced to the use and control of its natural assets, which have not been enjoyed equally by all its people.

Despite the presence of several large cities, according to the 1990 census more than half of northern New England's 2.9 million residents lived in nonmetropolitan counties with slightly more people living in areas adjacent to metropolitan centers than in nonadjacent regions. Many of these nonmetropolitan residents commute for work to metropolitan areas both in and out of the three-state region. The bedroom communities characteristic of suburban sprawl indicate where these people are concentrated. Other nonmetropolitan residents live and work in the region's numerous rural communities. The large majority are employed in nonunionized jobs that offer wages generally below the national average. In addition, scattered throughout the area is yet another segment of the region's population, the forgotten poor. These people for the most part remain invisible to the majority. They tend not to be noticed because they are dispersed over an expansive and sparsely settled area (cf. Fitchen, 1981). A spate of recent novels, television documentaries, and articles in the popular press have provided anecdotal evidence of entrenched poverty in many of the rural areas of northern New England. Carolyn Chute's novels *The Beans of Egypt, Maine* (1985) and *Letourneau's Used Auto Parts* (1988) and the recent video *Back Country Blues* (WCVB-TV, Boston) have powerfully depicted the human suffering and angst of those living in persistent poverty. For some, the consequences are bitterness, anger, and violence; for most, a quiet desperation ensues from the feeling that the causes of one's poverty lie "out there," outside of one's own community and control (cf. Gaventa, 1980). According to Peter Anderson in the *Boston Globe Magazine* (16 September 1990) these people include

the pregnant woman who slept in a cardboard box in back of a new factory-outlet store in North Conway; the father, mother, and children who lived for a time on berries, dandelion greens, and horned pout caught nightly in Umbagog Lake in Errol; the young mothers like Sharon, of Leeds, who didn't have enough money to have her teeth extracted; elderly women such as Delphine, of Monmouth, who was poor long enough to think it normal to live without electricity; and the elderly woman in Jonesport who heated her house with a kerosene burner and had a well and pump but no bathroom. She used a bucket, which she emptied each day in a little field behind her house near the shore.

How indicative of normal daily life are such accounts of human misery in late twentieth-century northern New England? Are they merely vignettes of unusual or rare instances of poverty? Or do they perhaps point to a more pernicious social malady of the area? To answer these questions we look now at the history and current reality of northern New England.

Uneven Development: A Historical Sketch

An important and sometimes overlooked factor in northern New England's development and history is the role of the last glacial retreat, which left this land in an inhospitable condition. Much of the area was covered with large deposits of unconsolidated till composed of clay, sand, gravel, and boulders, contributing to the sparseness of agricultural lands. At the same time glaciated soils provided productive aquifers and valuable mineral resources; sand, gravel, granite, marble, limestone, and clay were mainstays of the early mineral industry (New England Regional Plan, 1981; Luloff, 1989). The denser vegetation found in the valleys, coupled with their soils' higher fertility and the annual deposits of humus, made these inland areas attractive sites for agriculture. But the glaciers, with a wryness prescient of Yankee culture, buried in these same valleys great quantities of stones and boulders, at depths of several feet, which the frost heaves to the surface each year making productive agricultural use difficult (Labaree, 1982).[2]

The region's forests included a variety of species. In the colonial era, the coastal plains were dominated by oak-hickory, white pine, occasional coastal red spruce, and scattered Atlantic white-cedar swamps. As one moved inland, in Maine, balsam firs and white and black spruce predominated, especially at higher elevations. Moving westward into New Hampshire and Vermont, one increasingly encountered northern hardwoods (sugar maple, beech, birch) with large components of white pine and eastern hemlock intermixed. At mid to high elevations (above 1,500 feet) these gave way to spruce and fir forests once again (Eckert, 1991).

Coastal waters and inland rivers and lakes also played an important role in the region's early development. Many of its fast-flowing streams and rivers facilitated early development of water-powered industries. Plentiful stocks of shellfish and finfish were found along the New Hampshire and Maine coasts. The colder waters of the area supported fertile beds of clams, mussels, and lobsters. New England coastal waters were home to great schools of migrating cod, herring, sardines, mackerel, and tuna (Greenwood, 1991). Each spring, shad, alewives, and Atlantic salmon made their way up the brackish waters of the major rivers to spawn, and the numerous ponds and lakes supported several species of trout (Labaree, 1984).

Early settlement in the three northern states occurred along the coastal waterways and accessible river valleys. The dominant stream of early migrants was composed of farmers, foresters, and fishermen who came from the southern New England states. Because the soils were marginal in Connecticut, Massachusetts, and Rhode Island, large stands of softwoods had been cleared to expand productive tillable areas, depleting both the soil and forest resources. Migrants from that area brought with them to their new settings both these "soil-mining" practices and the names of their previous towns (Luloff and Frick, 1986). The vast majority of these people remained engaged in extractive industries; fishing, forestry, and mining supplemented the dominant agricultural sector.

Population growth during the early period of settlement was relatively slow. By 1770 barely 103,000 people resided in the three states, with 60 percent in New Hampshire, 30 percent in Maine, and 10 percent in Vermont. The region's enduring dependence on its natural resources was established in the small hamlets of settlement and reinforced by the need for external capital for development during this period. This external linkage, however, allowed many of the new seacoast communities to join in the emerging international trade, particularly in timber and wood products, ships, salt cod, and early artisan-produced goods.

From 1800 to mid-century, the aggregate population of the three states grew to 1.2 million, with half in Maine and the rest divided roughly equally between Vermont and New Hampshire. Port activity increased, bringing many raw materials to the rapidly developing industries of the urban centers. In addition, a large rural industrial manufacturing economy developed, based primarily on local natural resources; its products included textiles and footwear. This industrial expansion resulted in further settlements along the region's inland waterways, which were the lifeblood of the settlements, providing both the power to manufacture and the transportation necessary to deliver products to market.

It was the forests, however, which played the dominant role in the region's early development. Large quantities of timber were readily available for use by early settlers in housing, heating, creating home utensils, and for protection (stockade fencing). These resources were also important for shipbuilding and for use in shipping the products of the region. The large stock of white pine, formerly claimed by the British Parliament for use as masts by the Royal Navy, now served the important and growing American shipbuilding trade. With increasing settlement the demand for building products increased enabling a more diversified and stronger lumber industry to develop. This resulted in further clearing of forested lands.[3]

Infusion of external capital, especially in the post–Civil War years, stimulated industrial, agricultural, and residential development. But, in the largely unrestrained capitalistic development of those years, control of resources became concentrated in the hands of absentee owners (cf. Irland, 1989).

The post–Civil War era has generally been viewed as the beginning of modern rural New England. Several important interrelated factors occurred here at this time. The widespread adoption of both waterpower and steampower in factories hastened the growth of manufacturing and facilitated advancements in textile technologies. Both communities and industrial mill complexes, especially paper manufacturers, were constructed on tidewaters and at major falls. In 1860, New England accounted for about half of the value of output of the paper industry in the United States (Eisenmenger, 1967). This growth in early manufacturing created a niche for the excess of population from the agricultural areas, particularly for daughters and for second born (and later) sons, and for the flood of immigrants to the region.

The building of the railroads and canals also hastened the integration of the relatively isolated communities of northern New England into a more coherent whole. The region became linked not only with the southern New England states, but with the growing population base and developing industrial infrastructure of the Mid-Atlantic states. These transportation improvements brought changes in the demand and distribution of indigenous products. Cottage industries producing shoes, processed foods, and other articles gave way to large-scale factories which turned out many of these same products, in addition to canned and metal-worked goods. Farm products enjoyed wider and more dependable markets, enhancing their early advantage of proximity to large population centers. The railroads also facilitated migration, both into and out of the region, and initiated the beginnings of seasonal and recreation-based community economies. Public transportation to the early spas in Sheldon Springs and Hot Point, Vermont, to the Lakcs region of New Hampshire, and to coastal areas of Maine, including Rangely and Bar Harbor, helped to foster the region's tourist industry (Judd, 1988).

With the growth and development of the industrial infrastructure, numerous job opportunities were created, and workers moved to the large mill complexes. The unseemly side of this growth was reflected in the increasing numbers of children and women working long hours for relatively low wages. As a result of growing concern over this problem, New Hampshire became one of the first states to establish child-labor laws, to impose a ten-hour work day, and to affirm the principle that states had the right to regulate business—including the charters of state-granted monopolies (Morrison and Morrison, 1976:138; see also Howe, 1988). Of course, children and women continued to be major factors in the success of industry in the region.

In spite of industrial growth, the region was never densely populated. In 1800 both Vermont and Maine had population densities lower than the national average of 19.9 persons per square mile (16.9 and 5.1 respectively). This pattern of low person-to-land ratios existed throughout most of the nineteenth century. During the last half of the 1800s, many farmers left northern New England and relocated to the southern three New England states and to the West in search of better employment opportunities (Brown and Zuiches, 1986). At the same time, the area's other primary industries, especially fishing, mining, and forestry also suffered declines, reducing the numbers of people gainfully employed in extractive work.[4]

This out-migration resulted in the diminution of many of these states' agricultural communities and the concomitant increase in abandoned land. Peak acreages in farmland occurred in 1870 in New Hampshire and in 1910 in both Vermont and Maine (see Figure 7.1).[5] With the out-migration of these people, the most unproductive agricultural land, especially that which was "improved" during the mid-1800s, reverted to second-growth forest. Much of this land was only marginal for production in the first place; as Black (1950:180) has suggested, "[The region is] not even moderately well endowed with natural soil resources."

These declines, coupled with the relatively slow growth in the rural industrial towns of the region, restricted northern New England's total population increase to roughly 50 percent during the period 1850–1950 (an average annual rate of growth of only .41 percent). Thus, despite the restructuring of the region's agricultural economy in an extremely short time and the emergence of a strong industrial infrastructure, the early history of northern New England is one of general population

Figure 7.1. Farmland and Population in Northern New England,
1850–1990

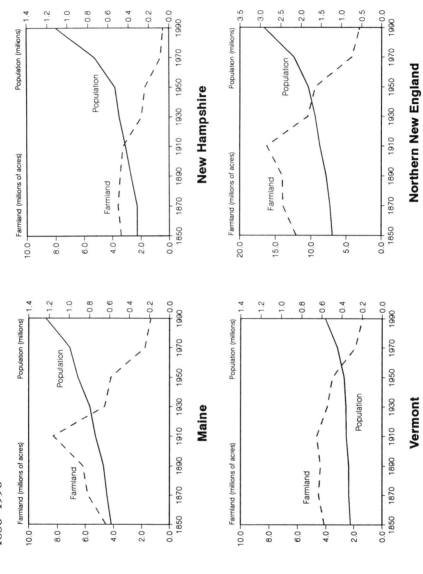

stability and the emergence of distinct class lines between owners and workers, the latter of whom earned their keep with either skilled or relentless labor.

Uneven Development: The Current Reality

An examination of recent economic and social indicators provides a more comprehensive picture of conditions in these three rural states. The 1981 report of the New England Governors' Commission called attention to the distressed rural areas of the region. This report, the New England Regional Plan, stated: "These [rural] areas have often been overlooked for both public and private investment, a situation that has begun to change only in the past several years. As a result of disinvestment and remoteness, these areas have chronically suffered a disproportionate share of poverty" (New England Regional Commission, 1981:92). The report identified ten distressed counties as representative of the thirty-six fully rural counties of New England. Nine fell within northern New England. These counties are very rural indeed, with population densities ranging from ten persons per square mile in Essex County, Vermont, to fifty-two in Bennington County, Vermont (U.S. Bureau of the Census, 1988a).[6]

In these nine counties, poverty and unemployment rates have been substantially and persistently higher than those of the region as a whole. The 1970 average poverty rate in these counties was nearly twice that of the New England region (14.7 percent versus 7.8 percent). By 1979 this rate had declined only slightly to 14.1 percent, remaining half again as high as the regional average (unweighted county averages, U.S. Bureau of Census, 1988a). In 1979, both Waldo County, Maine, and Essex County, Vermont, were marked by almost one in five people living in poverty.[7] In addition, the unemployment rate (1977–1979) in these nine counties (7.5 percent, U.S. Bureau of Census, 1988a) was 50 percent higher than the regional average (5 percent, New England Regional Commission, 1981). Since Lichter and Costanzo (1987) have demonstrated that economic underemployment in rural areas tends to be substantially worse than is indicated by simple unemployment counts, there is reason to believe that the disadvantage was even greater than these figures revealed. This portrait of uneven development is also evinced by the quality of the region's housing. The median value of occupied housing in 1980 was substantially lower in the nine distressed counties than in New England as a whole. It ranged from just 51 percent of the regional median in Essex County, Vermont, to

82 percent in Bennington County, Vermont (U.S. Bureau of Census, 1988a).

Of course there is more to the forgotten region of northern New England than these nine representative counties. Inferential information suggests that at least two-thirds of the forty counties in the three states share the same fate as the nine selected by the Governors' Commission. To demonstrate this, we have analyzed a number of indicators comparing these thirty-nine "forgotten counties" with the more "urban counties" of the area. We classified as forgotten all but the six counties on the I-95 corridor of Maine, all but the four central and southeastern counties of New Hampshire, and all of Vermont except Chittenden County (see Map 7.1). These counties form a contiguous block encompassing the northern three-fourths of the three-state region (plus two coastal enclaves in Maine), stretching 450 miles from Pawnal, Vermont, to Madawaska, Maine.[8]

The poverty rate in the forgotten counties in 1979 was 13.2 percent, compared with 9.7 percent in the urban counties (see Table 7.1 and Map 7.2); average per capita income in the forgotten counties in 1979 was only 87.5 percent of their urban counterparts (U.S. Bureau of Census, 1988b). In 1980, 49 percent of the housing stock in the forgotten counties was more than forty years old (U.S. Bureau of the Census, 1988c). Such were the conditions in rural northern New England at the end of the 1970s, and as in decades past, there was little to be optimistic about.

For New England as a whole, however, the 1980s were a decade of remarkable growth and development. According to the Federal Reserve Bank of Boston (1990):

> Employment grew vigorously and unemployment rates, consistently lower than those in the nation, fell to 3% in late 1987 and early 1988. Per capita income jumped from 104% of the national average in 1979 to more than 120% in 1988 and 1989. . . . New England's economic performance through most of the 1980s was truly extraordinary. . . .
>
> Total personal income, perhaps the best single measure of regional economic success, grew at an annual rate of 9.3% between 1979 and 1989. (iv)

Were the benefits of this growth realized throughout New England? Did the increase in regional prosperity translate into improved well-being in rural northern New England? At the national level, Henry, Drabenstott, and Gibson (1988) have shown that the rural-urban

Map 7.1. The Forgotten Counties of Northern New England and the NERC Representative Sample

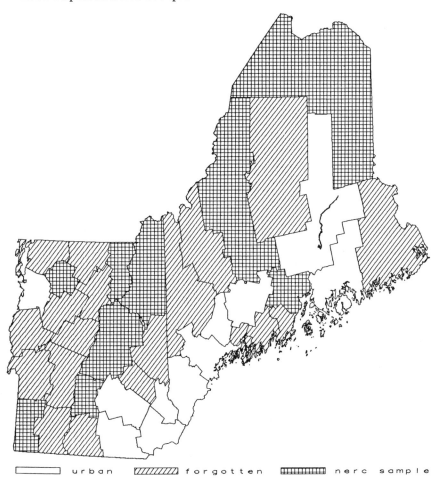

| | urban | | forgotten | | nerc sample |

gap in per capita income *widened* during the 1980s. This pattern was quite evident in northern New England as well (see Table 7.2). The unweighted average of per capita incomes for the nine distressed counties stood at 75 percent of the New England regional average in 1979. It had fallen to 70 percent of the regional average by 1985 and fell even further, to 69 percent, by 1987. Growth in real per capita income from 1979 to 1985 for the nine counties was only about one-third that of the region (3.9 percent versus 11.4 percent). Within northern New England, the gap in average per capita income between the forgotten counties

Table 7.1. Poverty Rates in Northern New England, 1979

State	Urban	Forgotten
Maine	11.5	15.7
New Hampshire	7.6	10.7
Vermont	10.3	12.5
Combined	9.7	13.2

Source: U.S. Bureau of the Census, 1988a.

Poverty rates (percentage of population below poverty level) are weighted averages of 1979 county poverty rates weighted by 1980 county population. Urban/forgotten residence is by county; status as defined in this study.

Map 7.2. Poverty Rates by County, Northern New England, 1979

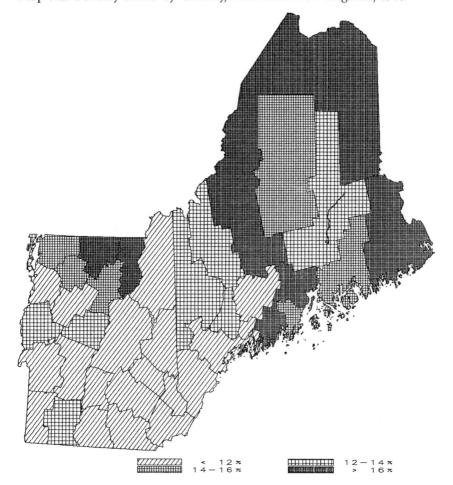

< 12 %   12 − 14 %
14 − 16 %   > 16 %

Table 7.2. Annual Per Capita Money Income in Nine Rural Counties of Northern New England

County	Annual per capita money income (Percentage of New England average)		
	1979 (constant 1985 $)	1985 (current $)	1987 (current $)
Maine			
Aroostook	7,127 (65)	7.556 (62)	8,577 (60)
Somerset	7,176 (65)	7,505 (61)	8,670 (61)
Waldo	6,949 (63)	6,992 (57)	8,269 (58)
New Hampshire			
Coos	8,516 (77)	9,060 (74)	10,249 (72)
Grafton	9,489 (86)	10,207 (83)	11,925 (84)
Sullivan	9,612 (87)	9,575 (78)	10,985 (77)
Vermont			
Bennington	9,686 (87)	9,829 (80)	11,524 (81)
Essex	7,305 (66)	7,472 (61)	8,267 (58)
Lamoille	8,278 (75)	8,715 (71)	10,148 (71)
Average[a]	8,226 (75)	8,546 (70)	9,846 (69)
New England average	11,020	12,271	14,232

Source: U.S. Bureau of the Census, 1988a and 1990a.

[a]Calculated as the simple unweighted average of the per capita income for the nine counties.

and the urban counties widened for all three states (see Table 7.3). Average per capita income in the forgotten counties of Vermont, for example, stood at 85 percent of that of Chittenden County in 1979, but fell to 81 percent in 1985. In many rural places this was not just a relative loss; it was an absolute loss. Real average per capita income *declined* from 1979 to 1985 in 28 percent of the minor civil divisions (MCDs) in the forgotten counties of Vermont, in 24 percent of MCDs in Maine, and in 10 percent of those in New Hampshire (U.S. Bureau of Census, 1988b).

Analysis of data on poverty rates from the 1988 Current Population Survey microdata file (U.S. Bureau of Census, 1988d) indicates that there was only a marginal improvement in state level poverty rates for the period 1979 to 1988 in Vermont and Maine (10.0 percent from 12.1 percent and 12.6 percent from 13.0 percent, respectively), whereas New Hampshire experienced substantial improvement (down to just 4.1 percent from 8.5 percent in 1979); (1979 data from U.S. Bureau of Census, 1988a). The rural economic disadvantage continued; in each of the three states, nonmetropolitan areas experienced higher poverty

Table 7.3. Per Capita Money Income in 1979 and 1985 (in current $)

State	1979				1985			
	Urban	Forgotten	Forgotten Urban		Urban	Forgotten	Forgotten Urban	
Maine	6,084	5,179	.851		9,632	7,910	.821	
New Hampshire	7,193	6,419	.892		12,251	10,150	.829	
Vermont	6,973	5,931	.851		11,277	9,118	.809	

Source: U.S. Bureau of the Census, 1988b.

rates than metropolitan areas. This was particularly true in Maine, where 13.7 percent of the nonmetropolitan population was below the poverty level, whereas their metropolitan counterparts experienced a 10.8 percent rate. By 1986 the unemployment rates in the six counties in Maine and Vermont identified by the Regional Commission as distressed had declined to an average of 7.6 percent, but they remained at nearly twice the regional average of 3.9 percent. There was, however, significant improvement in the New Hampshire employment situation. In all three of its distressed counties unemployment rates were near or below the regional rate.

Participation rates in government assistance programs also indicate high rates of distress in many rural counties. In April, 1990, in the forgotten counties of Maine and Vermont, 9.7 percent of the population received food stamps, compared to 7.2 percent in the urban counties of those states (Maine State Planning Office, 1991; Vermont Department of Social Welfare, 1991; New Hampshire data was not comparable). In Washington County, Maine, 20.1 percent of the residents received food stamp assistance (this marks an improvement over 1980, when 27

Table 7.4. Per Capita Money Income in the Lowest-Income Towns in Nine Counties of Northern New England, 1987

| | | Average Per Capita Money Income ($) (Percentage of County PCI) | |
	County	Lowest Income Town (%)	Average of Towns in Lowest Decile of PCI (%)
Maine			
Aroostook	8,577	4,609 (54)	6,171 (72)
Somerset	8,670	6,300 (73)	6,401 (74)
Waldo	8,269	6,640 (80)	6,664 (81)
New Hampshire			
Coos	10,249	9,036 (88)	9,042 (88)
Grafton	11,925	6,215 (52)	8,330 (70)
Sullivan	10,985	8,491 (77)	9,002 (82)
Vermont			
Bennington	11,524	8,602 (75)	9,074 (79)
Essex	8,267	5,161 (62)	5,161 (62)
Lamoille	10,148	6,781 (67)	7,214 (71)
Average[a]			7,290

Source: U.S. Bureau of the Census, 1990a.

[a]Unweighted average of the 26 towns

percent of the population of Washington County was receiving food stamps). The four counties with the next highest participation rates were Orleans (13.7 percent) and Essex (12.6 percent) in Vermont, and Somerset (13.0 percent) and Aroostook (12.5 percent) in Maine.[9] All of these are among the counties we have classified as forgotten, and all except Orleans are among the nine representative "distressed" counties identified by the New England Regional Planning Commission. As with measures of underemployment, recent evidence suggests that participation in government programs as a measure of distress tends to understate rural compared to urban poverty (Jensen, 1989), which further underscores the severity of the situation in these counties.

The unevenness of economic well-being in this region is substantially greater than these county level data indicate. Further disaggregation of 1987 county level per capita income data into MCD level information reveals considerable variation. Among MCDs in the nine distressed counties we found the average per capita income for the lowest-income town to be only 52 percent of the *county* average. The unweighted average of per capita income for the lowest decile of towns in each county ranged from 62 percent of the county average in Essex County, Vermont, to 88 percent in Coos County, New Hampshire (see Table 7.4). Average per capita income in some towns, then, was as low as 32 percent of the New England regional average of $14,232 and the unweighted average for the lowest-income decile of towns (26 towns in the nine counties) was only $7,290, barely half of the regional average.

Uneven Development: The Roots

What factors produce and maintain this unevenness of economic well-being in northern New England? Why are poverty and hardship concentrated in the more remote rural areas? These are essentially questions regarding two variables: space and poverty. To address questions of the association between these two, intermediary factors, associated with both variables, need to be interposed. We propose two such factors: spatial patterns of human settlement and of economic activity. We then pose three questions: (1) What factors account for the spatial distribution of human activity and human population? (2) What is the nature of economic relationships between urban and rural areas? (3) How do these patterns of human settlement and economic conditions and relations interact with other attributes of places to distribute poverty spatially in specific ways?

Spatial Distribution of Human Activity

There have been two great ebbs and flows of economic activity in the rural areas of northern New England. Early settlements were agriculturally based, and extractive activities (farming, forestry and fishing) dominated the New England landscape through the first half of the nineteenth century. Farming declined steadily beginning in the late 1800s, but the decline was partially offset by growth in manufacturing concentrated in nondurable industries. As recently as mid twentieth century, northern New England's labor profile was dominated by employment in textile, rubber, shoe, paper, and paper products industries. With the transfer of these traditional industries out of northern New England communities (first to the American South and then to the Pacific Rim) many communities shrank to mere shells of their former selves. Labor-intensive industries metamorphosed into capital-intensive industries, leaving many people with no employment opportunities in a region marked by its limited range of opportunities to begin with.

What were the social, economic, and environmental forces that brought about these great ebbs and flows of people and enterprises? Human ecology theory suggests three interrelated factors to explain the spatial patterns of human settlement and human activity: (1) interdependence among people draws them into concentrated settlements; (2) the dependence of activities or functions upon various characteristics of the land tends to disperse people across the landscape; and (3) the "friction of space," that is, the costs of moving goods, people, and information, relates the first two factors to one another and to the specific landscape. The overall result is a pattern of regular clusters of human activity and settlement. The first two factors account for the tendency of settlement patterns to be dispersed around scattered nuclei; the third affects the size and specific shape of the pattern (Hawley, 1950:236).

Since it is the dependence of activities or functions upon various characteristics of the land that tends to spread human activity (and consequently people) out across the landscape, it follows that where there are relatively few land-dependent economic activities only a few people will be scattered in the area. Obviously, in any locality there are many employed people resident whose jobs do not depend directly on characteristics of the land. Generally, such people provide services to those whose jobs do require residence in the locale. Those people in turn also require goods and services, so that a multiplier operates, resulting in a population substantially larger than that directly dependent on place-specific characteristics of the land. Nevertheless, the entire population depends on the base of those who are there because of the characteristics of the land. If that base shrinks, not only those directly dependent on the base will leave but also (over time) those who depend on them through the multiplier effect. If the base disappears, the entire population may disappear, a fact to which the western ghost towns bear mute testimony.

The friction of space is also an important factor in determining the size and shape of the clustered settlement pattern. As this friction is reduced by improved transportation and communication, people can acquire their daily and occasional necessities from greater distances. Normally, as the size of the effective hinterland of a trade center increases, small communities lose out to larger area and regional centers (cf. Kraenzel, 1980).

These two factors, the decrease in location-dependent jobs and improved transportation and communications, account quite well for the long gradual decline in population in many northern New England communities. In the mid 1800s the farming base deteriorated due to exhaustion of the land and to the opening of better lands in the Midwest (Barron, 1984). The remaining agriculture often used marginally productive soils and became less labor-intensive. Timber and pulp extraction and processing also became more mechanized, requiring a smaller resident work force. In Maine, fishing became more mechanized. Also, total catch declined from the late 1950s (Pease and Richard, 1983:27) as a result of overfishing and competition from foreign fishing vessels. Manufacturing, which had been location dependent in its use of waterpower, moved out of the northern parts of New England as electrical power replaced water power. Each of these factors resulted in a decrease in the number of jobs directly dependent on characteristics of the land. Taken together, along with improved transportation and communications, they have resulted in a slow and steady decline in population in many communities of northern New England for over 150 years.

Unfortunately, population decline in rural communities often produces a vicious cycle of poverty. Bunce (1982:99) describes the logic of the downward spiral as follows:

> Low incomes and limited employment opportunities weaken the community infrastructure and lead to reductions in local investment and to the exodus of the population. This causes further decline in the economic, social and demographic structure and a slide further down the spiral. The most direct symptoms and,

at the same time, causes are personal and institutional poverty. . . . Direct results are decay in physical structures and facilities and depopulation.

In the last two decades a reversal of migration in certain places in rural New England has occurred. This reversal is also related to special characteristics of the land—specifically the fact that rural areas are pleasant places to live or recreate. Steahr and Luloff (1986) found that residential amenity was a principle cause of the migration turnaround of the 1970s, and that the turnaround (in New England, at least) affected primarily those areas adjacent to metropolitan areas. In effect, improvements in transportation allowed the size of the "central places" to grow. The recreation-and-tourism boom has also affected some parts of northern New England and should provide a solid base for a limited amount of long-term, location-specific employment. It remains to be seen, however, whether this will be stable, adequately remunerated employment or primarily low-paying, seasonal jobs vulnerable to fluctuations in the economy.

A comparative analysis of county business structures between 1969 and 1988 clearly shows the shift of the economy away from the manufacturing of non-durables into services (see Figure 7.2). In the forgotten counties, personal income share from nondurables manufacturing declined from 14.8 percent of total earnings in 1969 to 8.9 percent in 1988. During the same period the income share of services increased from 15.8 percent to 23.2 percent (Bureau of Economic Analysis, 1990). This service sector growth in the area is atypical of rural America in general. Henry, Drabenstott, and Gibson (1988) found the shift to services to be much slower in rural than in urban areas. But in northern New England the growth is surprisingly consistent between urban and forgotten counties over the period 1969 to 1988, occurring even in those counties most dependent on natural resources. In fact, the service sector share in 1988 was slightly larger in the forgotten than in the urban counties (23.2 percent, compared to 22.4 percent). This growth in services is consistent with increasing tourism and amenity-related residence in the forgotten counties.

Corroborative information is provided by recent data compiled by the Federal Reserve Bank of Boston. Total annual average nonagricultural employment in the three states in 1987 was 1,259,000. By November 1990, the average number of those in nonagricultural employment had increased by about 46,000 to a total of 1,305,000 (a 3.7 percent gain). The number of those involved in manufacturing declined in both New Hampshire and Vermont (a total of about 15,000 less jobs

Figure 7.2. County Business Structure, Northern New England, 1969 and 1988

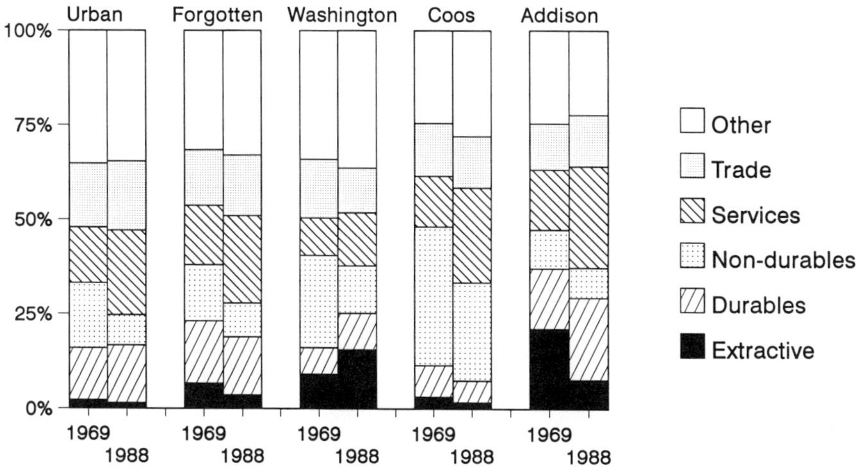

Source: Bureau of Economic Analysis, 1990.

in 1990) and stayed about the same in Maine. Employment in non-manufacturing (1,052,000 in 1990, compared with 988,000 in 1987) therefore, accounted for this change. Within this sector, services employment accounted for the vast majority of the increase in the number of employed, realizing a net gain of almost 75,000 jobs (Federal Reserve Bank of Boston, 1991).

To further explore changes in population in northern New England, we analyzed preliminary 1990 census data. Although only three counties showed a decline in population (Aroostook and Washington counties in Maine, and Coos County in New Hampshire), overall population growth was much lower in the forgotten counties than in the urban counties (7.2 percent compared to 15.7 percent, see Map 7.3). Moreover, a substantial number of MCDs lost population. Almost two-thirds of the MCDs (65 percent) in Aroostook County, Maine, 55 percent of those in Coos County, New Hampshire, and 46 percent of those in Essex County, Vermont, lost population during the last decade. In five other forgotten counties, at least 30 percent of the MCDs lost population. The MCDs which lost population were concentrated in the remote areas whereas the fastest growing MCDs were generally just outside the urban fringes (see Map 7.4).

The relationship between size of place and population change from 1980 to 1990 was rather surprising, however. On average, the

Map 7.3. Population Change, Northern New England 1980–1990

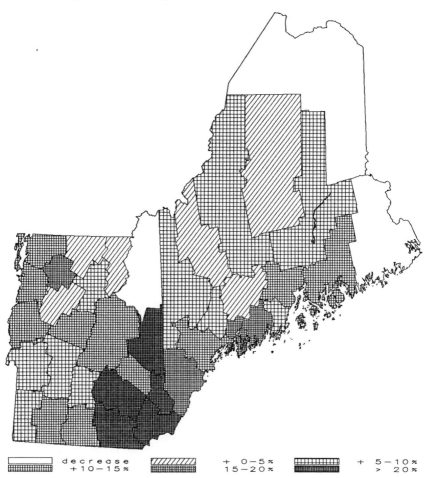

| decrease | +10−15% | +0−5% 15−20% | +5−10% >20% |

smaller places grew fastest during the decade. This is true for both forgotten and urban counties, and the pattern is quite consistent in all three states (see Figure 7.3). In the forgotten counties, MCDs with populations of less than 250 experienced an average population increase of 17.6 percent during the decade, while those between eight and sixteen thousand experienced an average *decline* in population of 2.8 percent.[10] Such a pattern is consistent with the attractiveness of the small rural community as places to live. It is difficult to imagine any business-related, land-dependent activities which would produce this growth pattern. Among MCDs of the same population size, those in "urban" counties generally grew substantially faster, with the only exception found among the very small communities in Maine.

This pattern of population change is even more striking when viewed in light of the relationship between per capita income and size of place (see Figure 7.4). This relationship is essentially monotonic with income in the largest MCDs in the forgotten counties being, on average, a full 25 percent more than those in the smallest places. The pattern is generally consistent among the three states, and in both forgotten and urban counties. For MCDs of the same population, those in urban counties generally have higher average per capita incomes

Map 7.4. Population Change, Northern New England, 1980–1990

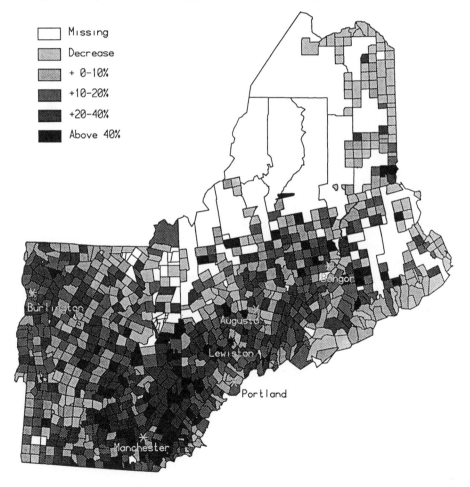

Figure 7.3. Average Population Growth by Size of Place, 1980–1990

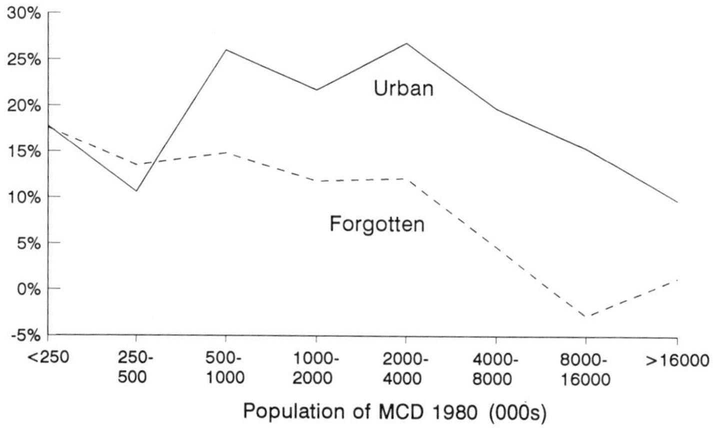

Sources: U.S. Census Bureau, 1990a, 1990b.

than those in the forgotten counties. The exception is again the smallest communities in Maine (<500), in which incomes in the forgotten counties are higher than those in the urban counties. Map 7.5 shows that high per capita income was generally concentrated in and around the urban areas, though there were also scattered high income MCDs in the remote areas.

Economic Relationships Between Urban and Rural Areas

The land-dependent, natural resource–dependent, and space-dependent activities that still remain in the region's rural areas often do not provide employment stability or significant local income opportunities. This spatial inequality can be seen as a logical outcome of capitalistic development as rural resources have come under the control of the urban industrial complex. Development through this process results in spatial inequality (Lefebvre, 1976; Harvey, 1973; 1982; Wilkinson, 1989). In addition, the political economy of advanced capitalism is seen to result in regional inequalities and to reflect exploitive relations between capital and labor (Howes and Markusen, 1981; Markusen, 1985). Capital that operates from the center is mobilized to extract and then concentrate surplus production from labor. Rural areas are particularly vulnerable since natural resources, which are plentiful, and labor, which is cheap, are both exploited (Krannich and

Luloff, 1991). In this process three devices are used which produce spatial inequality in the periphery:

1. *Capital mobility*—Capital is moved from area to area in search of profits; local labor is less mobile and comes to depend on these investments for employment. The investments tend to come and go, however, not so much to balance supply and demand in the local labor market, but to maximize profits for the capital holders.

2. *Assignment of special uses to space*—To maximize profits, capital concentrates narrow ranges of commercial activity in each place according to the natural competitive advantages of that place. This narrow range of activity produces local instability as demand for the specialty fluctuates in the larger economy.

3. *Selective use of reserves*—Underdevelopment in the periphery may actually contribute to profitability of capital. Reserves of labor, natural resources, and sites for operations are thus maintained ready, available, and at low price.

We would therefore anticipate that in rural areas where a large majority of the productive resources are owned and controlled by

Figure 7.4. Per Capita Income by Size of Place, 1985

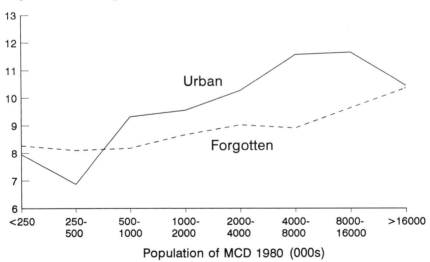

Sources: U.S. Census Bureau, 1990a, 1990b.

Map 7.5. Per Capita Money Income in Northern New England, 1985

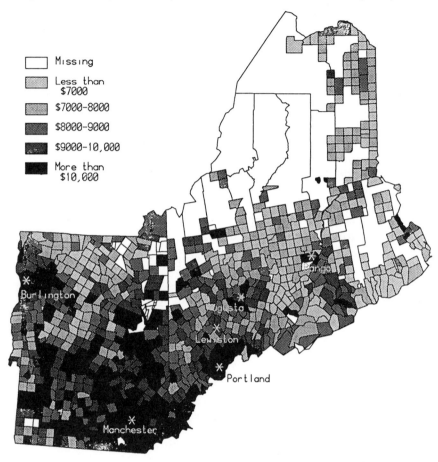

persons or corporations located outside of the area, high levels of employment instability, low wages, and consequent poverty would obtain. This mechanism produces more serious levels of local economic distress when industry ownership is concentrated in a few hands and where the industrial mix is narrowly specialized.

Both of these conditions exist in northern New England. A recent report to Congress prepared by the USDA and the Governors' Task Force on Northern Forest Lands (Harper et al., 1990:4) included this analysis of property and capital ownership in roughly the same geographic area[11] we are discussing in this chapter:

Commercial forestry is the dominant land use on 60 percent of the private land. Owners of this land hold more than 13 million acres in tracts larger than 5000 acres. The majority of the commercial forest is owned by about 45 companies and families. . . .

Industrial landowners own both wood processing facilities and forest land, totaling almost 10 million acres. Roughly 90 percent of the industrial owners are paper manufacturers; the other 10 percent are companies with sawmills or specialty product plants. Several of the paper companies also own sawmills. Since these owners hold both land and processing facilities, their primary objective is to grow timber and supply raw materials to their operations. Several are Fortune 500 corporations whose main objective is profits from the land and timber.

Based on such structural and spatial inequality we should anticipate counties which are dependent on natural resource extraction and processing to have low incomes and high poverty rates. This condition would appear, in principle, to be met in northern New England. To demonstrate this we analyzed natural resource dependence using county level data on sources of personal income by industrial category (Bureau of Economic Analysis, 1990). As a measure of natural resource dependence we used income share from natural resources–related activities, which included the extractive industries (farming, fishing, mining, forestry) plus the manufacturing subcategories of paper and lumber. Income from natural resources–related activities as a percentage of total income was surprisingly low in the forgotten counties as a group, accounting for only 8.7 percent of the income in 1969 and declining to only 5.9 percent by 1988. There was a great deal of variability in natural resource dependence, however. In 1988 it ranged from over 24 percent in Somerset and Washington counties in Maine to under 1.5 percent in Belknap County, New Hampshire, and Chittenden County, Vermont. The bivariate correlation between natural resource dependence and average per capita income in 1979 was very strong ($r = -.70$). The correlation between natural resource dependence in 1979 and poverty rate in 1980 was also strong ($r = .58$).

The strong relationship between natural resource dependence and poverty in northern New England is consistent with Ford's (1969) finding that primary production industries based on renewable natural resources have the greatest percentage of workers earning substandard incomes. He found that 75 percent of the workers in this sector were poor, compared with 14 percent in mining, 17 percent in manufacturing, and 30 percent overall in all industries. This is consistent with the theory we have outlined above linking poverty to external ownership and control of capital, although it does not decisively demonstrate that link.

The Spatial Distribution of Poverty

There is often implicit in questions about the localization of poverty the assumption that there must be something wrong in the locales where poverty is concentrated—some factor or factors which produce the poverty. This assumption is the result of a careless joining of what are really two quite separate questions. The first is, "Why do people become poor?" The second is, "Why do poor people go where they go or stay where they stay?" An uncritical amalgamation of these questions can lead us to look for the causes of poverty *in the locality where poor people are found.* But of course, poverty need not necessarily be produced where it is concentrated. By explicitly separating the question of the *production* of poverty from that of the *localization* of poverty we are better able to address both more fruitfully.

We are then led to ask, how important is migration (and nonmigration) in determining local concentrations of poverty? The preliminary results of research now in progress (Nord et al, 1992) suggest that it is very important indeed. Analysis of poverty and migration data from the 1987 and 1988 Current Population Surveys (U.S. Bureau of Census, 1987; 1988d) reveal that in an average rural county, 10 percent of the poor population migrate into and out of the county in a single year. Following migration theory (Lee, 1966; 1970; Ritchey, 1976) we assume that migration decisions by the poor, like those of anyone else, are based on their assessments of many factors. One of these factors is the probability of finding employment; through this mediating factor local economic conditions presumably do affect migration of the poor into and out of the area. Notice, however, that this factor should tend to *deconcentrate* poverty. That is, where employment opportunities are poor, we would expect high out-migration and low in-migration.

A local economic factor which may tend to *concentrate* poverty is the predominance of employment which requires relatively little education and specialized skill. An area with a predominance of such jobs may be more likely to attract and hold disproportionate numbers of poor persons even when unemployment is relatively high. When persons in more highly skilled occupations lose their jobs, they may be able to move to lower-skilled, lower-paying jobs if they are unable to get work in their specialty. But people who lose their employment of last resort have little hope of finding work elsewhere. It seems likely that jobs of this sort are concentrated in counties that are highly dependent on natural resources extraction and processing and in manufacturing. If so, this causal chain could help account for the strong relationship observed in northern New England between natural resources dependency and poverty.

Another factor that could well affect migration of the poor in such a way as to produce the observed concentrations of poverty in rural areas is the availability of low-cost housing.[12] Housing considerations figure very prominently in the decision making of those near and below poverty (Fitchen, 1981; 1991). Poor people go where housing is cheap. In many cases they have no choice. Eviction (or threat of eviction) for overdue rent makes it impossible to stay in other areas where employment possibilities may be better. In many rural areas housing is cheap for several reasons: (1) In areas of recent (or even much earlier) economic downturn, low demand for housing drives prices down; (2) in many rural areas building codes are nonexistent or not enforced or do not apply to old, existing houses; (3) land values, a substantial part of housing costs, are lower than in cities; (4) where there are already substantial numbers of poor people, it may be possible to share accommodations. The crowding may not be healthy or pleasant, but it helps keep everyone's housing expenses low; and (5) housing values are lower where there are already many people living in poverty. Wealthier people do not want to move into such an area; this lowers housing demand and depresses prices.

Cheap housing attracts poor people to rural areas and discourages rural poor from moving out. The concentration of poverty in rural (and inner-city) northern New England is, then, in part a direct result of zoning ordinances in the balance of the New England region. Indeed, as suburbanization and exurbanization (cf. Zelinsky, 1978) increase and as more of the rural communities adopt land-use plans and zoning laws, the poor are being progressively squeezed into a diminishing supply of substandard housing (Fitchen, 1981:205). Zoning does not solve the problem of poverty. It simply tends to push the poor out of sight—mainly into forgotten places.

Federal Efforts to Improve Human Resources and Infrastructure in Northern New England

Unlike other regions of the nation with similar incidences of poverty, northern New England has not benefited from a series of targeted federal antipoverty programs. Excluded from minority-oriented programs (this area is perhaps the whitest of America, with only 0.7 percent nonwhite in Vermont, 1.1 percent in New Hampshire, and 1.2 percent in Maine in 1984 [U.S. Bureau of Census, 1988a])[13] and from participation in regional programs, such as the Appalachian Regional Commission, this area has had to make do with other nontargeted programs. It has been particularly creative and successful in using funds allocated under the old Revenue Sharing formulae, Community Development Block Grants Program, Head Start Programs, Community Action Programs, and programs offered under both Farmers Home Administration (FmHA) and Small Business Administration (SBA). Other programs, including Aid to Families With Dependent Children (AFDC) and Women, Infants, and Children (WIC), have experienced increased requests for assistance, and McKinney Homeless Assistance has been increasingly applied to rural situations.

Although no uniform federal program has provided organization and guidance to address the region's problems, it is clear that some efforts have materialized, largely as a result of good, old-fashioned New England ingenuity and resolve. Maine, for example, has been extremely aggressive in attempting to utilize uncommitted FmHA funds from other states to help remedy some of its pressing rural economic development problems.

Maine's FmHA staff has been involved in numerous economic development projects over the past several years. It has aggressively sought and received millions of dollars more than its basic allocation (roughly $6 million). According to one source, this occurs because potential lenders agree to work with the FmHA in developing their applications even when no money is currently available to be loaned. As a result, when and if money does come available, Maine is able to seize that moment by applying. For example, in FY 1989 the FmHA staff accounted for between $30 and $32 million in grants and loans; in FY 1990 some $43.5 million; and in 1991, despite problems associated with the federal budget, about $17 million had been committed by February. Such a level of activity reflects the willingness of this organization to work very closely with other federal, state, and local agencies, and the private sector where appropriate, to assist in community economic development. Through a policy of person-to-person contacts, this small group of individuals have funneled financial support to a variety of projects, including construction, expansion, and improvements to community infrastructure, especially water and sewer projects.[14] Two specific efforts merit some additional attention: 1) an intermediary loaning program; and 2) an industrial development grant funds effort. As a result, several organizations representing rural areas of Maine, for example, have been able to establish revolving loan programs. These programs were targeted at helping small businesses expand and have been used to support local women's efforts at creating businesses (including daycare centers).[15]

A similar situation arises with respect to SBA's Business Lending Program funds. During the last several years, this office has been able to generate almost $25 million in new loans annually. The vast majority of these loans are made in rural Maine. According to a key individual in this office, the SBA works extremely closely with other federal and state programs, particularly in supporting the Governor of Maine's Job Opportunity Zones Program. This program identified four areas suffering particular hardships (Belfast, Waldo County; Millinockett-Medway, Penobscot County; Great Presque Isle, central Aroostook County; and Calais-Downeast, eastern Washington County). Through the combined efforts of federal and state agency resource teams, counseling and training vehicles to assist small businesses in these areas were realized. As a result, numerous firms have been able to retool or engage in buyouts enabling local firms to stay in business. In FY 1990, the SBA assisted 154 businesses with over $28 million in loans (the average loan was $174,000 and the average business employed 14). As in the case of FmHA, in both cases, aggressive state management of this program has been quite helpful in improving the welfare of Maine's rural economies.

Another successful and innovative use of federal allocation is that by the Maine Cooperative Extension. In their efforts at assisting rural areas in economic development, they have adapted a once primarily farm and farm-family service organization into one that now attempts to serve the business and commercial sectors of rural areas as well. The Trade Area Analysis Program, for example, attempts to bring a diverse group of individuals together to discuss and consider the development of a retail strategy for the community. The program first provides a basic review of the economic history of retail trade and traces out its patterns over the last ten years. Then, through the use of a trade surplus and linkage model (McConnon and Deller, 1990) gaps in the retail trade sector are uncovered. Subsequently, as a result of this overview, a core group of community members initiates some action designed to facilitate the closing of a gap. The initial applications of this new effort in Maine have been highly successful. Four areas have had experience with Trade Area Analysis: Ellsworth, Hancock County, Belfast, and Greenville. Preliminary reports indicate considerable success, and much interest has been shown by other local and county governments in conducting studies in their areas.

In Vermont, a well-developed and integrated network of agencies exist that address issues related to economic development. All of these efforts are linked to the Vermont Agency of Development and Community Affairs. This Agency has two divisions: the Department of Housing and Community Affairs and the Economic Development Department. The former administers Act 200 (among the nation's foremost planning laws), Regional Planning, Housing Programs, and the Vermont Community Development Program whereas the latter has responsibility for administering Industrial Recruitment, Marketing, the Regional Development Corporation Program, and the Job Training Program. In the Northeast Kingdom of Vermont (Caledonia, Essex, and Orleans counties), no fewer than two regional planning commissions, four industrial development corporations or councils, and one development association provide economic and community development assistance to area communities. In addition to these agencies, there are several Community Action Agencies which operate with federal funds, and seven other organizations[16] that together provide technical assistance, support, and resources for local economic development.

Local Attempts at Economic Development

There have been many indigenous efforts at economic development. Indeed, some might argue that the strength of New England has been its history of entrepreneurship based on local product development. Blessed with an abundance of colleges and universities which attract the brightest and best students from this nation and elsewhere, the region has had an intellectual wealth to draw upon, especially since so many of these students never abandon their newly acquired homes (Howell, 1984; Garreau, 1981). As a result, it is not surprising that the much heralded high technology revolution had its birth here. Many of the products of this revolution are assembled in factories throughout northern New England. And these factories have often been built with venture capital. California and New England together accounted for almost two-thirds of the investment capital made available during the 1970s.[17] This talent and money were augmented by the presence of decentralized mill complexes throughout the region that made incubator space readily available.

At the same time, this entrepreneurial spirit is found in traditional enterprises. Less than twenty years ago Vermont Castings began production of a line of air-tight wood stoves. Its products, named "Defiant," "Resolute," and "Vigilant," were model stoves and quickly captured an increasingly large share of the growing market of homes that heated with wood. At about the same time, a couple of Burlington, Vermont, retreatists sent away for a correspondence course in producing ice cream. Their success story is as well known as their famous first names: Ben and Jerry. They started with only a few flavors and an old service station shop from which to market their product. Soon demand required expansion of both. Searching the files of business incorporation, Ben and Jerry used a piece of legislation written years before to restrict the sale of shares in their business only to Vermonters. From this original effort, Ben and Jerry's has grown into a publicly held corporation with an image that capitalized on a rugged independence and social conscience.

Of course these are only two of the major private enterprises which arose and helped stabilize local economies in northern New England. As with most business enterprises, fortune breeds imitation, and numerous other homespun efforts arose. However, the general experience is not characterized by the success stories of individuals. Rather, northern New England has been able to capitalize on a more collective spirit to improve the local conditions of many of its communities.

In a soon-to-be-released report by the Economic Research Service (ERS) of USDA, a series of nonmetropolitan community self-development success stories is presented. This study, undertaken by Cornelia and Jan Flora, Gary Green, and Fred Schmidt, identifies five efforts in northern New England. Each is characterized by the investment of substantial local resources, the expansion of locally controlled enterprises, the active involvement of local organizations and governments, and the creation of jobs and the generation of income for the area. By focusing on these aspects of self-development, this study excludes as successes the capture of branch or absentee-owned industries or of state government entities like prisons or of federal entities like regional offices of some agency; the development of infrastructure; the securement of state or federal grants to support development activity; or the efforts of a single individual or firm acting alone in the development process. The result is a set of economic development activities that aligns with several theoretical perspectives of community development (cf. Wilkinson, 1991; Kaufman, 1985; Luloff and Swanson, 1990).

In Vermont's Caledonia County (part of the Northeast Kingdom) a group of organic farmers in 1978 organized themselves into the Vermont Northern Growers Co-op to market their products and provide locally grown vegetables for area residents. To initiate their efforts, they purchased an old potato warehouse and a carrot planter and harvester, and hired a manager to run the facility and oversee marketing. The original effort was financed by borrowing $14,000. Through an annual fee, plus a commission on produce sold, the Co-op is able to secure sufficient finances to continue its efforts. It has also been able to sell equity shares in the Co-op to local residents, gain guaranteed loans through the state of Vermont, and secure contributions from various organizations, including a local church. Members of the cooperative raise organic carrots, potatoes, and rutabagas and have been able to achieve a good deal of success in marketing their products. As a result of this effort, additional agricultural jobs were created in the area, and members were able to secure higher incomes.

In Hancock and Waldo counties, Maine, a cooperative was formed to sell products for artisans who worked at home. Initiated in 1970, this cooperative is often cited by area professionals, government workers, and politicians as the best example of indigenous efforts, to date, in Maine. This cooperative, H.O.M.E., Inc., was originally designed to help people help themselves through job training and education. Early successes led to an expanded store, the opening of a market stand, pottery and weaving studios, a woodworking shop, flea market, and food bank. At the same time, increased efforts were devoted to the creation of human capital through increased learning opportunities, including adult education courses and a two-year, Associates Degree program. Day-care was offered to encourage participation of the many low-income residents who without it would be unable to take advantage of this new chance for learning. In addition, H.O.M.E., Inc., began building shelters for the homeless and abused and developing programs for women prisoners to enable them to better move into society when they complete their sentences. In 1978, the Covenant Community Land Trust was organized. It has helped build fourteen family-farm houses, each of which comes with ten acres for use in supplementing the owners' income. The wood products for these homes are made in H.O.M.E.'s own shops. The success of this worker-controlled enterprise is evident in the total sales volume of its stores, its successes in winning grants from various agencies, and the increased confidence of its members.

Berlin, New Hampshire, is the home of the Berlin Economic Development Council (BEDCO), an example of an indigenous project that has helped this community prepare for its future. This north-country city, insulated from the population boom to its south and separated from markets by the White Mountains, has been caught in a steady economic decline coupled to significant population losses for almost twenty-five years. In 1979 Converse Rubber announced the closing of its plant in Berlin, causing an immediate increase in unemployment of 15 percent, which exacerbated an already high level due to losses of jobs in other textile, shoe, and paper and pulp businesses. To combat this problem, BEDCO established a revolving loan program using Community Development Block Grants and Economic Development Administration funds. BEDCO had some limited success in attracting new businesses into Berlin, but enjoyed its greatest achievement in establishing a business incubator, New Ventures North, in 1987, which is now running at capacity (and contains four service and light manufacturing businesses). At about the same time, the Berlin Industrial Development Park Authority joined with BEDCO to help get a new firm, J. P. Stitching, established in an old fire station owned by the city. Both of these developments created almost twenty jobs and a new sense of optimism for Berlin and the entire north-country region.

Also in New Hampshire, south along the Connecticut River, the Charlestown Economic Development Association (CEDA) was formed in 1983 to help build the local economy and create jobs. In 1987, CEDA was approached by a prominent New Hampshire developer who wanted to assist them in providing a more stable economic base for the community through the development and use of an idle industrial park. With the huge financial assistance of the developer's family, and a $350,000 loan, the twenty-seven-acre park was purchased and subdivided. As industrial subdivisions were sold, CEDA was able to retire its debt, pay for improvements in its properties, and amass a new economic development war chest for future efforts. An unanticipated consequence of the success of CEDA was realized when a neighbor subdivided his property into industrial lots, and found tenants willing and eager to fill these openings. Almost a hundred jobs were created as a result of these efforts.

The final indigenous effort identified in the ERS-sponsored research was the Rochester Industrial Park. Rochester lies along the Maine–New Hampshire border and is part of the Portsmouth-Dover-Rochester Metropolitan Area. During the mid-to-late 1980s Rochester was the home to rapid residential development, and its growth rate exceeded that of its two sister cities. By 1988 local leaders believed that the private sector was not doing enough to encourage industrial growth to help provide a sense of balance to the community. As a result, the city—through its Economic Development Commission—the local public utility, and a group of private developers purchased land in the city and developed an industrial park. With an aggressive local leader, this park was able to secure tenants very quickly, including companies which were located elsewhere in its metropolitan area. Together the park has provided 250 jobs and generated an estimated $100,000 in property taxes.

Toward a Future Scenario for Northern New England

Traditionally, and somewhat narrowly, two explanations of poverty have dominated the sociological literature—the culture of poverty thesis and the structural explanation of poverty (see O'Hare, 1988). The former focuses on individual and cultural factors that make and keep individuals poor. It stresses a lowering of expectations, slackening of the work effort, lowering of educational attainment, increased reliance on government welfare programs, and cultural norms and values which perpetuate these conditions (O'Hare, 1988). This perspective is associated with the work of Lewis (1966) and Banfield (1968).[18] By contrast, the premise of the structural approach is based, not on a set of intrinsic qualities of poor people, but rather on the inability of the social structure to provide the necessary opportunities for the poor to improve their plight (Harrington, 1962; Wilson, 1987).

Throughout this paper we have adopted a structural framework for the study of the forgotten of northern New England. We do not completely reject the culture of poverty thesis. Writ large, it is quite capable of supplying some reasonable explanation of individual experiences, particularly why some are more apt to be poor than others, and why individuals in poverty situations find it difficult to escape. But we find the culture of poverty thesis inadequate to provide insight into and prescription for amelioration of large-scale poverty. The thesis fails to provide an explanation of macrolevel conditions which exclude a large segment of the population from the economy.[19]

Viewing poverty from a structural perspective shifts the focus to a community and societal level. It argues for an understanding of poverty that emphasizes the inability of the existing socioeconomic structure to apportion adequate resources relative to needs. By moving from a cultural and social psychological framework to one which encompasses a macro-, societal level, using the structural approach, we become capable of pointing to public policies aimed at the amelioration of pervasive social poverty.[20] Such policies will focus on opportunity structures, particularly in terms of education and jobs. More importantly, to the extent that the society as a whole fails to provide employment opportunities adequate to solve problems of poverty at a societal level, the structural approach clearly places responsibility for the welfare of the unemployed and underemployed poor[21] on the *society as a whole*, not on the residents or governments of the local areas where they reside.

It is the unfortunate plight of the forgotten people of northern New England that the major factors affecting their future are not under their control. As in other natural resource–dependent areas, the health of the local company depends largely on decisions made by nonresident owners, on the structure and fluctuations of the national and regional economies, as well as on international trade and tariff agreements, the value of the dollar, and other issues decided in Washington and in overseas capitals (O'Hare, 1988).

The residents of this area, individually as well as cooperatively, have shown themselves adept at stretching resources and making the best of what is available. But most of the determinants of their future are simply not under local control. For this reason, among others, projecting the future of the area is difficult. There are, however, several trends that seem clearly established and that provide both threats and opportunities to the forgotten people of northern New England.

The first of these is the shifting pattern of ownership of the region's natural resources. For many decades, the relationship between the landowners and the citizens of this region have remained relatively stable. Recent changes, however, such as Diamond Occidental Forest's sale in 1988 of more than 400,000 acres in New Hampshire and Vermont, portend a greatly altered future. Purchase of forest land by owners less interested in the land's natural resource value than in its investment and subdivision value poses a real threat to local residents. They are likely to suffer loss of employment opportunities, lower environmental quality, and diminished recreational access as a result of changes in land ownership and land use (Luloff, Schmidt, and Echelberger, 1990). And the government may not protect the interests of the local residents. As a result of the recent ownership shifts, the United States government initiated a study of how best to protect the forest resources of the region. This study in its original design, however, failed to include any focus on the human dimensions of land management policies. Yet changing ownership structures also creates windows of opportunity for the north-country residents. First there is the opportunity of tying extralocal development funds to improvements in community services and infrastructure and to forms of resource development sensitive to the existing human needs of the area. Second, long-standing inequities in tax structures may be redressed so that a larger share of the area's natural resources benefit the local population.

The second trend is the increase in amenity-residence value of successively more remote parts of northern New England. With rapid growth and residential development, costs of housing and services increase. For the poor, an even more serious threat resulting from this growth is the specter of zoning ordinances. Such ordinances act to force the poor first to the fringes of their communities, and then to yet more remote, isolated, and poorer areas. This second trend also creates an opportunity, however—the opportunity to manage such growth. With adequate management representing local interests, the in-migrants can be made to bear a healthy share of the costs of local infrastructure development and provision of services. Opportunities also exist for the creation of sufficient public housing during the period of expansion, especially as decisions about private housing projects came before the community. Properly managed, growth and development do not need to be the bane of north-country existence—they can result in a more adequate population on which to base services and infrastructure.

The third trend is the increase in tourism. The new business opportunities created by increasing tourism are likely to also come under the control of nonresidents, thus repeating the earlier cycle of dependence on extralocally controlled natural resources (Krannich and Luloff, 1991). The employement opportunities created under these conditions will be seasonal, poorly paid, lacking in benefits, and uncertain. Yet this increase in tourism also creates an opportunity to enfranchise the indigenous population in business ventures. These people know their areas better than anyone else; with targeted credit and management assistance, locally owned tourism and service-related businesses can be nurtured. It may also be possible for local development agencies and communities, as collectives, to enter into the tourism business, thereby creating additional employment opportunities under local ownership.

A key factor in responding to the threats and opportunities created by these three trends will be the level of organization of the local people. They will need to collectively address these issues of development, lest a repeat of earlier development patterns occurs. Community organization will be needed to protect the local interests with regard to zoning, planning, taxation, and development issues. Regional organization will be needed to prevent outside developers from playing one community against another in their efforts to tap the resources of this area. Better cooperation and coordination of the efforts of state and multistate agencies are needed to ensure that the costs of alleviating poverty are not borne by those least able to pay.

Local, county, and regional responses to these threats and opportunities will be important in shaping the future of northern New England. But they will not by themselves be sufficient to solve the problems of poverty among these forgotten people. Whether a mature (Chapman, 1982) and equitable economy emerges in New England will depend largely on the degree to which the region as a whole accepts responsibility for the welfare of the rural poor and for supporting community economic development in the forgotten areas of Maine, New Hampshire, and Vermont. The residents of the forgotten counties are doing their part, both at individual and, in many cases, at community and area levels. But they cannot lift themselves up by their bootstraps when the rest of the region is standing on their toes. Their situation is well reflected in the poignant words of a person struggling against the constraints of poverty:

> If people would only recognize that we are trying, that we are struggling with everything we've got. If they would encourage us when we're doing something to better ourselves, instead of faulting us for the way we have to live. . . . (Fitchen 1981:102)

Notes

1. These rankings were based on a study by the National Center for Economic Alternatives, which adjusted per capita income for the cost of living in each state.

2. Traditionally these same stones provided the raw material for stone walls; their presence today has regenerated a demand for such walls on the property of many new in-migrants.

3. Much of the land in northern New England was converted into small farms during this period, greatly reducing forest cover. This cutting resulted in today's second growth cover, which in composition, of both mix and frequencies of species, has remained about the same.

4. The sardine industry was at its height at the turn of the century. More than a hundred smoking plants existed along the coast of Downeast Maine, largely to serve the increasing demand for smoked herring, the staple barfood of this era. As a result of Prohibition, however, by the end of the 1920s only three or four plants remained. This decline reverberated throughout the local, coastal rural economies.

5. Other sources including Irland (1989) put the peak year in agricultural land for Maine at 1880, whereas Stanton and Plimpton (1979) set 1880 as the peak year for land in farms for Vermont. These dates would suggest that all three states' peak amounts of land in agriculture more or less coincided. Some of this difference is attributable to the statistical incorporation of forested lands on farms into the total for agricultural lands. Despite this, in order to have a comparable base of information for each of these states we have made use of data developed by the Economic Research Service of the United States

Department of Agriculture. The essential point for agricultural land is not greatly altered by differences in dates. By the turn of the century, northern New England agriculture began to succumb to the advantages of the newly opening and mechanized agricultural settlements of the midwestern and western states.

6. These nine counties are: Aroostook, Somerset, and Waldo in Maine; Coos, Grafton, and Sullivan in New Hampshire; and Essex, Lamoille, and Bennington in Vermont.

7. These people are not voluntarily poor either. It has been in vogue for some time to associate New England with a fashionable level of poverty—one characterized by the bohemian, well-heeled college graduate who earns a living doing menial labor so that she or he can enjoy a certain quality of life. The forgotten people are not included in this scenario. The fact that they often choose not to leave the area in search of better opportunities may well reflect a preference for the safety of what is known. Unfortunately, too much attention has been placed on the bohemian at the expense of the forgotten.

8. An argument can be made that the forgotten region of northern New England includes northern New York, which is ecologically, sociologically, and economically of a piece with the areal focus of this paper.

9. Food stamp participation rates are calculated from caseload data provided by the Vermont Social Welfare Department and the Maine State Planning Office. Participation rates were weighted by county population according to the U.S. Bureau of Census, 1990b.

10. The variability in population change is also higher for the smallest MCDs; both the fastest-growing and -declining MCDs are found among the smaller communities.

11. The only major exception is that a large amount of land in northern New York is also included as part of the land study.

12. A growing liberal concern over the conditions that contributed to city blight—including but not limited to the crime and drug use rampant in dilapidated buildings in run-down areas of central cities, which in turn has been popularly accepted as a major cause of white flight from these cities—may also have contributed to the problems of homelessness in rural areas. Burt and Cohen (1988) have estimated that the homeless are composed of one-third released mental patients, one-third alcoholics and drug users, and one-third people who are homeless for purely economic reasons. Part of the concern over the presence of tired old buildings was reflected in the increased pressures placed on local and state governments by city residents to rid central cities of single room occupancy (SRO) motels or hotels as one means of reducing the numbers of beggars, public drunks, and other unseemly street people. Often these pressures were placed on a housing market already constrained by a significant number of housing regulations. Further, as money for housing rehabilitation, particularly through urban renewal programs, was directed toward the SROs, one immediate impact was the increase in numbers of homeless people on city streets (cf. Tucker, 1991). What perhaps was unanticipated was the increased presence of the homeless in small and rural towns, where the problem hadn't been as noticeable or as severe. This is the case in many rural areas of northern New England (Luloff, Zaso, and Vissing, 1991).

13. This, however, does not vitiate the fact that the stigmatization and separation that result from being poor is as insidious as that which results from racial differences.

14. The level of commitment of the dedicated FmHA staff of Maine, who not only work with the loan candidates during the time of application but who maintain contact with these people thereafter, is unique. So, too, is the apparent sense of responsibility to debt service in Maine. Grantees feel an obligation to pay their bills, and as a result, despite the large volume of grants and loans made, there have been few delinquencies.

15. Two of the ones most often cited as recipients of these FmHA funds are Coastal Enterprises and Eastern Maine Development.

16. These include five funded locally, one which uses both state and federal resources, and one privately funded regional effort.

17. According to a recent listing of 755 venture capital firms in the United States, more than 100 were located in New England, with the vast majority headquartered in Boston (Venture Capital Journal, 1988). Indeed, Boston is the home of American Research and Development, the original venture capital firm which began operations in the 1950s (Wetzell, 1988).

18. This is tantamount to blaming the victim (Ryan, 1971).

19. At the same time, local efforts and programs aimed at alleviating or ameliorating the effects of individual and family poverty must take local culture very seriously.

20. This does not diminish the continued need for programs geared toward alleviating the poverty of individuals. Such need will exist for quite some time. The key, however, is the ability to utilize scarce resources in a more efficient manner and thereby counter the difficulties associated with concentrations of poverty found in many communities.

21. We use "underemployed" to capture those who work insufficient hours or are paid too low a wage to provide an adequate standard of living.

References

Anderson, Peter. 1990. "The Rural Poor: Misery on the Back Roads of New England." *Boston Globe Magazine*, 16 September: 21–28.

Banfield, Edward C. 1968. *The Unheavenly City.* Boston: Little, Brown.

Barron, Hal. 1984. *Those Who Stayed Behind: Rural Society in Nineteenth Century New England.* New York: Cambridge University Press.

Black, John D. 1950. *The Rural Economy of New England: A Regional Study.* Cambridge, Mass.: Harvard University Press.

Brown, David L., and James J. Zuiches. 1986. "New England's Population in Historical Perspective." Pp. 19–36 in Thomas E. Steahr and A. E. Luloff (eds.), *The Structure and Impact of Population Redistribution in New England.* University Park, Pa.: Northeast Regional Center for Rural Development.

Bunce, Michael. 1982. *Rural Settlement in an Urban World.* Guilford, Eng.: Billing and Sons.

Bureau of Economic Analysis. 1990. *Personal Income by Major Source and Earnings by Industry: 1969–1988* (county data file on computer tape).

Chapman, M. Perry. 1982. "The Mature Region: Building a Practical Model for the Transition to the Sustainable Society." *Technological Forecasting and Social Change* 22:167–82.

Chute, Carolyn. 1985. *The Beans of Egypt, Maine.* New York: Ticknor and Fields.

———. 1988. *Letourneau's Used Auto Parts.* New York: Ticknor and Fields.

Eckert, Robert. 1991. Personal communication.

Economic Research Service. 1991. Land use data provided by Ken Krupa.

Eisenmenger, Robert W. 1967. *The Dynamics of Growth in New England's Economy, 1870–1964.* Middletown, Conn.: Wesleyan University Press.

Federal Reserve Bank of Boston. 1990. *New England Economic Indicators: First Quarter 1990.* Boston: Federal Reserve Bank.

———. 1991. *New England Economic Indicators.* January Report. Boston: Federal Reserve Bank.

Fitchen, Janet M. 1981. *Poverty in Rural America: A Case Study.* Boulder, Colo.: Westview Press.

———. 1991. *Endangered Spaces, Enduring Places: Change, Identity and Survival in Rural America.* Boulder, Colo.: Westview Press.

Flora, Jan L., James J. Chriss, Eddie Gale, Gary P. Green, Frederick E. Schmidt, and Cornelia Flora. 1991. *From the Grassroots: Profiles of 103 Rural Self-Development Projects.* Washington, D.C.: Agriculture and Rural Economy Division, Economic Research Service, Department of Agriculture.

Ford, Thomas. 1969. "Rural Poverty in the United States." Pp. 153–76 in Task Force on Economic Growth Through Opportunity (ed.), *Rural Poverty and Regional Progress in an Urban Society.* Washington, D.C.: U.S. Chamber of Commerce.

Garreau, Joel. 1981. *The Nine Nations of North America.* New York: Avon Press.

Gaventa, John. 1980. *Power and Powerlessness: Quiescence and Rebellion in an Appalachian Valley.* Urbana: University of Illinois Press.

Greenwood, Peter. 1991. Personal communication.

Harper, Stephen C., Laura L. Falk, and Edward W. Rankin. 1990. *The Northern Forest Lands Study of New England and New York.* Rutland, Vt.: Forest Service, USDA.

Harrington, Michael. 1962. *The Other America.* New York: Macmillan.

Harvey, D. 1973. *Social Justice and the City.* Baltimore: Johns Hopkins University Press.

———. 1982. "Urbanization as a Process." Pp. 3–26 in D. Street and Associates (eds.), *Handbook of Contemporary Urban Life.* San Francisco: Jossey-Bass.

Hawley, Amos H. 1950. *Human Ecology: A Theory of Community Structure.* New York: Ronald Press.

Henry, Mark, Mark Drabenstott, and Lynn Gibson. 1988. "A Changing Rural Economy." Pp. 15–37 in Mark Drabenstott and Lynn Gibson (eds.), *Rural America in Transition.* Kansas City, Mo.: Federal Reserve Bank of Kansas City.

Howe, Gerald. 1988. "The Natural Resources of New England." Pp. 5–23 in Gerald Howe, A. E. Luloff, and Louis Ploch (eds.), *New England as a Region: Its Resources, Its People, Their Interaction.* Kingston, R.I.: New England Regional Leadership Program.

Howell, James M. 1984. "America's Regions in Transition: Who Will Benefit?" Paper presented at Demographics for Business Development Conference, Boston, Mass.

Howes, Candace, and Ann Markusen. 1981. "Poverty: A Regional Political Economy Perspective." Pp. 437–63 in Amos H. Hawley and Sara Mills Mazie (eds.), *Nonmetropolitan America in Transition.* Chapel Hill: University of North Carolina Press.

Irland, Lloyd. 1989. *Maine's Economic Heritage.* Report prepared for the Commission on Maine's Future. Augusta, Maine: The Irland Group.

Jensen, Leif. 1989. "Rural-Urban Differences in the Utilization and Ameliorative Effects of Welfare Programs." Pp. 25–39 in Harrel R. Rodgers, Jr., and Gregory Weiher (eds.), *Rural Poverty: Special Causes and Policy Reforms.* New York: Greenwood Press.

Judd, Richard W. 1988. "Reshaping Maine's Landscape: Rural Culture, Tourism, and Conservation, 1890–1929." *Journal of Forest History* 32(4):180–90.

Kaufman, Harold F. 1985. "An Action Approach to Community Development." Pp. 53–65 in Frank Fear and Harry Schwarzweller (eds.), *Focus on Community.* Research in Rural Sociology and Development, vol. 2. Westport, Conn.: Greenwood Press.

Kraenzel, Carl F. 1980. *The Social Cost of Space in the Yonland.* Bozeman, Mont.: Big Sky Books.

Krannich, Richard S., and A. E. Luloff. 1991. "Problems of Resource Dependency in U.S. Rural Communities." *Progress in Rural Policy and Planning.*

Labaree, Benjamin W. 1982. "An Historical Perspective." Pp. 24–58 in Carl Reidel (ed.), *New England Prospects: Critical Choices in a Time of Change.* Hanover, N.H.: University of New England Press.

Lee, Everett C. 1966. "A Theory of Migration." *Demography* 3(1):47–57.

———. 1970. "Migration in Relation to Education, Intellect, and Social Structure." *Population Index* 36(4):437–44.

Lefebvre, H. 1976. *The Survival of Capitalism: Reproduction of the Relations of Production.* Translated by Frank Bryant. London: Allison and Busby.

Lewis, Oscar. 1966. "The Culture of Poverty." *Scientific American,* (April): 19–25.

Lichter, Daniel T., and Janice A. Costanzo. 1987. "Nonmetropolitan Underemployment and Labor-force Composition." *Rural Sociology* 52(3):329–44.

Luloff, A. E. 1989. "The Changing New England Landscape: A Sociodemographic History." *New England Landscape* 1(1):54–65.

Luloff, A. E., and George E. Frick. 1986. "Population Growth and Economic Development." Pp. 71–78 in Dale Jahr, Jerry W. Johnson, and Ronald C. Wimberley (eds.), *New Dimensions in Rural Policy: Building Upon Our Heritage.* Washington, D.C.: Government Printing Office.

Luloff, A. E., and Louis E. Swanson. 1990. *American Rural Communities.* Boulder, Colo.: Westview Press.

Luloff, A. E., F. E. Schmidt, and H. E. Echelberger. 1990. "Attitudes and Resource Use: A Study of North Country Citizens." Pp. 203–7 in *Proceedings of the 1990 Northeastern Recreation Research Symposium.* Radnor, Pa.: Northeast Forest Experiment Station.

Luloff, A. E., Gus C. Zaso, and Yvonne Vissing. 1991. *Community and Case Studies for the Education of Homeless Children and Youth: A Typological Approach.* Final Report to Department of Compensatory Education, New Hampshire Department of Education. Durham: Department of Leisure Management and Tourism, University of New Hampshire.

Maine State Planning Office. 1991. Internal report of cases and persons covered by food stamp and AFDC programs by month, 1979–1990.

Markusen, Ann. 1985. *Profit Cycles, Oligopoly, and Regional Development.* Cambridge, Mass.: MIT Press.

McConnon, James C., and Steven C. Deller. 1990. *Trade Area Analysis of Retail*

Sales. Agricultural and Resource Economics Staff Paper No. 412. Orono: University of Maine.

Morrison, E. F., and E. E. Morrison. 1976. *New Hampshire—A Bicentennial History.* New York: W. W. Norton.

New England Regional Commission. 1981. *The New England Regional Plan: An Economic Development Strategy.* Hanover, N.H.: University Press of New England.

Nord, Mark, A. E. Luloff, and Leif Jensen. 1992. "The Localization of Poverty: A Model and Preliminary Empirical Application." Paper presented at the annual meeting of the Rural Sociological Society at Pennsylvania State University.

O'Hare, William. 1988. "The Rural Poor and the Economic Transformation of Rural America." Paper presented at the Rural Sociological Society meeting, Athens, Ga.

Pease, Allen, and Wilfred Richard. 1983. *Maine: Fifty Years of Change, 1940–1990.* Orono: University of Maine Press.

Ritchey, P. Neal. 1976. "Explanations of Migration." Pp. 253–304 in Alex Inkeles (ed.), *Annual Review of Sociology 2.* Palo Alto, Calif.: Annual Reviews.

Ryan, William. 1971. *Blaming the Victim.* New York: Vintage Books.

Stanton, B. V., and L. M. Plimpton. 1979. "People, Land, and Farms: 125 Years of Change in the Northeast." Pp. 3–23 in Hugh Davis (ed.), *Proceedings of the Northeast Agricultural Leadership Assembly.* Amherst, Mass.: Center for Environmental Policy Studies.

Steahr, Thomas E., and A. E. Luloff. 1986. *The Structure and Impact of Population Redistribution in New England.* University Park, Pa.: Northeast Regional Center for Rural Development.

Tucker, William. 1991. "How Housing Regulations Cause Homelessness." *Public Interest* 102 (Winter):78–88.

U.S. Bureau of the Census. 1987. Current Population Survey, March Supplement (machine-readable microdata file on tape). Washington, D.C.: Bureau of the Census.

———. 1988a. *County and City Data Book.* Washington, D.C.: Government Printing Office.

———. 1988b. Current Population Reports: Local Population Estimates: Northeast 1986 Population and 1985 Per-capita Income Estimates for Counties and Incorporated Places (machine-readable data file on tape). Washington, D.C.: Bureau of the Census.

———. 1988c. County and City Data Book (machine-readable data files on tape). Washington, D.C.: Bureau of the Census.

———. 1988d. Current Population Survey, March Supplement (machine-readable microdata file on tape). Washington, D.C.: Bureau of the Census.

———. 1990a. *Current Population Reports: Local Population Estimates: Northeast 1988 Population and 1987 Per-Capita Income Estimates for Counties and Incorporated Places.* Washington, D.C.: Government Printing Office.

———. 1990b. 1990 Census Preliminary Counts.

Venture Capital Journal. 1988. "Special Report: Record Growth in Ventures Industry Resources in 1987 Brings Capital Pool to $29 Billion." *Venture Capital Journal* (April):8–16.

Vermont Department of Social Welfare. 1991. Internal reports on Food Stamps and Aid to Needy Families with Children: households, families, recipients, and benefits by Vermont county, 10/85 to 10/90.

WCVB-TV. 1989. "Back Country Blues." Television Documentary for *Chronicles*, WCVB-TV, Boston.

Wetzell, William E. 1988. Personal communication.

Wilkinson, Kenneth P. 1989. "Community Development and Industrial Policy." *Rural Sociology and Development* 4:241–54.

———. 1991. *The Community in Rural America*. Westport, Conn.: Greenwood Press. Forthcoming.

Wilson, W. J. 1987. *The Truly Disadvantaged*. Chicago: University of Chicago Press.

Zelinsky, Wilbur. 1978. "Is Nonmetropolitan America Being Repopulated? The Evidence from Pennsylvania's Minor Civil Divisions." *Demography* 15(1):618–33.

8 | Ontonagon: A Remote Corner of Michigan's Upper Peninsula

Harry K. Schwarzweller and Sue-Wen Lean

MICHIGAN'S UPPER PENINSULA (UP), a part of the historically underdeveloped upper midwestern area of the United States known as "the Great Lakes Cutover Region," has been and is, even today, socioeconomically distinct from the Lower Peninsula. To the "Yoopers," as people from the UP are often called, "downstate" means government, taxes, wetland restrictions, unnecessary constraints on development, and a flood of tourists during the summer months. A few years ago the antagonisms, misunderstandings, and conflicts of interest between the UP and downstate again became so intense that a movement to join with the northern areas of Wisconsin and Minnesota (together constituting the old "cut-over region") to form a separate governmental entity—"the great state of Superior"—was reinstituted. The statehood movement, which first surfaced in the mid-1800s, still simmers (Carter, 1980). But in fact the upper and lower segments of Minnesota, Wisconsin, and Michigan have become so integrated, through shared history, economic exchanges, migration, and tourism, that it is quite unlikely that this effort to attain statehood will gain political momentum. Nevertheless, at least in Michigan, where the north country is a peninsula that stands geographically apart from the state's industrial heartland, this region, once regarded as a major problem area in America (Beck and Forster, 1935), continues to struggle for recognition and respect.

As one drives across Michigan's Upper Peninsula, perhaps from the Mackinac Bridge and Sault Ste. Marie to Duluth in Minnesota or down along the west side of Lake Michigan to Milwaukee and Chicago, it is rather easy to bypass Ontonagon (see Map 8.1). Located on the shores of Lake Superior in the far northwestern section of the UP—500 miles by road from the state capitol in Lansing—the Ontonagon area, which currently has about 8,800 residents, in many ways represents the Upper Peninsula rather well. Its problems reflect some of the developmental issues that have plagued this region since it was first drawn into the mainstream of contemporary America.

Map 8.1

Ontonagon County

The Early Years

Michigan became a state in 1837 and at that time acquired the Upper Peninsula in return for Ohio's takeover of the Toledo/Maumee River Strip. Eventually too, in 1842, the Indians ceded the region to the United States. Until the mid-1800s the far western part remained largely a wilderness area visited mostly by Chippewa Indians, French trappers, and English explorers. But then massive deposits of copper were discovered in the Keweenaw area and some rich iron ore was discovered in the Marquette Range in the central UP. Reports of a huge copper boulder discovered not far from the Ontonagon River added to the excitement and attracted many adventurers and fortune-seekers. (The boulder still survives—though somewhat mutilated—in the Smithsonian Institution.)

In 1843 the town of Ontonagon was formally laid out along the east bank of the Ontonagon River by James K. Paul. He had been drawn there by the lure of mass "float" copper (Jamison, 1939), and he actually "found" and subsequently sold the great Ontonagon boulder, which had been in the possession of Indians since at least the 1700s. Others came to search for copper and silver; numerous small mines were started. Copper prices rose during the Civil War and continued to be high after the war, as copper telephone and telegraph lines were stretched across America; fortunes awaited the lucky. Ontonagon Village grew; by 1896 there were 2,300 residents, many community amenities, and even an opera house. After the federal government induced railroads to build in the region through a system of land grants, the southern part of the county was also opened up to more intensive settlement.

There were vast stands of white pine and mixed hardwoods throughout the region, and when logging operations in the lower peninsula could no longer meet the burgeoning demand generated by the country's rapid urbanization, exploitation of the Upper Peninsula's timber, along with its mineral resources, attracted entrepreneurs seeking investment opportunities and workers seeking jobs. Many of the newcomers were immigrants from northern Europe, particularly from Finland, other Scandinavian countries, and Cornwall in England. Often recruited for labor in the mines and lumber camps, many later became farmers, clearing the land, pulling the stumps, and planting crops that could be marketed locally. Farming conditions in the UP are harsh and not unlike what many of the newcomers had experienced as youngsters in the "old country"—the soils are poor, the growing season short, and the winters cold.

From the very beginning Ontonagon's socioeconomic development and growth depended on mining and timber (and, more recently, pulp.) These extractive industries attracted eastern capitalists, Chicago investment bankers, absentee landlords, adventurers, and immigrants from the Old World. As mining exploration and lumber mills moved inland and west, and as roads and rail lines linked this remote region more closely with the major population centers downstate, new communities were formed. Greenland, Mass City, and Rockland (where the Victoria mine was located) are situated southeast of Ontonagon. Silver City (site of an early silver mine) is west of Ontonagon. All less than fifteen miles from the town of Ontonagon, these places are now integral parts of the Ontonagon service area, only a short commute from supermarkets and the variety of shops along Ontonagon's main street. But in the old days, when the Ontonagon River was the only gateway to the outside world, these settlements were small, self-contained communities that, in such a rough, stony country, were quite isolated from one another. White Pine, five miles south of Silver City, however, is a rather new town with an enclosed shopping mall, a modern high school, and a multineighborhood, suburban-style complex of individualized homes—projects that were subsidized and built in 1970 by the mining corporation. Only a few miles west of White Pine are the Porcupine Mountains and "Lake of the Clouds," one of Michigan's most scenic tourist attractions.

The emergence of communities in the southern part of Ontonagon County, which occurred somewhat independently of the formation of communities bordering Lake Superior in the northern part, was also primarily associated with the exploitation of timber and the construction of railroads and automobile roads for transporting logs and copper. Bergland (on Lake Gogebic), Ewen (the main railroad terminal), Bruces Crossing, and Trout Creek were founded to provide services to logging camps, sawmills, and lumber-related industries; they grew into small towns. When the virgin pines had been slashed and hauled away, the cutover flat land, which had greater agricultural potential than land to the north, was sold very cheaply for cultivation and grazing; a number of dairy farms were established. Pulp logging and wood chipping for an expanding pulp-and-paper (cardboard) industry gradually gained importance after the stands of big timber had been depleted. These activities and other jobs associated with the pulp-and-paper industry became a critical source of supplemental income for many struggling families during the long periods of economic depression. The years from 1921 through 1954 were especially difficult; copper prices had plummeted, mining exploration had almost ceased, all commercial mines were closed, and the economy of Ontonagon and the western UP was stagnant. Work in the pulp woods helped many households to survive, particularly those that had been dependent on mining or on small, marginal farming operations. In 1954 the socioeconomic transformation of Ontonagon County and the western Upper Peninsula area was dramatically advanced when Copper Range Corporation opened its modern, technologically-sophisticated mining and smelting facility at the site of the old White Pine copper mine.

Contemporary Developments

Over the past thirty-five years a number of major economic developments within the area have had a profound impact on the lives and fortunes of Ontonagon residents. Most impressive, with far-ranging consequence, was the construction of the White Pine Copper Mine, smelter, and ore refinery complex, which quickly became a focal point for employment in the region. This was paralleled by a general expansion and modernization of the pulp-and-paperboard industry, attempts to strengthen tourism, and more recently, the location of a large manufacturing firm in Ontonagon Village. Often referred to as "rural industrialization" or "rural revitalization," these contemporary developments, like earlier intrusions of the commercial world into this region, are the outcome of concerted efforts by many people and agencies both within the region and elsewhere to exploit the available natural resources and to utilize the underemployed human capital in this rather remote area of Michigan.

Copper Mining

Mining in this area began over a century ago. During World War I over 300 men were employed and production was stimulated; the mine was closed soon after the war, however, when the price of copper fell to an extreme low, and the original mine was sold in 1929. The quality of this Lake Superior chalcocite is low; the big problem was to devise a technique for extracting copper more efficiently from the ore. With the outbreak of the Korean War the federal government financed more intensive research and subsidized construction of the present operation, and the first ore was taken from the new mine in 1953. The smelter was completed and functional by 1955. Eventually, in 1981, immediately prior to a veritable collapse of the industry, a modern, high-technology ore refinery was built to purify the copper, to recover the contaminating silver, and to help the mine "to survive in the copper market." As it turned out, despite herculean efforts by management and workers, falling copper prices in the late 1970s and early 1980s again brought mining operations almost to a standstill.

Workers got angry, and there was a protracted strike. Ownership changed hands a number of times (first to a Louisiana firm and then to a Canadian one); in 1985 the state and union arranged a worker takeover (to become the only worker-owned mine in the country). A few years later the workers sold their shares to a German company (Copper Range Company is owned by Metall Mining Company of Toronto, a subsidiary of Metallgesellschaft of Germany). Currently, mining operations are proceeding at about 50 percent of capacity.

The White Pine mine was designed as a large-scale industrial operation. At its peak in 1974, there were over 3,000 employees with a payroll of over $35 million. Although some workers commuted from as far away as eighty miles (by company bus, called locally "the White Pine Sleeper"), about half were from Ontonagon County (and these accounted for nearly two-thirds of the county's employed persons). As copper prices tumbled, the work force was reduced. The biggest layoff occurred in 1976, when half of the employees were let go. By 1982 there were only about 900 employees, and during the strike period of 1983–1984 only a caretaker crew was retained (mining operations were suspended for three years). After the worker takeover was implemented, employment rose to about a thousand; currently, it remains at about that level.

Many "spin-off jobs," especially in the service sector, were and are associated with the ebb and flow of employment in the mine. Community amenities too, particularly in the company-built town of White Pine, were and continue to be dependent upon the economic viability of the mine. Indeed, the socioeconomic impacts of these huge layoffs reverberated throughout the region. Within a year of the big layoff in 1976 many younger families in White Pine, Ontonagon, and elsewhere in the area opted to move elsewhere in search of jobs; the tax base and school enrollments eroded, and it is very unlikely that the affected communities will ever recoup these losses. So it is with a local economy that is overwhelmingly dependent upon one industry. And so it has been historically throughout the Upper Peninsula of Michigan.

Pulp/Paper Industry

The Diamond Match Company (DMC), a national corporation, dominated the lumber industry in the western Upper Peninsula during the early 1890s. Some of the local pine was used to make wooden matches, but most was milled into boards and shipped out for construction purposes. In 1896 a huge fire reduced the DMC mills and facilities to ashes and swept through Ontonagon Village, destroying most of the homes and businesses (Cooper, 1983). Thereafter, logging and timber milling activities in the region were mainly small-scale, relying on part-time and temporary laborers for "work in the woods." The earlier logging operations (with clear-cutting practices and periodic fires) had devastated the forests; a wasteland was left. Only gradually, and in response to the growing demand for pulp and paper products, did the woods resources of the western Upper Peninsula regain significant economic value.

A small pulp/paperboard mill, built at the outskirts of Ontonagon Village in the early 1920s, operated irregularly over the years and barely survived the Great Depression; forced to close in 1953, it was reopened in 1956 and since then the number of employees and the volume of production has grown rather steadily. There has been a succession of owners: National Container Corporation, 1945–1953; Huss Ontonagon Pulp and Paper Company, 1956–1962; Hoerner Box Company, 1962–

1967; Hoerner-Waldorf, 1967–1976; Champion International, 1976–1986; and, currently, Stone Paper Company. Large doses of outside developmental capital and smooth but tenacious linkages to national and international markets are absolutely essential for maintaining a reasonably successful pulp/paper enterprise.

Over the years, spurred by persistent competition within the industry (both foreign and domestic) and the pressures to increase the scale of operation, to capture a large share of the market, and to reduce unit costs by maximizing efficiency, the industry has become almost totally mechanized. Earlier, the mill would purchase pulp logs or a stand of pulp trees from local farmers, logging crews, or land owners and the woods work was low-technology and labor-intensive. Basic to this was "a good man with an axe," a team of horses, and often, the man's wife and children. Delimbing, debarking, and the stacking of logs were hard work. Hauling, of course, was done by truck, but the loading was a muscle-intensive task. At the mill, the work, too, was very physical. Then came power saws, hydraulic loaders, "skidder" tractors, "grapple" skidders, mobile heavy-duty chippers, semitrailers for hauling chips, automatic unloading systems at the plant, and scores of other laborsaving devices. In short, the pulp/paperboard industry, in a relatively short period of time, became technologically sophisticated and almost completely automated.

According to Rieger and Schwarzweller (1991), "the arrival of mechanization has reduced the number employed in woods work in the Ontonagon County area to under a hundred." We well might ask, as does Rieger: "What has happened to the families that were once dependent upon this industry?" Concomitant with the large decrease in woods jobs, there has been an increase, though of lesser magnitude, in employment at the mill and in the chipper/hauling businesses now so essential to the pulp industry (currently, 1000 tons of wood chips are processed daily). The number of employees at the Ontonagon plant has doubled during the past decade, to over 300 workers. Additionally, the two principal independent "suppliers" (essentially, contractors for chipping and hauling) employ a large number of equipment operators, drivers, technicians, and accountants. The pulp/paper industry, like the copper mining industry, has evolved rather rapidly into a high-technology business that demands from its workers not brawn, but skills and educated intelligence. And it, too, as an industry dependent upon the exploitation of natural resources (though more self-sustaining than mining), is subject to marketing disorders and the sometimes erratic fluctuations of prices (the pulp-and-paper market is notoriously volatile, not unlike the copper market).

Shipbuilding/Manufacturing

In 1979 construction was begun on a $9 million shipbuilding plant that represented an effort by the community and its fledgling development program to diversify the economy of Ontonagon. It was an ambitious undertaking, and the negotiations that led to it are, even to this day, not altogether clear. Backing from the state was involved. Initially, the plan was to build tugboats and barges that could be operated on the Great Lakes. Contracts were drawn up, facilities constructed, and work begun. But, for various reasons, the original deal fell through. An overseas buyer for the business (Japanese) was found, but this arrangement also collapsed. Then, amidst all the confusion, a New York–based firm bought out the entire operation with the intention of building pontoon causeways for the U.S. Navy; a contract with the Navy was in hand. The enterprise was quite successful; about 200 people were employed (many of whom were trained as welders through a special program administered by the local high school and its state-financed vocational training center). A second contract was negotiated with the Navy in 1985 for more causeways. Ontonagon's Economic Development Corporation was pleased, for the manufacturing firm added much needed diversity and income to the local economy (which has always been constrained by its dependence on the mining and pulp/paper industries).

As it turned out, Wedtech Corporation, in 1986, was caught up in a rather awkward and somewhat bizarre scandal that involved allegations of influence peddling at the highest levels of the United States government. The Ontonagon facility was closed for a time until the complexities of this situation could be sorted out. Now under new management (Lake Shore Inc., an Oldenberg Group Company based in Michigan), operations have resumed, the company is manufacturing cargo-handling and lifeboat equipment for the U.S. Navy, and there are about 130 persons employed. The workers and Ontonagon's Economic Development Corporation are optimistic about the future of the facility.

Tourism

Porcupine Mountain State Park, in the western corner of Ontonagon County, is one of Michigan's most scenic tourist attractions. There are good fishing streams, well-marked hiking and nature trails, beautiful vistas, and, during the winter months, excellent downhill and cross-country skiing. But, because "The Porkies" and the many other recreational and tourist attractions in the area are a long, long way from major downstate population centers, it is difficult for the Ontonagon business community to derive significant economic gains from additional investments in tourism. Nevertheless, numerous serious attempts have been made in recent years to develop a tourist industry more fully.

Federal funds were obtained during the 1970s to build a marina; it was argued that a marina was needed here to provide safe harbor for boats cruising between the Apostle Islands off Wisconsin to the Keweenaw. Moreover, a local group promoting tourism managed to get a snowmobile trail laid out, with federal assistance, from Ontonagon to the Porcupines. And in the early 1970s trails were cleared for another major downhill ski area; unfortunately, the private company went bankrupt before the project could be completed, and currently there is talk about venture capital from as far away as Hawaii being enticed into this snow country business. Most of these, and the many other tourist-oriented projects—often strongly supported by local groups and state or federal subsidization—have failed to lure a flood of tourists and their dollars.

Ontonagon and the western Upper Peninsula of Michigan, in planning development projects related to tourism or to any other commercial enterprise, must cope with what has been called "the tyranny of distance" (Blaney, 1966). A high school principal in the area with whom we spoke expressed the problem quite clearly: "Ten years ago I would have said that tourism was a bright hope on the economic horizon. But now it doesn't look nearly as promising. We are missing some key things necessary to make it really take off. Some outlying islands to interest the boaters, for instance. It's also an awful long distance to come for things that can be found closer to where people are coming from. Take skiing: we haven't got any facilities that are any better here than people can get closer to their homes."

Livelihood Patterns

These contemporary economic developments within the Ontonagon area are reflected in the changed livelihood patterns of its people. Subsistence farming, of course, has long passed from the scene; this is not to say, however, that the few remaining farms and agricultural enterprises are operating at far above the marginal level. But with the coming of industrialized mining, mechanized pulp harvesting, assembly-line welding in the manufacture of naval equipment, and an

Table 8.1. Ontonagon: Industry Composition of Labor Force, 1940–1980 (in percentage of total persons employed)

Industry	1940	1950	1960	1970	1980
(Total Persons Employed)	(3,064)	(2,850)	(3,145)	(3,369)	(3,310)
Agriculture[1]	40.8	30.4	11.2	4.8	3.9
Mining	0.3	0.5	28.8	30.7	16.5
Construction	4.7	5.3	5.5	4.8	4.9
Manufacturing	21.9	25.8	14.8	14.0	14.7
Distributive services[2]	15.3	18.7	16.9	19.5	23.6
Producer services[3]	2.1	3.5	3.3	2.8	3.9
Personal services[4]	4.7	3.8	4.6	2.4	2.4
Social services[5]	9.0	10.3	13.4	21.0	30.1
Not reporting	1.2	1.7	1.5	*	*
Total	100.0	100.0	100.0	100.0	100.0

Source: U.S. Census Reports, 1940–1980.
*Data not reported.
[1]Includes forestry and fishery.
[2]Includes transportation, communications, utilities, wholesale and retail.
[3]Includes finance, insurance, real estate, business and repair services.
[4]Includes personal services, entertainment and recreation.
[5]Includes public administration, education, professional, health, and welfare.

increased emphasis on tourism, the character of the Ontonagon labor market has changed dramatically.

Between 1940 and 1980 there has been an enormous decrease in the percentage employed in agriculture and forestry (probably only 2 percent in 1990); the services sector has expanded greatly, to nearly two-thirds of the labor force, with much of that increase due to the huge growth in social services; and employment in the mining industry has followed rather closely the fluctuations of copper prices and White Pine Copper's corporate history (see Table 8.1).

There has also been a rapid decrease in farming and forest work since the late 1960s and a steady increase in numbers of service workers, sales and clerical jobs, and professional/technical/managerial employment (Table 8.2).

Especially interesting and relevant is the fact that total size of the Ontonagon labor force has not changed very much over the years, hovering between 3,000 and 3,400. As we noted previously, in the early 1970s about half of the Ontonagon labor force was employed by White Pine Copper; thus, the big layoffs and protracted strike in the late seventies, and the failure to get the mine into full production by now (1991) had, and continue to have, serious negative impacts on the Ontonagon economy.

Table 8.2. Ontonagon: Ocupational Distribution of Labor Force, 1940–1980 (in percentage of total persons employed)

Occupation	1940	1950	1960	1970	1980
Professional, managers, technicians	13.0	15.6	16.9	19.8	21.6
Sales, clerical	7.0	9.0	10.8	13.9	18.6
Crafts, operatives	20.8	26.8	43.0	43.5	31.7
Service workers	7.3	7.4	10.7	14.8	17.9
Laborers, nonfarm	21.6	10.9	5.1	4.1	5.6
Farm, forestry (all levels)	29.1	28.8	10.1	3.9	4.6
Not reporting	1.2	1.5	3.4	*	*
Total	100.0	100.0	100.0	100.0	100.0

Source: U.S. Census Reports, 1940–1980.

*Data not reported.

Not surprisingly, unemployment rates over the years (Table 8.3) have been relatively high, except for the early 1970s, and have always been much higher than in Michigan generally, especially for men; even in 1980, the unemployment rate for men in Ontonagon and throughout the Upper Peninsula was over twice as high as that in downstate Michigan. Moreover, a rather large segment of the Ontonagon adult population of both men and women, a significantly larger segment than downstate, was not and is not a regular part of the labor force, whether employed or actively seeking employment. We surmise that the Ontonagon population is somewhat older on average, that there is more chronic underemployment, and that livelihood problems and intrafamily dependency burdens are probably more severe in the Ontonagon situation than downstate.

Are livelihood patterns any different in the Ontonagon County situation than in Michigan's Upper Peninsula generally? Historically, economic development of the Ontonagon area has been shaped by the copper and forest products industries. Other areas of the UP also have been affected by close interaction with these industries; for instance, the Keweenaw Peninsula (Houghton/Hancock and Calumet) was at one time a major mining center, and the pulp-and-paper industry in concentrated in various places.

Years ago, before the White Pine Copper Mine came into production, mining, although an active industry in other parts of the UP, was unimportant in Ontonagon (Tables 8.1 and 8.4). On the other hand, proportionately twice as many persons were engaged in farming and forestry in Ontonagon as in the UP generally. Now (prior to the big decline in copper), the composition of the labor force of Ontonagon is basically similar to that of the UP, except for the larger proportion of persons employed in mining (White Pine Copper) and in manufacturing (jobs deriving from the smelting operation and from welding jobs at the local shipyard). Indeed, in the distribution of occupatinal types or skill/status levels, the Ontonagon labor force is now remarkably similar to that of the UP as a whole (Tables 8.2 and 8.5.) Workers employed in the modernized mining-and-smelting and pulp-and-paper industries are now skilled, semiskilled operatives, and clerical workers, and no longer laborers with pick and shovel or ax and saw.

Thus, the livelihood patterns of people in this remote corner of Michigan's Upper Peninsula have changed dramatically over the years. Self-sufficiency and small-scale, independent commercial operations (in farming and pulp/lumber enterprises, especially) are now a thing of the past. The people of Ontonagon and their economic activities have

Table 8.3. Ontonagon County, Upper Peninsula, and Lower Peninsula: Labor Force Participation and Unemployment as Percentage of Total Population, 1940–1980

	1940	1950	1960	1970	1980
Ontonagon County					
Participation	53.3	46.3	49.3	52.3	51.0
Male	81.0	69.3	71.3	72.4	62.9
Female	14.0	16.8	23.2	31.3	38.9
Unemployment	33.3*	17.4	12.6	7.1	11.7
Male	34.3*	19.7	14.4	6.9	12.9
Female	25.5*	5.5	5.7	7.5	9.7
Upper Peninsula					
Participation	50.3	46.6	46.1	46.4	51.5
Male	77.6	71.3	65.7	60.4	62.3
Female	17.9	19.8	25.4	32.1	40.7
Unemployment	32.3*	9.0	10.5	8.9	12.3
Male	33.6*	10.0	11.6	9.8	13.4
Female	25.3*	4.9	7.5	7.1	10.6
Lower Peninsula					
Participation	52.8	54.0	55.1	58.3	61.6
Male	80.7	80.2	78.3	77.6	75.4
Female	23.6	27.7	33.0	40.4	49.0
Unemployment	13.0*	5.2	6.8	5.8	6.6
Male	13.2*	5.2	6.7	5.3	4.3
Female	12.4*	5.4	7.2	6.6	9.9

Source: U.S. Census Reports, 1940–1980.

For 1940, 1950, and 1960 censuses, participation rate was calculated against those 14 years and older; the other censuses were based on those 16 years and older.

*Includes those on public emergency work such as WPA.

Table 8.4. Upper Peninsula: Industry Composition of Labor Force, 1940–1980 (in percentage of total persons employed)

Industry	1940	1950	1960	1970	1980
(Total Persons Employed)	(83,185)	(93,824)	(88,703)	(90,037)	(109,818)
Agriculture	19.6	12.3	5.4	2.9	2.5
Mining	11.9	10.8	11.6	8.2	5.6
Construction	4.2	5.0	7.1	5.9	6.0
Manufacturing	16.3	22.6	18.6	16.2	15.6
Distributive services	23.3	25.9	26.5	29.1	27.4
Producer services	3.2	3.8	3.8	4.4	5.7
Personal services	7.0	5.2	6.2	5.1	4.2
Social services	13.1	13.2	18.5	28.2	33.0
Not reporting	1.4	1.2	2.3	*	*
Total	100.0	100.0	100.0	100.0	100.0

Source: U.S. Census Reports, 1940–1980.

* Data not reported.

been incorporated into the mainstream of American industry and, consequently, the well-being of the people of Ontonagon, always tenuous at best, is now far more dependent upon the economic viability and bureaucratic scheming of two or three firms.

Whether these changes in livelihood patterns have effected a narrowing of income differentials (and the gap in life chances) between Ontonagon families and their downstate counterparts—the "bottom line," so to speak, in our assessment of the contemporary situation in this troubled region—must be considered. But before turning attention to this critical and complex issue, it is appropriate to explore, very briefly, some of the concomitant changes in population growth and in the social organization on Ontonagon communities.

Population and Community

The copper boom of the Civil War period brought a rush of people to Ontonagon; the 1860 census reported over 4,500 persons in the county. But it was a short-lived spurt of prosperity and many of the newcomers were adventurers, with no intentions of remaining as permanent residents; it wasn't until the timber boom of the 1980s that the population again climbed to over 4,000. In the early 1900s there was a huge influx of Finnish settlers; the population peaked at about 12,400 in 1920. From that time until 1980 the population remained at between 10,500 and 11,000. But White Pine Copper's troubles in recent years generated a stream of out-migration; the 1990 census counted only 8,854 residents in the county (and only about 2,000 in the village of Ontonagon). If population growth is an indicator of development, then we'd probably conclude that Ontonagon is once again experiencing hard times.

Within the county too, as one would expect, there has been an ebb and flow of population, depending on the locational placement (and luck) of economic development. For the most part the shift has been toward Ontonagon Village and the lakeside, where the industrial plants are located; the interior of the county has been losing population. Many hamlets have almost disappeared, and many of the smaller villages, once relatively independent, have become satellites of Ontonagon Village. School consolidation, of course, had an enormous effect on the social integrity of these places and the social ecology of the region; in 1957, for instance, there were eleven high schools in the county, but now only three remain.

One of the significant characteristics of the Ontonagon community (the village of Ontonagon and the network of settlements that constitute this community)—and of rural communities generally throughout the Upper Peninsula—is a distinct separation of spheres of consumer services and consumer-oriented markets from those of other settlement clusters in nearby counties, and from the cities of this region. As a trading area, the Ontonagon community stands apart; it is a relatively self-contained entity. Community trade areas downstate, where the countryside has been urbanized and where metropolitan centers are a short drive from most places, overlap considerably and in many diverse ways, often in a seemingly chaotic fashion. But in more

Table 8.5. Upper Peninsula: Occupational Distribution of Labor Force, 1940–1980 (in percentage of total persons employed)

Occupation	1940	1950	1960	1970	1980
Professional, managers, technicians	16.5	16.7	19.6	21.5	22.5
Sales, clerical	12.6	14.5	16.3	20.2	22.8
Crafts, operatives	33.5	37.3	37.3	33.5	28.2
Service workers	11.0	9.3	12.8	17.2	18.5
Laborers, nonfarm	11.9	9.9	5.9	5.4	4.9
Farm, forestry (all levels)	13.6	11.2	4.5	2.2	3.1
Not reporting	0.9	1.1	3.6	*	*
Total	100.0	100.0	100.0	100.0	100.0

Source: U.S. Census Reports, 1940–1980.

*Data not reported.

sparsely populated rural regions, like Michigan's Upper Peninsula, community boundaries and their service areas are more distinct; in effect, the reality of "community" is manifest.

Over the years community amenities in the Ontonagon area have improved enormously. Although Ontonagon Village boasted an opera house in the late 1890s, after the great fire of 1896 and after the copper and timber booms, the people of Ontonagon became resigned, it seems, to a relatively Spartan existence. It was not until recent years that any community recreational facilities were introduced. (The lack of recreational facilities was an especially irksome issue for the young people; it was a matter often mentioned as a reason for leaving the area.) Now there are three bowling establishments; two golf courses; an indoor public swimming pool; two sets of tennis courts; a huge recreational center in Ontonagon Village for indoor ice skating, ice hockey, dances, parties, etc.; two smaller recreational centers elsewhere in the county; a downhill ski area; snowmobile trails, and many related activities. Also, there are a variety of social organizations and a full slate of youth programs. Shopping centers and stores carry most items that families need to maintain a comfortable lifestyle; larger shopping malls are located in Houghton/Hancock, only 60 miles away, and Marquette City, 125 miles away. Yet, despite the fact that the people of Ontonagon are linked very directly to mainstream America in many ways and accept the urban, consumer-oriented values of middle America without great hesitation, there is still an aura of remoteness. It is a long drive to the "bridge"; it is a longer one still to the state capitol in Lansing. Downstate is another world.

Upstate/Downstate

The Lower Peninsula of Michigan is a vital part of America's industrial heartland; not long ago Detroit was the automobile capital of the world. Early in the state's development the cities of lower Michigan began to grow and prosper through the unique interplay of investment capital, shrewd business deals, stable labor force, reliable power sources, excellent location (relative to raw materials and markets), and other factors that have been noted by economic historians. Much like what happened in Minnesota and Wisconsin (and as well in New York, the New England region, and Ontario, Canada), socioeconomic development of the lower segment of Michigan spurted ahead; development of the upper segment, which could not and did not share equally in the transformation to a manufacturing-based economy, lagged.

Table 8.6. Lower Peninsula: Industry Composition of Labor Force, 1940–1980 (in percentage of total persons employed)

Industry	1940	1950	1960	1970	1980
(Total persons employed, in 000s)	(1,742)	(2,298)	(2,638)	(3,162)	(3,640)
Agriculture	11.8	6.6	3.3	1.8	1.6
Mining	0.3	0.2	0.2	0.2	0.2
Construction	4.0	4.9	4.5	4.8	4.1
Manufacturing	39.2	41.7	38.7	36.4	30.8
Distributive services	21.6	23.8	23.4	24.6	25.8
Producer services	4.5	5.1	5.6	6.6	8.5
Personal services	7.7	5.6	5.5	4.2	3.4
Social services	9.6	10.8	15.5	21.4	25.6
Not reporting	1.3	1.3	3.3	*	*
Total	100.0	100.0	100.0	100.0	100.0

Source: U.S. Census Reports, 1940–1980.

*Data not reported.

The greater historical emphasis on manufacturing industries in the Lower Peninsula than in the Upper Peninsula persists (see Tables 8.4 and 8.6). Indeed, according to the 1980 census, the proportion of persons employed in manufacturing in the Lower Peninsula is twice that of the UP. Conversely, a somewhat greater proportion of persons in the UP are employed in agriculture and mining and, surprisingly, also in social services. But patterned variations in kind of occupations (and in occupational status levels) in the UP and in the Lower Peninsula, although distinguishable, are by no means startling (see Tables 8.5 and 8.7). Today, it appears, differences in occupational composition of the downstate and upstate labor forces are relatively slight (there is a greater proportion of service workers in the UP and a greater proportion of sales/clerical workers in the Lower Peninsula). Farming, forestry work, and laborer jobs were far more common in the UP in earlier times. Apparently the industry composition of the UP labor force has been slower to change (and to diversify) than has the occupational composition. Today most jobs, even those associated with mining and forestry in the UP, require specialized skills, training, and education.

The occupational composition of Ontonagon's labor force too, as noted, has been evolving in much the same direction as that of the UP region—leaning more toward professional, technical, and sales/clerical occupations—a pattern that typifies downstate Michigan and American society generally.

Ontonagon County and the Upper Peninsula had very similar rates

Table 8.7. Lower Peninsula: Occupational Distribution of Labor Force, 1940–1980 (in percentage of total persons employed)

Occupation	1940	1950	1960	1970	1980
Professional, managers, technicians	14.8	16.4	18.8	21.2	24.4
Sales, clerical	17.1	19.5	21.5	23.8	26.3
Crafts, operatives	38.7	42.4	37.6	36.8	30.1
Service workers	10.6	9.3	10.8	12.7	13.8
Laborers, nonfarm	6.5	4.8	3.9	4.0	3.8
Farm, forestry (all levels)	11.4	6.3	3.1	1.5	1.6
Not reporting	0.9	1.3	4.3	*	*
Total	100.0	100.0	100.0	100.0	100.0

Source: U.S. Census Reports, 1940–1980.

*Data not reported.

of labor force participation and unemployment in the 1980s (Table 8.3). This was not always so, for in earlier years, when the White Pine Mine was booming, employment was much easier to come by in Ontonagon than elsewhere in the UP. But when the mine ran into trouble, unemployment again became more serious in Ontonagon, and now, as in the UP generally, is about twice as high (for males) as in the Lower Peninsula; an unemployment rate of 12 percent is stressful for a community, particularly one that is as geographically isolated from alternative employment opportunities as is Ontonagon.

Income differentials, many would say, represent the bottom line in comparing the economies of downstate and upstate Michigan and in assessing the economic life chances of families in these regions. One must take into account, of course, that there are some variations in the industrial and occupational compositions of these labor markets. A temporal stability in the pattern of per capita income is evident. Incomes in the UP (and in Ontonagon County) average about 70 percent of incomes in the Lower Peninsula (see Table 8.8), not unlike differences observed generally in the United States between metropolitan and nonmetropolitan areas (Fuguitt, Brown, and Beale, 1989:338, 431). Residents of Michigan's Lower Peninsula clearly enjoy a comparative advantage (at present, about $3,200 more per person per year). But of course, cost of living and lifestyle norms are not the same in Ontonagon or Marquette (Upper Peninsula) as in East Lansing or Ann Arbor (Lower Peninsula).

Compared with downstate, a larger proportion of families are living under the poverty level in Ontonagon County and the Upper Peninsula (Table 8.9). But the regional differences in percentages are minor,

Table 8.8. Ontonagon County, Upper Peninsula, and Lower Peninsula: Income per Capita, Selected Years

	Income per Capita ($)					
	1959	1969	1974	1979	1985	1987
Ontonagon	1,323	2,342	3,461	5,599	7,531	8,904
(% of Lower Peninsula)	(67.4)	(69.0)	(72.1)	(72.1)	(68.4)	(73.6)
Upper Peninsula	1,392	2,360	3,509	5,654	7,661	8,296
(% of Lower Peninsula)	(70.9)	(69.6)	(73.1)	(72.9)	(69.5)	(68.6)
Lower Peninsula	1,962	3,392	4,797	7,761	11,017	12,101

Source: County and City Data Book, 1962–1988.

especially if one takes account of differences in material standards of living and lifestyle norms, and if one recognizes as well that there are many, many poor, "forgotten" families struggling for survival in deteriorating urban neighborhoods in some of Michigan's largest cities. Most certainly, no families in contemporary America should be left to flounder along in poverty, whether in urban metropolitan centers or in more remote situations in the Upper Peninsula; a poverty rate of 8 percent is unconscionable!

Thus, we observe some significant differences between the Upper Peninsula and the Lower Peninsula in labor market structure (industrial composition of the labor force), availability of work (unemployment rates), and the opportunity of individuals and their families to generate good incomes (as evidenced by per capita income comparisons). The chances of finding employment (especially for a young man or woman starting out on a work career), acquiring an upper-level position (professional, technical, managerial, administrative, skilled), and drawing a decent wage or salary, are better downstate. Such downstate/upstate labor market disparities, long a characteristic of the Great Lakes Cutover Region relative to mainstream America, are re-

Table 8.9. Ontonagon County, Upper Peninsula, and Lower Peninsula: Percentage of Families below Poverty Level

	1969	1979
Ontonagon	8.2	9.5
Upper Peninsula	11.7	8.6
Lower Peninsula	7.1	8.2
Michigan	7.3	8.2

Source: County and City Data Book, 1973–1988.

flected in comparative statistics on population growth. Until World War I, the UP and Ontonagon populations were growing much faster than the downstate population (see Table 8.10). As a result of the copper boom stimulated by the war, Ontonagon County drew a large influx of people during the decade of 1910–1920, while the UP at that time was losing population. But from 1940 on, the Upper Peninsula's population remained at slightly over 300,000, whereas the downstate population continued to grow. Ontonagon County, during this period, began a steady decline.

It is clear that there has been a large flow of out-migration from Ontonagon and from the Upper Peninsula since World War II. The pull of better wages and more diverse job opportunities downstate induced many (particularly young people) to move out of the UP to metropolitan centers in lower Michigan, lower Wisconsin, and elsewhere. This consistent and persistent stream of migration from north to south—readily absorbed, until recently, by industrial and business expansions in the Lower Peninsula—reinforced an interdependency between the two regions that is too easily overlooked by social analysts. To be sure, the socioeconomic development of Michigan's Upper Peninsula, in terms of community amenities and material style of life, has not attained parity with the Lower Peninsula. But, many "Yoopers" have become, through migration, participating members of the downstate economy and of metropolitan American.

Pathways Out

For over thirty years we have been following the careers of three cohorts of Ontonagon County high school graduates. (The research, initiated in 1957 by J. A. Beegle and H. Goldsmith, was expanded into a follow-up study by J. Reiger and J. A. Beegle in 1968 and, since then, has been continued periodically by H. K. Schwarzweller and J. Rieger.) Information was obtained by self-administered questionnaires from all high school seniors in the county just prior to graduation (classes of 1957/58, 1968, and 1974) and thereafter, via mailed questionnaires that were nudged along by telephone contacts and, quite often, too, by home visits and personal interviews (Lean, 1992). Our most recent follow-up was in 1985; at that time we surveyed the 1974 and 1968 cohorts (which were 11 years and 17 years, respectively, beyond high school graduation). The 1957/58 cohort is composed of two graduating classes, and both segments had been surveyed for a second time in 1974 (18 and 17 years, respectively, after graduation).

Table 8.10. Ontonagon County, Upper Peninsula, Lower Peninsula: Percentage Change in Total Population for Decades 1870–1880 through 1980–1990

	1870–1880	1880–1890	1890–1900	1900–1910	1910–1920	1920–1930	1930–1940	1940–1950	1950–1960	1960–1970	1970–1980	1980–1990
Ontonagon	-9.8	46.4	65.0	39.6	43.7	-10.6	2.2	-9.5	2.9	-0.3	-6.5	-10.2
Upper Peninsula[a]	94.6	51.4	103.0	24.6	2.1	97.9	-50.8	-6.4	1.9	-0.5	5.1	-1.8
Lower Peninsula	36.1	26.6	9.9	15.0	34.3	25.4	17.9	23.0	23.9	14.0	4.3	0.4
Michigan total	38.2	27.9	15.6	16.1	30.5	32.0	8.5	21.2	22.8	13.4	4.4	0.4

Source: U.S. Census Report, 1870–1990.

[a]Includes Ontonagon County

The locational (residential place) distrubtion of the three cohorts at a point in their life when many of the major career events—college, military service, "finding a good job," and marriage—had been completed and the individual career paths were essentially settled was determined (see Table 8.11). Only about a third or less of each of these cohorts were residing in the Ontonagon area at that time, and about half, approximately, had migrated away from the UP and were residing downstate or elsewhere. Clearly, the stream of out-migration of young people from Ontonagon and, as demonstrated by these data, from the region, has been consistent and persistent. If we consider that the economy of Ontonagon County during these years, with the copper boom and the expansion of the pulp/paper industry, was doing quite well relative to other parts of the UP, the scale of out-migration from the area and region is impressive.

The young people who moved away from Ontonagon were talented and well-educated. Historically, schooling was regarded with deference and respect, and perhaps because of ethnic competition or Old World values, very few Ontonagon young people were permitted by their families to drop out of high school. Furthermore, the State of Michigan subsidized primary and secondary schools in remote, relatively poor rural areas like Ontonagon. The Ontonagon schools were good and their graduates scored high on achievement tests. To some extent, "the cream of the crop," but mainly in the case of young men was likely to be exported downstate (see Table 8.12). To be sure, one should not expect it to be otherwise. Those more prepared for the challenge and stress of building a career in metropolitan America should be encouraged to compete. We observe virtually no difference in out-migration pattern by the young women relative to scholastic performance. This may be affected in part by the exigencies of marriage norms and by other traditional barriers to career achievements by women; it also may be due to the fact that in the Ontonagon schools (and elsewhere) women dominated the upper scholastic ranks, and consequently represented more diversity in socioeconomic background. Similarly, of those young people from Ontonagon County who were able to earn a college degree—and over the years there were a respectable number, from 18 to 29 percent of the various cohorts—far fewer returned to live and work in the Ontonagon area than opted to live elsewhere (see Table 8.13). Whether the long-term trends in locational distribution constitute evidence of a brain drain or simply represent an effective interdependency between the two segments of Michigan's economy is a question that needs to be addressed more directly in future research relating to the developmental potentials of

Table 8.11. Residence Place at "Settled Stage of Career," Three Cohorts of Ontonagon County High School Graduates, by Gender (in percentage)

	Males			Females		
	1974 (N=93)	1968 (N=86)	1957/58 (N=97)	1974 (N=95)	1968 (N=96)	1957/58 (N=115)
Ontonagon area	28.0	30.2	43.3	36.8	22.9	40.9
Other Upper Peninsula	12.9	8.1	18.6	16.8	13.5	9.6
Elsewhere	59.1	61.7	38.1	46.4	63.6	49.5
Total	100.0	100.0	100.0	100.0	100.0	100.0

"Settled Stage of Career" is 11 years after graduating from high school for the 1974 cohort, 17 years after for the 1968 cohort, and 18 and 17 years after, respectively, for the 1957 and 1958 graduating classes (which together make up the "1957/58 cohort").

Michigan's Upper Peninsula and its people. But there is no doubt that, insofar as its young people are concerned, education can and does serve as a bridge between relatively remote areas like Michigan's Upper Peninsula and the metropolitan mainstream of American society (Schwarzweller and Brown, 1962).

Toward the Future

In 1935 Beck and Forster reported on a survey conducted by the Federal Emergency Relief Administration under the direction of Dwight Sanderson (Beck and Forster, 1935). The research team had designated the "Lake States Cut-Over Area" of northern Minnesota, Wisconsin, and Michigan, as one of six major rural problem regions in America. "The future of this area," the team concluded, "depends on a rehabilitation program which can be developed around—the dominant industries—forestry, mining, agriculture and recreational projects" (Beck and Forster, 1935:97).

The depression era of the 1930s was indeed a tough time for people in Michigan's Upper Peninsula and in that relatively remote corner of the region, Ontonagon County. Copper prices had plummeted and mining activities had ceased. Work in the woods was also at almost a standstill. Families survived through subsistence farming, odd jobs, and government make-work programs. The frustrations of those dark days are still a part of the local culture and locked into the collective memory of the Ontonagon people.

World War II, of course, revived the American economy and stimulated some new developments in the Ontonagon area that essentially

Table 8.12. Residence Place at "Settled Stage of Career": Three Cohorts of Ontonagon County High School Graduates, by Graduation Rank (in percentage)

Males

	1974		1968		1957/58	
	Upper Half (N=39)	Lower Half (N=54)	Upper Half (N=27)	Lower Half (N=53)	Upper Half (N=31)	Lower Half (N=62)
Ontonagon area	30.8	48.1	29.6	45.3	45.2	72.6
Elsewhere	69.2	51.9	70.4	54.7	54.8	27.4
Total	100.0	100.0	100.0	100.0	100.0	100.0

Females

	1974		1968		1957/58	
	Upper Half (N=56)	Lower Half (N=38)	Upper Half (N=66)	Lower Half (N=27)	Upper Half (N=74)	Lower Half (N=38)
Ontonagon area	53.6	55.3	36.4	37.0	50.0	50.0
Elsewhere	46.4	44.7	63.6	63.0	50.0	50.0
Total	100.0	100.0	100.0	100.0	100.0	100.0

Table 8.13. Percentage with College Degree, Three Cohorts of Ontonagon County High School Graduates, by Residence Place at "Settled Stage of Career" and Gender (in percentage)

Residence	Males			Females		
	1974 $(N=89)$	1968 $(N=85)$	1957/58 $(N=97)$	1974 $(N=93)$	1968 $(N=94)$	1957/58 $(N=115)$
Ontonagon area	25.0	31.8	39.3	28.6	32.0	15.0
Elsewhere	75.0	68.2	60.7	74.1	68.0	85.0
Total cohort	18.0	25.9	28.9	22.8	26.6	17.4

implemented recommendations made years earlier by the Federal Emergency Administration. Economic expansion was organized around "the dominant industries": forestry, mining, and recreational projects. Agriculture in the UP, however, is not and never was in a good position to compete effectively with downstate commercial agriculture. Subsistence farming gradually faded from the scene. Families have become dependent upon wage jobs for their livelihood. But despite the rapid economic transition to industrialized forestry and mining and to a specialized labor force, the local economy continues to be driven by the circulation of income from persons employed in the few major industries of the region. When the economy goes sour, as it can where the industrial base is not diversified and where two or three firms control a region's destiny, the entire community is vulnerable. In Ontonagon and in similar communities in Michigan's Upper Peninsula the possibility of economic collapse and chronic unemployment is a very real threat.

Since long before World War II there has been a great stream of out-migration from Ontonagon and the Upper Peninsula. This southward movement, mostly young people seeking employment, was not unlike the movement to northern industrial areas by people from eastern Kentucky and the Appalachian region (Schwarzweller, Brown, and Mangalam, 1977). In many of the industrial areas of destination, such as Detroit (Michigan) and Racine/Milwaukee (Wisconsin), these two streams of migration found themselves in direct competition for jobs. But the migrants from Ontonagon and the Upper Peninsula, collectively, had a decided advantage: the school systems in communities like Ontonagon had been strongly supported and nurtured by the downstate governments. There had been greater investment in the human capital represented in the remote, rural communities of the cutover region than there had been in the southern Appalachian region. Regional development, too, for those left behind, benefited from these investments in education by the cutover region states.

Looking ahead, one can see difficulties for Ontonagon and many Upper Peninsula communities. On one hand, there is the age-old problem of lack of industrial diversity. If one or the other of Ontonagon's two major industrial facilities locks its gates, Ontonagon, as a viable, self-contained community will be, for all intents and purposes, dead. On the other hand, there is the associated problem of community sustainability. When a small, relatively remote community like this loses population, perhaps as a result of industrial strife or as a consequence of a business deal made elsewhere that runs counter to the well-being of the local populace, attracting new industry and new families becomes very difficult. Ontonagon's future is very uncertain.

In any event, it is clear that the stream of migration from upstate to downstate and the easy absorption by the expanding industries of lower Michigan of migrants from Ontonagon and other communities in Michigan's Upper Peninsula served as a mechanism that facilitated development in the northern region. Population growth in the Upper Peninsula (and in Ontonagon County) stabilized long ago, and it seems the upstate and downstate disparity in per capita income has also stabilized (at 70 percent). Whether or not this evidences the attainment of an economic equilibrium, there is little doubt that the economic future of Michigan's Upper Peninsula and the well-being of its people are inextricably tied to the economy not only of downstate Michigan but also of the nation and world.

Acknowledgments

The initial surveys of Ontonagon County high school seniors, in 1957, 1958, 1968, and 1974, and the series of follow-up surveys over the years, were sponsored by the Michigan State University Agricultural Experiment Station. We gratefully acknowledge the support that was provided and, as well, the patience and good offices of the various Directors of the MSU Agricultural Experiment Station. A longitudinal project, spanning more than three decades, is unusual.

J. Allan Beegle, now Professor Emeritus of Sociology at Michigan State University, and Jon Rieger, now Professor of Sociology at the University of Louisville, initiated the follow-up phases and had much to do with establishing the research foundations for our long-range study of the people of and from Ontonagon County. We sincerely appreciate their efforts, their contributions, and the directions of research that were set under their leadership. We owe a special debt of gratitude to Professor Reiger for his careful assessment of technological changes coming about in the pulp/paper industry, a topic overviewed in our present paper. We extend our thanks also to Mr. K. J. Moilanen of Ewen, Michigan, Ontonagon County Extension Director for many years, now retired and very active in regional development efforts, for providing us with information on current development activities in the area.

Above all, we wish to acknowledge the kindness and patience of Ontonagon residents who helped us enormously and in many ways over the course of this long-term project.

References

Beck, P. G., and M. C. Forster. 1935. *Six Rural Problem Areas.* Research Monograph no. 1. Washington, D.C.: Federal Emergency Relief Administration.

Blaney, Geoffrey. 1966. *Tyranny of Distance: How Distance Shaped Australia's History.* New York: St. Martin's Press.

Carter, James L. 1980. *Superior: A State for the North Country.* Marquette, Mich.: Pilot Press.

Clay, Daniel C. 1976. "Parental Rapport and the Changing Patterns of Educational Mobility among High School Seniors in Rural Michigan County." Master's thesis, Department of Sociology, Michigan State University.

Cooper, Jim. 1983. "The Great Ontonagon Fire." Chapter 21 in *A Most Superior Land,* vol. 4 of the Michigan Heritage Series. Lansing, Mich.: Two Peninsula Press (Michigan Natural Resources Magazine).

County Business Patterns: Michigan. 1951–1987. Washington, D.C.: Department of Commerce, Bureau of the Census.

Fuguitt, Glenn V., David L. Brown, and Calvin L. Beale. 1989. *Rural and Small Town America.* New York: Russell Sage Foundation.

Gates, William B., Jr. 1951. *Michigan Copper and Boston Dollars: An Economic History of the Michigan Copper Mining Industry.* Cambridge, Mass.: Harvard University Press.

Horan, Patrick M., and Charles M. Tolbert II. 1984. *The Organization of Work in Rural and Urban Markets.* Boulder, Colo.: Westview.

Jamison, James J. 1939. *This Ontonagon Country: The Story of an American Frontier.* Ontonagon, Mich.: Ontonagon Herald Company.

Labor Market Letter: Upper Peninsula. 1958–1973. Lansing: Michigan Employment Security Commisison, Department of Labor, State of Michigan.

Labor Market Review: Upper Peninsula. 1974–1991. Lansing: Michigan Employment Security Commission, Department of Labor, State of Michigan.

Lean, Sue-wen. 1992. "Pathways Out: Career Patterns of Three Cohorts from a Remote County in Michigan." Ph.D. diss., Department of Sociology, Michigan State University.

Martin, John Martlow. 1986. *Call It North Country: The Story of Upper Michigan.* Detroit: Wayne State University Press.

Rieger, Jon. H. 1971. "Geographical Mobility and Occupational Achievement of Rural Youth: A Ten Year Longitudinal Study of an Upper Michigan Sample." Ph.D. diss., Department of Sociology, Michigan State University.

Rieger, Jon H., J. Allan Beegle, and Philip N. Fulton. 1973. *Profiles of Rural Youth: A Decade of Migration and Social Mobility.* East Lansing: Michigan State University Agricultural Experiment Station Research Report 178.

Rieger, Jon H., and Harry K. Schwarzweller. 1991. "Mechanization in the Western Upper Peninsula Pulp-Logging Industry." Manuscript.

Schwarzweller, Harry K., and James S. Brown. 1962. "Education as a Cultural Bridge between Eastern Kentucky and the Great Society." *Rural Sociology* 27:363–65.

Schwarzweller, Harry K., James S. Brown, and J. J. Mangalam. 1977. *Mountain Families in Transition.* University Park: Pennsylvania State University Press.

Verway, David I. 1975. *County Income and Employment Patterns in Michigan's Upper Peninsula: An Analysis of 1969–1972 Data with Forecasts for 1975 and 1976.* East Lansing, Mich.: Graduate School of Business Administration, Michigan State University.

Zuiches, James J., and Jon Rieger. 1978. "Size of Place Preference and Life Cycle Migration: A Cohort Comparison." *Rural Sociology* 43:618–33.

9 | The Failure of Sustained-Yield Forestry and the Decline of the Flannel-Shirt Frontier

Michael Hibbard and James Elias

IN 1948, POPE AND TALBOT, INC., started up their new mill in Oakridge, Oregon. It was a time of unparalleled optimism in the Pacific Northwest timber industry. The postwar housing boom was in full swing, and the demand for lumber seemed unlimited. Opportunities for expansion were restricted only by plant capacity and the availability of raw material. The new mill was a response to the first restriction. To address the raw material problem, Pope and Talbot purchased 32,000 acres of timber land in the area, which it aimed to manage cooperatively with national forest lands on a sustained-yield basis to provide a continuous supply of raw material for the mill.

According to the firm's semiofficial centennial history, Pope and Talbot envisioned "permanent operations at Oakridge" (Coman and Gibbs, 1949:343). In his remarks at the opening ceremonies, company president George A. Pope, Jr., stated that "here we have built not for the next few years but for the next century" (Pope and Talbot, 1951:3). "Permanent" turned out to be forty-two years. In 1989, Pope and Talbot sold their Oakridge mill to the Bald Knob Land and Timber Company. The following year, Bald Knob closed the mill and filed for bankruptcy protection.

Oakridge exemplifies the crisis faced by the small towns of the Pacific Northwest timber belt. Forty years ago, the future seemed boundless in timber-dependent communities from northern California to British Columbia and the southeastern panhandle of Alaska. After decades of struggling through booms and busts, insecure employment, and temporary settlements, the region finally seemed to have achieved a level of stability. Now its livelihood is disappearing again.

In the late 1970s there were 534 timber mills, employing almost 200,000 workers, in the Pacific Northwest region of the United States. They produced about 11 billion board feet of lumber. By 1988, following a downturn because of the recession of the early 1980s, production had increased to 16.5 billion board feet. But because of automation and other technological changes in the industry, the 1988 output was achieved by fewer than 160,000 workers in just 453 mills (Western Wood Products Association, in Murphey, 1990).

The economic base of Pacific Northwest timber towns was not supposed to collapse. Since the 1940s, federal timber management policy has had long-term stability as one of its central goals. The cycle of booms and busts, the abandoned settlements, and the itinerant way of life that had characterized the American timber industry were supposed to have been eliminated through the sustained-yield management of timber lands. The adoption of sustained yield as the new conventional wisdom, as reflected in tne rhetoric heard in Oakridge in 1948, exemplified the shift from frontier status to the modern era in the timber belt. And the events of the early 1990s in Oakridge exemplify the end of the modern era. To understand what happened in the Pacific Northwest timber belt during that forty-year period and to gain some perspective on the probable aftermath, it is useful to begin by exploring the policy debates that shaped the conventional wisdom of 1948.

The Timber Culture Debate

Itinerant Mills and Floating Workers

Logging and lumber milling began in the Pacific Northwest in the 1850s in response to the gold rush and subsequent boom in California. However, the industry did not achieve prominence in the region until the early 1900s. At that time the last stands of white pine were being logged in the western Great Lakes states—the old "North Woods." The common claim of timber industry analysts was that "it is mainly from [the Pacific Northwest] that the future supply of timber must come," since that region contained more than half the standing timber in the United States (Ise, 1920:318). In addition, completion of the northern transcontinental railroad routes in the 1890s and the Panama Canal in 1912 provided access to eastern markets.

In response, the American timber industry migrated to the Pacific Northwest at the turn of the century and began "logging off the last great belt of timber in the United States" (Holbrook, 1926:19). In 1890, nearly 40 percent of the timber cut in the United States came from the western Great Lakes states; by 1914, it was less than 10 percent. In the same period, the harvest in the Pacific Northwest rose from less than 10 percent to more than 20 percent of the U.S. total (MacKaye, 1919).

And by 1936, the region accounted for over 60 percent of the American timber harvest (Kotok, 1938).

The timber industry was intrinsically unstable. It suffered all the economic problems characteristic of natural-resource-based industries—a competitive situation that encouraged overproduction, resulting in glutted markets, depressed prices, and cyclical booms and busts (Greeley, 1917). As Benton MacKaye of the Forest Service wrote, "the lumber industry, as now generally conducted, is 'timber mining,' not timber culture" (MacKaye, 1919:77).

Timber mining consisted of cutting down all the marketable trees in any given watershed or logging unit, exhausting the entire stand of timber just as a vein of ore is mined to exhaustion. A mill, the focus of several logging operations, was located at some central point and formed the center of a sawmill camp. Logging operations fed timber to the mill. Each operation was conducted from a temporary logging camp. An operation was usually located in any one place for only a few months, until the adjacent timber was exhausted, then it would move to a new stand. In a few years all the timber tributary to the millsite would be removed and the whole enterprise—sawmill and logging operations—would move or go out of business.

The itinerant operation and economic instability of the industry became a matter of public concern because the migration of the timber industry to the Pacific Northwest was accompanied by a series of "waves of business depression" in 1893, 1903, 1907, and 1913 (O'Hara, 1914). In a report to the Secretary of Agriculture, Assistant U.S. Forester William Greeley wrote that

> where lumbering is the dominant industry, as on the West Coast, . . . hard times react critically upon labor and all business and community life. Unemployment becomes serious. The failure of many sawmills causes bank failures and the widespread upsetting of business and financial security. Worst of all perhaps is the demoralizing effect of wholesale failures and business instability. Recklessness on one hand and lack of confidence on the other cut deeply into the economic well-being of large regions and large numbers of people. (Greeley, 1917:64)

The most serious issue was the large "reserve of labor" required by the industry (Parker, 1920), "casual" or "floating" laborers who were the subject of numerous policy studies. In 1913, the Washington State Bureau of Labor Statistics estimated peak employment in the timber industry at 31,268, but the number "regularly employed" was 26,290, a "surplus" of 4,978 or nearly twenty percent of the total number employed, "a transient mass of workmen who . . . form this state's 'army of the unemployed'" (Olson, 1914:51).

A somewhat different methodology was used to try to estimate the size of the timber industry's floating worker problem in Oregon and California. In Oregon, in the peak month of June, 1910, timber industry employment was 16,462; but in the month of lowest employment, January, 1910, the industry employed 11,545 workers, only seventy percent of peak employment (O'Hara, 1914:15). In California in 1909, peak employment in the timber industry was 29,003 and the low point was 14,325, less than fifty percent of the peak (Hanna, 1917:11).

By comparison, the 1910 census found that for the United States as a whole the total number of wage earners in the month of minimum employment was 89 percent of those working during the month of maximum employment (U.S. Bureau of the Census, 1912:8:282).

Floating workers were a major concern because the timber industry was such an important proportion of the overall economy of the Pacific Northwest. The industry provided 63 percent of all the manufacturing jobs in Washington and 52 percent in Oregon; even in highly urbanized and diversified California, 20 percent of the manufacturing jobs were in timber (Hanna, 1917:8).

One study estimated that there were at least 100,000 casual workers in California, Oregon, and Washington (Hanna 1917:15). This amounted to slightly over 3 percent of all the residents aged fifteen and over, and 5.5 percent of all rural residents in the three West Coast states. The annual turnover rate in the timber industry among these "womanless, voteless, and jobless" men was over 600 percent (Parker, 1920; President's Mediation Commission, 1918:14).

Contemporary studies found that the strikes, lockouts, and riots which had become commonplace were intrinsic to the organization of the industry. The timber industry, "being itself a tramp industry, is a breeder of tramps; it is an industry of homeless men" (MacKaye, 1919:22). The social consequences of the tramp industry were unavoidable. "Permanent homes and normal family life have been the exception rather than the rule, and the standard of citizenship has been lowered" (Dana, 1918:22).

Men who are out of work and out of funds for a considerable length of time deteriorate in quality as workmen and as citizens. (O'Hara, 1914:5)

No one who has the interest of America at heart can look forward with tolerance to the growth or continuance of a body of migratory workers who in the nature of the case must have . . . a hatred for the law which they have never known except in its repressive aspect. (U.S. Department of Labor, 1918:221–22)

The direction in which solutions should be sought was clear, at least in principle.

The lack of staple industries operating day in and day out the year around . . . lie at the heart of whatever labor problem there exists, [and the solution] is to establish steady employment by attracting and fostering such industries as will offer permanent work in all seasons of the year. (Olson, 1914:13)

All of these analyses pointed to one conclusion, that the path to permanent employment and community stability in the timber belt lay in the transformation of the industry from timber mining to timber culture (Dana, 1918; MacKaye, 1919). The basic idea of timber culture had three elements. First, the forest was to be managed for continuous production, "sustained yield," by limiting the average amount of timber cut annually to the amount grown. The economic and environmental benefits of sustained-yield forestry were numerous. Most Pacific Northwest forest land was unsuitable for any purpose other than growing trees; it did not make good farming or grazing land. And cutover areas were highly susceptible to fire, erosion, and stream-flow disruption. Moreover, cutover land was extremely expensive to reforest. Sustained yield minimized these problems and at the same time promised the industry an indefinite timber supply.

From an economic and environmental viewpoint, the area within which the annual cut was maintained—a rural neighborhood, a watershed, a state, or even a multistate region—was not relevant. Thus a second, social, element of timber culture recognized that sustained yield needed to be practiced in such a way that it provided permanent forest employment for itinerant workers. "Working circles" or "working units" were proposed, sustained-yield management areas that would allow a worker to "always reach the same spot at the end of the day's work, (so) he can establish a home there and a family life" (MacKaye, 1919:81).

The third element of timber culture was the establishment of stable forest communities. The bases of community stability were the continuous timber supply and permanent jobs. It was argued that fixed homes and a healthy family life, along with the associated expansion of social and educational opportunities, would "develop the more civilized virtues without destroying the courage, vigor, alertness, and physical prowess that always have been characteristic of the typical woodsman" (Dana, 1918:33).

Timber Culture and Community Stability

A variety of attempts were made to solve the problem of overproduction and depressed prices throughout the 1920s, most notably by developing new markets on the East Coast and in Asia and Europe. They failed because, as Greeley (1917) had argued, in the absence of production controls the harsh competitive environment soon led to a glut, even of the new markets (Clark, 1952). As a result, rural communities and their timber and mill workers continued to· suffer from cyclical unemployment and the chronic instability of the industry. It was only the collapse of the regional economy at the onset of the Great Depression that compelled the industry to acknowledge the need to consider an alternative to timber mining.

In the peak year of 1926, total lumber production for Oregon and Washington was 11.75 billion board feet. By 1932 it had fallen to 3.86 billion board feet, less than one-third of peak production (U.S. Forest Service, 1936: Table 26). The social impact of this collapse was catastrophic. The industry accounted directly for nearly 60 percent of all the industrial jobs in the region, more than 126,000 in Oregon and Washington in 1929. And indirectly, through dependent manufacturing and service industries, it supported an additional 187,000 workers (U.S. Forest Service, 1936: Table 41). With the collapse of the timber industry between 1929 and 1933, employment in Oregon and Washington declined by more than 20 percent, from 1,035,000 jobs to 814,000 jobs. During the same period the number of unemployed workers increased from 21,800, about 2 percent of the workforce, to 290,100, a rate of more than 26 percent (Herring, 1951).

But it was the threat to the firms themselves that brought on a willingness to think beyond their traditional commitment to exploitive short-term practices. Efforts to stabilize the industry through cooperation, mergers, consolidations, and acquisitions, and by voluntary reductions in production failed. From 1930 through 1935, the industry as a whole lost money. By 1933 nearly 90 percent of the timber firms in Oregon were near bankruptcy, and even the largest firms were on the brink. Taxes were delinquent on at least half the timber land in the state (Dembo, 1985; Lowitt, 1984).

In the cold light of fiscal crisis the image of timber culture as an alternative to timber mining took on a different perspective. Industry leaders continued to think of the forest as a commodity to be exploited for private gain. The problems of itinerant mills and floating workers that had been exacerbated by the depression did not move them. But they began to appreciate how public policy to limit the amount of timber cut annually, a sustained-yield policy, would help restrain production and force more rational market behavior. They were largely indifferent to the elements of timber culture that proposed the creation of stable forest communities based on working circles (Robbins, 1987; Schallau, 1987).

As the discussion moved toward serious policy proposals, the competing views of sustained yield—as a response to social versus industrial problems—became apparent. *A Master Plan for Forestry in Washington*, prepared by the Washington State Planning Council, called for sustainable development "so that all activities dependent upon [the forests] may have assurance of permanency; that men may find stable employment . . . ; that communities may look forward to continuing stability" (quoted in Washington State Planning Council, 1945:17). And in comments remarkably reminiscent of those twenty years earlier, E. I. Kotok, director of the University of California Forest and Range Experiment Station, spoke of sustained yield as a solution to "lost industries, ghost towns, stranded populations, tax delinquency and the social and economic ills that spring from these" (Kotok, 1938:90).

Industry representatives contended that community stability would follow from a stable timber industry. David T. Mason, leading industry advocate for sustained yield, based his appeal on the need to create favorable conditions for timber firms (Loehr, 1952: passim). Mason was echoed by Stuart Moir, a forester with the Western Pine Manufacturers Association, who called sustained yield "a constructive and logical method of solving many difficulties of the lumber industry" (quoted in Robbins, 1987).

Even after the passage of the principal sustained-yield legislation, the Sustained Yield Forest Management Act of 1944 (Public Law 273), there was widespread disagreement over what it meant. The stated purpose of PL 273 was to "promote the stability of forest industries, of employment, of communities and taxable forest wealth, through continuous supplies of timber." It also permitted the Forest Service to pool federal and private lands into cooperatively managed sustained-yield units where communities depended on trees from federal land. In a 1944 memorandum discussing its implementation, Chief U.S. Forester

Lyle Watts wrote that PL 273 "is an act to obtain community stabilization through sustained yield by federal-industry cooperation." President Voye of the West Coast Lumbermen's Association responded by pointing out that the first objective mentioned in PL 273 is "stability of forest industries . . . ; social gains [are] incidental and not primary" (quoted in Robbins, 1987).

The press to meet the rising civilian demand for wood products in the wake of fifteen years of depression and war allowed the participants to paper over the controversy. Discussions focused on community and industry stability as two sides of the same coin—reciprocal and interdependent (Loehr, 1952).

The first Cooperative Sustained Yield Unit to be formed under PL 273 was established in December 1946, through a one-hundred-year agreement between the Forest Service and the Simpson Logging Company of Shelton, Washington. It included 111,000 acres of national forest and 159,000 acres of private land. It guaranteed Simpson a monopoly on timber harvested from the public land; in return, Simpson agreed to allow its own land to be pooled with the public land and managed as a single unit. It was estimated that the agreement would provide a continuous supply of timber to Simpson's mills in the towns of Shelton and McCleary. "The cooperating company now employs about 1,400 workers. The sustained yield agreement assures these workers permanent jobs" (U.S. Forest Service, 1947:28).

Thirty or forty firms expressed interest in forming cooperative sustained-yield units in the years immediately following World War II, including Pope and Talbot's proposed project in Oakridge. Discussions revolved around the monopolistic nature of the units. In a public hearing in Eugene, Oregon, in September 1948, Mason presented the case for monopoly as a source of community stability (U.S. Congress, Senate Subcommittee Hearing, 1949).

> The greater the plant investment in a given project, the greater the assurance to the community that the private cooperator will afford stable long-continued support to the community. The greater the investment by the cooperator, the greater the economic pressure on the cooperator to place additional forest land on the sustained yield management basis. (203)

> The maximum contribution to the security and stability of the community is to be secured [by] . . . larger, efficient mills [that] operate much more steadily throughout the year and especially in

times of economic depression; their employees average more days work per year per employee. (205)

[A] company, in order to assure a long-time timber supply would undertake many costly and unusual burdens required by the [cooperative sustained yield] contract. . . . In my opinion the public gains by such an arrangement strongly outweigh the objections so far as the so-called 'monopolistic' practice is concerned. (355)

In the end no other cooperative units were established, despite Mason's argument that giving monopolies to large firms through cooperative sustained-yield agreements would best assure community stability. Small operators, few of which owned their own timberlands, depended for their livelihood on their access to public timber. Keeping them out of substantial portions of national forest land, as the cooperative agreements proposed to do, threatened to drive them out of business. Their vocal opposition discouraged the large firms from following through on their initial enthusiasm for cooperative sustained yield. Walter Lund, who was responsible for planning Forest Service timber sales, including potential cooperative units, in the late 1940s, explained that

there were a number of companies with whom discussions and investigations went quite a ways. Pope and Talbot, for example, at Oakridge, Oregon, considered making a formal application very seriously, and even prepared a brochure which examined the advantages of a co-operative unit involving their property. . . . Eventually the company dropped the idea, partly, I think, because they didn't want to be subjected to all of the opposition from their neighbors. (Lund, 1967:69–70)

But Pope and Talbot and the other operators of large mills in small, isolated communities didn't need PL 273. The timber culture debates had institutionalized sustained yield as a way of thinking about timber management on both public and private lands. It did not lead to sustained-yield practices—limiting the harvest to the amount of annual forest growth. Rather, it linked community stability to industry stability in the conventional wisdom: community stability was to be achieved by assuring mills a stable timber supply. Contemporary Oakridge is a product of that conventional wisdom.

Oakridge: Modern Mill Town

Like most Pacific Northwest mill towns, Oakridge is quite isolated. It is located at the base of the western slope of the Oregon Cascades, between a high ridge and the main fork of the Willamette River, on the uppermost portion of a thin finger of lowland connected with the Willamette Valley. The community was first settled by white people in the late nineteenth century as a rural agricultural district. The nearest population center is an hour's drive over a two-lane mountain road.[1]

In the early 1920s, when the Southern Pacific Railroad began construction of its Willamette Pass route, Oakridge became the main construction camp for the west side of the line, which was (and is) the only rail line through the Oregon Cascades. As the flatlands and lower valleys were logged off, the railroad provided access to an important new timber source. In 1923, in anticipation of completion of the line, the Western Lumber Company built a large mill and a company town —Westfir— about six miles downstream from Oakridge. And when the railroad was completed in 1926, Oakridge became a base for the helper locomotives that assisted trains over the pass and a maintenance center for the many tunnels and snowsheds on the line.

These two activities, the railroad and the Westfir mill, were the only substantial employers in the upper Willamette Valley until the coming of Pope and Talbot in 1948. As late as 1940, only 520 people lived in Oakridge.

The immediate postwar period was one of great optimism generally, and Oakridge greeted Pope and Talbot with much enthusiasm. The company planned to manage its own large timber holdings for sustained yield, and because of Oakridge's isolation, the only real competition for timber from nearby national forest land was the twenty-five-year-old Westfir mill. These factors, combined with its shining new state-of-the-art mill, gave Pope and Talbot a virtual de facto monopoly in Oakridge, cooperative agreement or not. The new employer stimulated a tripling of Oakridge's population between 1940 and 1950, to over 1,500; and this was thought to be just the beginning of a new era. New subdivisions and other developments were planned, and the population of the area was projected to reach 25,000.

This did not happen. The economy of the upper Willamette Valley never reached the self-sustaining level envisioned in 1948. However, the community did achieve a level of stability. The railroad replaced its steam locomotives with diesel and shut down its helper base, but Pope and Talbot expanded—eventually employing about five hundred workers. The old mill in Westfir declined and was eventually closed, but the Forest Service expanded as the demands for public-land management became more complex. The population doubled again during the 1950s, and then stayed in the 3,500–4,000 range through the 1960s and most of the 1970s. It seemed that industry stability had led to community stability in the modern era.

The first sign of trouble came in June 1978. Its Chicago-based owners decided that the Westfir mill was no longer profitable. They closed the mill, then sold it. The new owner leased the mill to an operator who reopened on a reduced scale. The mill was then closed and reopened at lower levels of production and employment several more times before it finally closed for good. This flickering phenomenon is common in the timber belt. Mill operations seldom come to a sudden and definite halt; most often they gradually fade away, as did the Westfir mill.

Closure of the Westfire mill was a blow to the small, isolated local economy—it had employed about 340 workers in June 1978—but Pope and Talbot's presence seemed to assure the basic stability of the community. However, in the same year as the Westfir closure Pope and Talbot began a modernization program that allowed their mill to maintain its former level of production with three hundred workers instead of the five hundred they had previously employed. The unemployment rate in Oakridge was over 15 percent in 1979. And then the deep national recession of the early 1980s struck.

The Pope and Talbot mill began flickering in 1981, in response to three factors. First, demand for Pacific Northwest wood products declined because of the recession; this was exacerbated by increasing competition from other regions of the world, especially Canada and southeast Asia. Second, even with the modernization program, the Oakridge mill was still marginal in comparison to newer, larger, more centrally located mills. And third, despite the stated commitment to sustained-yield management, raw material—trees—were becoming scarce in the upper Willamette Valley. The unemployment rate in Oakridge stayed over 15 percent.

During fall 1985, Pope and Talbot announced the indefinite layoff of all their Oakridge employees, and in December they announced the permanent closure of the mill. Following several months of negotiations the employees' unions agreed to significant reductions in wages and benefits. The mill reopened in spring 1986, at lower levels of production and employment. It continued to flicker, despite the fact that the market for Pacific Northwest wood products had bounced back and was at a historic high in terms of both output and price.

Three years later, in 1989, Pope and Talbot sold the mill. Bald Knob Land and Timber Company, a tiny firm with one other mill in Oregon, kept about one hundred workers employed in Oakridge. They continued the flickering operation for another year, then closed for good in September, 1990. The mill buildings, machinery, and equipment were sold at a bankruptcy auction. And in May 1991, everything that remained was burned in a fire started by sparks from the torch of a welder working on razing the site.

Current Social and Economic Conditions

The end of the Oakridge mill was more spectacular than most, but it was not an isolated event. The modern conventional wisdom, that policies directed at industry stability would produce community stability, has been undone completely. Not even the cooperative agreement with the Simpson Lumber Company worked out as planned. Most of the old-growth trees on Forest Service land were logged off by 1985. In that year Simpson closed its Shelton, Washington, old-growth mill and its last two logging camps. Simpson's employment shrank from 1,400 to 850, and the company is seeking changes in its agreement with the Forest Service that will further reduce the number of jobs in Shelton and McCleary: it wants permission to export unmilled logs from the sustained-yield unit or to ship them to mills outside the area for processing (Durbin, 1989).

Events such as those in Oakridge and Shelton have become common in the Pacific Northwest. For example, the Western Wood Products Association, the principal trade association, reported that the timber industry in Oregon experienced one of its best production years ever in 1989, and timber firms are reporting healthy profits (Robertson, 1990). At the same time, employment in the industry has steadily declined—from 81,400 workers in 1978 to 64,000 in 1990 (State of Oregon, Department of Human Resources, 1991). And it is estimated that by 1995, the timber industry will lose 11,100 more jobs—with an additional 13,900 jobs lost in nontimber businesses dependent on the timber industry (Miller, 1990).

Even those who keep their jobs are losing ground. Measured in constant dollars, average hourly wages in the wood-products industry have declined every year since 1979 (Steward, 1987). This trend is reflected in the drop in real earnings of manufacturing production workers—most of whom are timber workers—throughout the Pacific Northwest. Measured in 1982 dollars, average hourly manufacturing wages in Washington fell from $11.17 to $9.68 between 1978 and 1990; in Idaho, from $9.65 to $8.22; and in Oregon, the most timber-dependent of the states, from $10.68 to $8.38. This is in keeping with an overall drop in real earnings per hour among manufacturing production workers throughout the United States, but the national decline, from $9.11 to $8.14 was modest by comparison (Washington State Employment Security Department, 1991; State of Idaho Department of Employment, 1991; State of Oregon Employment Division, 1991; U.S. Bureau of Labor Statistics, Employment, Hours, and Earnings; all in *Pacific Northwest Executive*, 1991).

The trend toward fewer jobs and lower wages for Pacific Northwest timber industry workers has led to what is being called the "two Northwests." The region's urban economies—particularly the Puget Sound and Portland areas—are thriving at the same time that rural areas, home to most timber industry jobs, continue the steady decline begun in the late 1970s.

In a report to Oregon's Joint Legislative Committee on Trade and Economic Development, *The Two Oregons: Comparing Economic Conditions Between Rural and Urban Oregon* (1990), Tamira Miller outlines the differences between these distinctly different parts of the state, using the U.S. Census Bureau's definitions of rural and urban counties.[2] Unemployment in Oregon's urban counties averaged 5 percent in 1988 and ranged from a low of 4.5 percent to a high of 6.8 percent. Rural unemployment averaged 7.4 percent and ranged from 3.5 percent to 11.5 percent. Although 32 percent of the state's population live in rural counties, these areas hold only 26 percent of the jobs. At $10,744 (in 1982 dollars), rural Oregon's real per capita income in 1988 was only 77 percent of the urban per capita income of $12,804, and it was 25 percent below the national average of $13,451.

In addition to these standard measures of prosperity, Miller also notes that rural Oregonians are faced with other critical problems. With regard to access to health care, in the state's urban counties there are 401 persons for every doctor; in the rural counties there are 705 persons per doctor. And to the degree that education is an indication of the direction in which rural areas are headed, the outlook is not good. A rural Oregonian is 16 percent less likely to be a high school graduate and 33 percent less likely to have a college degree than an urban Oregonian.

Recent population trends show the effects of hard times on the rural Pacific Northwest. Between 1985 and 1988 urban Washington counties grew by 6.32 percent, from 3,566,000 to 3,791,500, while the rural population grew by only 1.73 percent, from 841,800 to 856,400;

urban Oregon grew by 3.85 percent, from 1,804,300 to 1,873,700, but rural counties grew by only 1.29 percent, from 881,500 to 892,900; and Idaho's urban area grew by 4.31 percent, from 192,400 to 200,700, while the rural parts of the state shrank by 1.17 percent, from 811,600 to 802,100 (U.S. Department of Commerce, Bureau of Economic Analysis, 1989).

As illustrative as these numbers are, they only tell part of the story. Net migration figures—the difference between the number of people who move into and the number who moved out of an area—are even more revealing. Net migration in Oregon's urban counties between 1980 and 1990 was +60,789, or 3.45 percent. During that same period, rural Oregon's net migration was −24,572, or a loss of 2.82 percent. Urban net migration consisted of gains of 46,986 people aged 0 to 64 and 13,803 aged 65 and over. But rural areas of the state experienced a net loss of 36,980, or 4.25 percent of people aged 0 to 64, and a gain of 12,408 (1.43 percent) people aged 65 and over (Center for Population Research and Census, 1991).

To go one layer deeper toward understanding the significance of population change in the rural Pacific Northwest we can examine specific counties that are especially dependent on the wood products industry. Three such counties are Oregon's Douglas, Lane, and Coos counties. All three experienced net out-migration during the 1980s, but again the figures are most revealing from the standpoint of age cohort population changes. Douglas County lost 5,941 or 6.34 percent of its population aged 0 to 64 while gaining 1,327 people aged 65 and over. Lane County experienced a net loss of 14,347 people, 5.21 percent of the total aged 0 to 64, while gaining 3,832 people aged 65 and over. And Coos County lost an amazing 10.68 percent—6,840 of its population aged 0 to 64, while gaining 472 people aged 65 and over (Center for Population Research and Census, 1991).

These counties are witnessing the loss of their working households and children, people who are not being replaced by the slight gain in the proportion of retired people. And it appears that many more working-age rural residents will likely be forced to move. In a household survey of six timber-dependent Oregon communities, respondents were questioned about economic conditions in their own household as well as their perceptions of the situation facing their community and its residents. When asked about problems in their own household in the last two years, 80 percent reported that at least one person in the household had been placed on indefinite layoff, nearly 90 percent that someone had been forced to change jobs, and just over 85 percent that a household member had had to move to find work. When asked how they thought the economy of their community compared with that of other communities of similar size, less than 10 percent thought their community's situation was better; about half thought the local situation was "about the same" as in other communities, and 40 percent thought their community was in worse shape. When asked about the future, about one-third expected that the economy of their community would be "a little better" or "much better" in five years; another third thought it would be the same; and one-third thought it would be "a little worse" or "much worse" (Hibbard et al., 1987).

In light of these gloomy perceptions and situations, it is unsurprising that nearly 20 percent of the residents of Oregon's small timber-dependent communities say they "definitely will" or "probably will" move away in the next five years, and another 25 percent report that they "might" move away. People's intentions mirror the migration data. Among retirees, about three-quarters say they intend to stay in their community, but among those not retired, half say they will move away. And when age and intention are correlated, the younger a respondent is, the more likely he or she is to intend to move. Finally, respondents with children at home are much more likely to say they will be moving (Hibbard, 1989).

The assumption of economic precariousness, especially among the young, might be interpreted to mean that itinerant mills and floating workers, not community stability, are still the expectation. However, when people are asked how they would feel about moving permanently away from their community, nearly half say they would "greatly prefer to remain," and another 30 percent say they would "prefer to remain but would not greatly mind leaving" (Hibbard, 1989).

To examine this issue more deeply, we explored the thoughts and feelings of laid-off timber workers and their families in a series of in-depth interviews (Elias, 1990). People's comments reflect a deep sense of betrayal.

> You talk to the old timers here and they'll tell you that [the timber company] said they had enough timber to last them for the next hundred years. Then they got greedy in the last four or five years and literally raped the ground, took all the trees and did very little planting. I've gone through two back surgeries from working in this mill. Now this happens [the mill closes]. Sure, I'm disgusted.

> It's a crying shame we can't keep a mill running here. The Willamette National Forest is the largest national forest in the whole Department of Agriculture in the United States. And yet [his

community], which sits right in the middle of it, can't keep its mill going. The timber industry itself has to take some of the blame because they're showing that they're not managing the forests like they should be. Even the Forest Service isn't doing all they should be.

There is also a great deal of fear, almost despair, about where the situation is leading.

When I worked at the mill, we always had ups and downs. The way I figured it, we all worked there so I didn't panic through the hard times. We were all in the same boat. I never let it get to me; I never worried about it. But, now that it really looks like the mill's not going to be there anymore, a lot of people have panicked and left. A lot of people are real distraught. You would almost expect to see a suicide.

I know a family with five kids, they had a beautiful home, and they lost everything. They had to move in with in-laws. It's sad; they've lost everything. These are people who've been good citizens, good church people. They've worked hard all their lives. Now there's nothing left. They can't afford to go somewhere else. There's nothing left for them. I don't know how to explain it any better than that.

The worry goes beyond financial concerns. People seem to derive their very identity from the local timber economy.

It doesn't take a Philadelphia lawyer to work in a sawmill, but you pick up some skills. There was this feeling that we were all in it together, 'nobody gets out of here alive' type of thing. We tried to stick together; it made work a lot more fun.

It doesn't make me feel bad to make my living off timber. Some people think we're a bunch of dumb hicks who just like to butcher trees, but they can't get through a day without using wood somehow. Why should I be ashamed to provide something that everyone needs?

I've always worked in the mill. I've never thought of doing anything else.

And with the small-town mills disappearing, there is concern that that important identity will disappear.

> With everybody migrating to the cities, nobody's going to know what it's like to be in the small towns anymore. Nobody's going to know what it was like for their forefathers. Small towns are either being engulfed by the cities or they're dying out. It's sad. What would be lost? A sense of permanency, a sense of roots, a sense of heritage.

In short, the communities of the Pacific Northwest timber belt have been hit hard by changes in the region's wood-products industry. Many timber workers have lost their jobs. Those who remain employed are making consistenly less money than they used to and face the constant threat of losing their jobs. Many people have been forced to leave the communities where they grew up, often where their parents grew up. Others acknowledge that although they do not want to move, they may have no choice.

It took thirty years, from the late 1910s to the late 1940s, to establish the conventional wisdom of the modern era—that industry stability creates community stability. For another thirty years, until the late 1970s, the conventional wisdom prevailed. But by the late 1980s, the industry was flourishing while communities were struggling again. And the region is searching for a path to stability in timber towns.

The New Localism in Community Development Policy

Events in the Pacific Northwest mirror the national trend in community development policy. Prior to the decade of the 1980s, the dominant view held that development is primarily a national policy issue in which the federal government should take the lead role. The policy debates surrounding the shift from timber mining to timber culture and its implications for community stability are a reflection of that view. During the 1980s, however, in response to the push of the Reagan administration's withdrawal of federal leadership and the pull of events such as the failure of industry stability to produce community stability, a paradigm shift has occurred in community development policy.

The emerging view is that contemporary socioeconomic problems are best addressed by public action at the state, substate region, and local levels (Weaver and Dennert, 1987). There has been a great deal of experimentation with state-level development policies in the 1980s (Osborne, 1988, Eisinger, 1988). Although no standard functions have yet emerged, some patterns are evident. Most of the attention has been focused on statewide initiatives in areas such as human resources, physical infrastructure, general quality-of-life, and overall "business climate" (Fosler, 1988). However, few states are economically homogeneous. They are made up of a variety of socioeconomic regions, each of which presents its own unique problems and opportunities. As in the two Oregons, they typically encompass thriving areas as well as distressed areas; they contain a variety of regional economies subject to various conditions of location, work force, economic base, and so on. How can state policy foster economic development in a multitude of local communities?

The general challenge of community development is to move beyond broad-gauge policies to create focused responses to specific issues facing specific locales (Shaffer, 1989). It is instructive to examine the attempts of one state to respond to that challenge. The rising threats to community stability in the timber belt make Oregon an especially interesting example. In addition to a typical array of statewide initiatives, Oregon has created the Community Initiatives program to try to address the problem of community stability by promoting community-level public action through local jurisdictions and private organizations. Because of its newness, it is risky to try to draw any firm conclusions about its effectiveness. However, it offers some indication of where community development policy is heading as responsibility shifts from federal to state governments.

Community Initiatives began in July 1989. It is based on the view that the stability of timber belt communities can be restored only by improving their problem-solving abilities. One lesson of the last forty years for timber towns is that they have simply been sites for the local operations of the timber industry. The communities have had little voice in the key decisions about the activities that constituted their economic base, and their citizens have had little experience in shaping the local economy and so have not had much opportunity to learn how to take an active role in community development. Now that the very survival of many of these communities is at stake, it is little wonder that people feel a sense of betrayal and despair, of helplessness. Facing such circumstances, the Community Initiatives program has as its primary objective the building of community capacity—to address the need for economic development while simultaneously training citizens for leadership and community problem solving in communities that have experienced mill closures. The approach has been used in nearly one hundred Oregon communities.

Community Initiatives has two analytic components. It puts a state-funded consulting economist in the community to prepare an economic base analysis and identify investment and entrepreneurial opportunities. At the same time, the program's own staff develops a strategic plan for the community.

Strategic planning in communities also have a process function. Residents are required to form a "community response team" which guides the strategic planning activities to their completion. And the planning activity involves a broad and deep cross-section of local residents in defining what they think are the strengths and weaknesses of the community and the opportunities and threats it faces. Community Initiatives staff help the community response team to use the information from the economic base study and strategic plan to identify specific goals for the community, assist in identifying and obtaining appropriate investment and loan capital and grant funds, and help work through bureaucratic and other barriers to meeting the community's goals. By engaging local residents in this fashion, Community Initiatives staff hope to overcome the prevailing sense of betrayal and despair and to facilitate local residents' design of realistic goals that are consistent with their own view of what the community is and should become. The community response team is a leadership cadre in the community; and the open-ended involvement of residents in creating the strategic plan builds ownership for the goals.

This program illustrates a good deal about the emerging role of states in local action. The new localism tries to address two closely related concerns: the importance of understanding that each local situation is unique, and the value of local control of the local development effort. Community Initiatives acknowledges that every local development effort is a unique project requiring a specific understanding of the characteristics of a particular place and its economy; it is the second concern that seems most problematic for timber towns. Helplessness breeds a conservatism that makes local action difficult. And state governments often have at least as much trouble as the federal government in dealing with local communities without attaching strings to the activities. But by focusing on the local communities as such, rather than considering them as a part of some larger political entity, the Community Initiatives program may actually be able to enhance local control of

the local development effort, if it can overcome the problematic characteristics of the local communities in which it is operating, and of those
that have typified other state and federal assistance programs.

The Future of Pacific Northwest
Timber Towns

The communities of the timber belt are trapped. Their mills—the
source of community stability since the 1940s—are shutting down.
From a larger perspective that may be a good thing. The overall efficiency of the timber industry is improving. But the places that depend
on the mills for their livelihoods face a different calculus. In the era of
footloose capital the rational decision for households in such places is to
move toward centers of industrial expansion. Thus, in purely financial
terms the next step for timber-belt residents seems obvious: find another line of work and move to where the jobs are. In doing so they will
presumably enjoy increased wealth and a higher standard of living. But
they pay a price for such instrumental rationality.

The long-sought stability that was finally attained in the 1950s and
1960s has led timber-belt people to believe they have achieved the kinds
of communities that were envisioned in the early years of this century—places where they have created "permanent homes and a normal
family life," communities "which contribute immeasurably to the development and welfare of the Nation" (Dana, 1918:33). Moving away
from such places in search of prosperity means more than departing a
town. It means abandoning places they created as they struggled to
move the fir belt from its pioneer mentality into modern times, places
that have sustained a way of life they created and now treasure. Yet
staying in these places means risking the very real possibility of im-
poverishment for oneself and one's children. It is a cruel choice.

Development approaches such as the Community Initiatives program, those that attempt to take into account the sense of identity
inherent in Pacific Northwest timber towns, seem to offer the only path
out. They may find means to build new economies without doing too
much violence to old ways. But it will be a difficult task and it is far too
soon to predict success.

Notes

Research for this chapter was supported in part by a grant from the University of
Oregon Office of Research and Sponsored Programs.

1. This section is drawn from Hibbard (1986) and Hibbard and Davis (1986).
2. This definition lumps the rural portions of many counties into the urban category. More precise definitions of rural and urban would show conditions in the two Oregons to be even further apart than Miller's study indicates.

References

Center for Population Research and Census. 1991. *Population Estimates for Oregon: 1980–1990.* Portland, Oreg.: Portland State University.

Clark, Donald H. 1952. "An Analysis of Forest Utilization as a Factor in Coloniz- ing the Pacific Northwest and in Subsequent Population Transition." Ph.D. dissertation, University of Washington.

Coman, Jr., Edwin T., and Helen M. Gibbs. 1949. *Time, Tide and Timber: A Century of Pope & Talbot.* Stanford, Calif.: Stanford University Press.

Dana, Samuel T. 1918. *Forestry and Community Development.* U.S. Depart- ment of Agriculture Bulletin 638. Washington, D.C.: Government Printing Office.

Dembo, Jonathan, 1985. "The Pacific Northwest Lumber Industry during the Great Depression." *Journal of the West* 24(4):51–62.

Durbin, Kathie. 1989. "Long-term Timber Deal Praised, Scorned." *Portland Oregonian,* December 3, E2.

Eisinger, Peter K. 1988. *The Rise of the Entrepreneurial State.* Madison: Univer- sity of Wisconsin Press.

Elias, James. 1990. "An Economic Culture in Crisis: A Community Study of a Pacific Northwest Timber Town." Master's thesis, University of Oregon.

Fosler, R. Scott (ed). 1988. *The New Economic Role of American States.* New York: Oxford University Press.

Greeley, William B. 1917. *Some Public and Economic Aspects of the Lumber Industry.* U.S. Department of Agriculture Report 114. Washington, D.C.: Gov- ernment Printing Office.

Hanna, Hugh S. 1917. *Labor Laws and Their Administration in the Pacific States.* U.S. Bureau of Labor Statistics Bulletin no. 211. Washington, D.C.: Department of Labor.

Herring, John P. 1951. *Labor Force, Employment, and Unemployment: Annual Estimates by States, 1900–1940.* Seattle: University of Washington Press.

Hibbard, Michael. 1989. "Issues and Options for the Other Oregon." *Commu- nity Development Joural* 24(2):145–53.

Hibbard, Michael. 1986. "Community Beliefs and the Failure of Community Economic Development." *Social Service Review* 60(2):183–200.

Hibbard, Michael, and Lori Davis. 1986. "When the Going Gets Tough: Eco- nomic Reality and the Cultural Myths of Small-Town America." *Journal of the American Planning Association* 52(4):419–28.

Hibbard, Michael, Edward C. Weeks, Helen Liggett, and Bryan T. Downes. 1987. "Taking Stock of Oregon's Rural Communities." Eugene: University of Oregon Department of Planning, Public Policy and Management.

Holbrook, Stewart H. 1926. "The Logging Camp Loses Its Soul." *Sunset* 56(6):19–21, 62.

Ise, John. 1920. *The United States Forest Policy.* New Haven, Conn.: Yale Uni- versity Press.

Kotok, E. I. 1938. "Some Economic Problems in Pacific Coast Forestry." Pp. 90–95 in *Proceedings, Pacific Coast Economic Association Seventeenth Annual Conference*, Berkeley, December.

Loehr, Rodney C. (ed.). 1952. *Forests for the Future: The Story of Sustained Yield as Told in the Diaries and Papers of David T. Mason, 1907–1950*. St. Paul: Forest Products History Foundation/Minnesota Historical Society.

Lowitt, Richard. 1984. *The New Deal and the West*. Bloomington: Indiana University Press.

Lund, Walter H. 1967. "Timber Management in the Pacific Northwest Region, 1927–1965." Interview by Amelia R. Fry. Regional Oral History Office, University of California, Berkeley.

MacKaye, Benton. 1919. *Employment and Natural Resources*. Washington, D.C.: Department of Labor.

Miller, Tamira. 1990. *The Two Oregons: Comparing Economic Conditions between Rural and Urban Oregon*. A Report to Oregon's Joint Legislative Committee on Trade and Economic Development. Salem: Oregon State Legislature.

Murphey, Michael. 1990. "Timber-r-r!" *Pacific Northwest* 24(1):28, 85.

O'Hara, Frank. 1914. *Unemployment in Oregon: Its Nature, Extent and Remedies*. A Report to the Oregon Committee on Seasonal Unemployment. Portland, Oreg.: Keystone Press.

Olson, Edward W. 1914. *Ninth Biennial Report of the Washington State Bureau of Labor Statistics and Factory Inspection, 1913–14*. Olympia: Frank M. Lamborn, Public Printer.

Osborne, David. 1988. *Laboratories of Democracy*. Boston: Harvard University Business School Press.

Pacific Northwest Executive. 1991. "Pacific Northwest Employment, Hours, and Earnings Indicators." *Pacific Northwest Executive* 7(2):12–13.

Parker, Carleton H. 1920. *The Casual Laborer and Other Essays*. New York: Harcourt, Brace and Howe.

Pope and Talbot. 1951. [Untitled pamphlet.] Portland, Oreg.: Pope and Talbot, Inc.

President's Mediation Commission. 1918. *Final Report*. Washington, D.C.: Government Printing Office.

Robbins, William G. 1987. "Lumber Production and Community Stability: A View from the Pacific Northwest." *Journal of Forest History* 31:187–96.

Robertson, Lance. 1990. "How Many Jobs? How Many Owls?" *Eugene Register-Guard*, May 7.

Schallau, Con. 1987. "The Commitment to Community Stability: A Policy or Shibboleth?" *Environmental Law* 17(3):429–81.

Shaffer, Ron. 1989. *Community Economics*. Ames: Iowa State University Press.

State of Oregon, Department of Human Resources, Employment Division. 1991. "Oregon Nonagricultural Wage and Salary Employment Statistics." Salem: Oregon Department of Human Resources.

Steward, Don. 1987. "Increased Earnings—Real or an Illustion?" *Oregon Labor Trends*, July: 6–7.

U.S. Bureau of the Census. 1912. *Census of the United States, 1910*. Washington, D.C.: Government Printing Office.

U.S. Congress. Senate. Committee on Interior and Insular Affairs. 1949. *Sustained Timber Yield: Hearings before a Subcommittee of the Committee on*

Interior and Insular Affairs: United States Senate. Testimony of David T. Mason. 80th Cong., 2d sess. 7, 8, and 9 September 1948, Eugene, Oreg. Washington, D.C.: Government Printing Office.

U.S. Department of Commerce, Bureau of Economic Analysis. 1989. *Local Area Personal Income* vol. 5: *Southwest, Rocky Mountain, and Far West Regions: Alaska and Hawaii.* Washington, D.C: Department of Commerce.

U.S. Department of Labor. 1918. *Sixth Annual Report of the Secretary of Labor.* Washington: D.C.: Government Printing Office.

U.S. Forest Service. 1936. *Forest Facts and Statistics for the North Pacific Region.* Portland Oreg.: Education and Information Section.

———. 1947. *Report of the Chief of the Forest Service.* Washington, D.C.: Department of Agriculture.

Washington State Planning Council. 1945. *Ten Years of Progress, 1934–1944.* Sixth and Final Report of the Washington State Planning Council. Olympia, Wash.: State Printing Plant.

Weaver, Clyde, and Marcel Dennert. 1987. "Economic Development and the Public-Private Partnership." *Journal of the American Planning Association* 53(4):430–37.

10 | In the Shadow of Urban Growth: Bifurcation in Rural California Communities

Ted K. Bradshaw

CALIFORNIA IS AN URBAN STATE on a scale of its own. Some 95 percent of the state's 30 million people live in metropolitan areas, yet the state is the nation's leading agricultural producer; the population has doubled every twenty years from gold rush days through 1970; the California economy is the sixth largest in the world; one of every six new jobs in the nation since 1979 has been in California;[1] the population increase of 5.4 million during the 1980s was equivalent to moving the state of Massachusetts to the west coast; and one of every three refugees and immigrants into the United States ends up in California.[2]

But behind the urban front is a significant, though often forgotten, rural backwater that has 2.2 million people (U.S. Bureau of the Census, 1991). If rural California were a state by itself its population would be larger than those of eighteen other states, and it would have four congressional representatives. The people in this rural state would be settled on about 95 million acres (out of California's total of 100 million acres), a land from which the urban population could obtain virtually all its water, recreation, and natural resources, including agricultural products, timber, energy, and minerals (see California Department of Forestry, 1988). Yet rural Californians compared to urban residents receive about 25 percent less per capita personal income,[3] and their poverty rate is a whopping 62 percent higher than the urban rate (California Department of Economic Opportunity, 1989). Rural communities are on average subject to more industrial plant closures, county governments are on the brink of bankruptcy, hospitals struggle to stay open (Bradshaw, 1987), and people worry about rising crime statistics. In addition, urban areas make many demands on the dispersed part of the state, establishing an urban agenda for their development. Yet rural areas receive few special resources and usually lack local leadership to structure their own future. Thus, the "forgotten California" is a valuable but vulnerable resource.

Behind the gross statistics lies a more challenging problem: a new urban-based rurality is transforming parts of rural communities as a sort of overlay, leading to a bifurcation of resources and opportunities. The term *bifurcation* is used to describe a two-pronged pattern of new and old rural development; the new pattern is tied to urban-global economic systems with considerable wealth and cultural advantage, whereas the old pattern is rooted in local indigenous or traditional community-centered opportunity structures, economic systems relying on agriculture and resource-based industries and resulting in high levels of poverty, declining opportunities, and dependency. Bifurcated development follows two separate tracks in which the traditional rural culture and economy remains separate from the new upscale rural overlay. Old-timers either leave, or are pushed to less desirable small towns, or are confined to run-down neighborhoods; they are excluded from expensive leisure, retirement, or security-gated "new towns." Bifurcation is a new layer of urban-based growth in rural communities that is significantly different from the old; it does not describe, for example, a process of industrial transformation that would create a two-tier economy, a dual class system, or a declining middle class (although each may be present).

With bifurcation, urban and rural development patterns are no longer spatially isolated from each other. Urban systems have come to rural communities for many reasons, including lower cost, attractiveness of rural life styles, escape from urban crime and racial tensions, and reliable labor forces (Bradshaw and Blakely, 1982). Rural communities and regions have welcomed them in the belief that the new companies and their employees will provide jobs, better incomes, and urban amenities. Many of the benefits the indigenous population expected fail to materialize, however, as responsible positions in the new industries are taken mainly by newcomers. As a consequence, the old rural part of the community is forced into deeper dependency and poverty, while new urban-based development gets most of the attention from statisticians, political leaders, economic developers, and service providers because it is linked to growing industries and the network of urban-global culture.

Development is problematic in both rural and urban areas. It requires inputs of economic resources as well as of human and organizational resources, which some groups and communities possess and some do not (Bradshaw, 1990). It is my thesis that rural areas, and particularly the indigenous rural populations, have identified and mobilized fewer of the resources that are needed in the modern economy, and they fail to develop in spite of the fact that outside development is coming into the community. Rural underdevelopment in modern society is caused less by conscious exploitation than by benign neglect; underdevelopment is perpetuated when less advantaged segments of the society fail to obtain or mobilize both economic and organizational resources necessary to trade what they have for what they need. In the case of rural bifurcation, resource mobilization and organizational strategies are set by newcomers rather than by the traditional rural population.

What will happen to rural areas like Firebaugh, Borrego Springs, Oakhurst, Patterson, Weed, or Crescent City in the next quarter century? Will they become collecting places for displaced people who cannot make it in changing and growing communities? Will they be overrun by commuters and urban refugees who bring their urban culture with them? Will they become resort playgrounds for the wealthy or open communities with opportunities for all social classes? When ethnic homogeneity is replaced by diversity will there be accommodation or tension? Will outside corporations set the terms of development or become local partners in community development? These are some of the questions that people in rural communities are asking, and often they have neither the answers nor the ability to determine their future. In short, California's rural communities are presently disadvantaged, and they will not find the transition to the twenty-first century easy. The purpose of this essay, therefore, is to identify the development challenge facing rural communities in California and to show how policy decisions made within the next few years will lead either to an increasingly depressed and dependent rural region, or to a region interdependent with other areas, and contributing to mutual well-being.

Tension between Cultures

Rural development problems are complex and interrelated, joining concerns about population growth, economic transformation, local needs, and global dynamics. The development problems of the indigenous rural population and their agricultural and forest resource industries stand in sharp contrast to the problems of containing new growth based on urban spillover and a new economy. For all of this, the existing governmental arrangement is hopelessly inadequate.

Rural California's natural resources have long been recognized as a unique asset. From the discovery of gold in 1849, which first made California a desired destination, until the present, California's unique combination of water, land, vegetation, and climate was recognized as a special resource for human technology to exploit. The state's resources have been available in practically unlimited bounty, and their exploitation became a technological and business challenge. By 1860 the value of wheat produced in California exceeded the value of all the gold produced, and soon agriculture was established as the preeminent state industry. Due to the shortage of labor, foreigners were recruited to work the fields, and new technology was invented. As Carey McWilliams (1949:120) pointed out, "in no other area have so many ingenious and man-made devices been invented to cope with an astonishing range of ecological factors. In the [eighteen] sixties and seventies California farmers experimented with steam-powered tractors, wheel plows, gang plows, rotary spades, and many similar devices, most of which were developed to cope with special conditions."

Waves of Chinese, Japanese, and Mexicans have all contributed to the building of California's rural economic infrastructure. Chinese laborers arrived in debt bondage and had to work in gold fields for years to repay their passage. Japanese migrants in the early 1900s were brought to the state to replace the Chinese as cheap farm laborers, but as they became successful farmers a wave of anti-Japanese sentiment led to legislation against Japanese land ownership. Mexican migration into California started during the Mexican Revolution of 1910–1920, and many Mexicans worked in the fields and in Los Angeles factories. Today, the vast majority of farm laborers are of Hispanic origin. Carey McWilliams chronicled the conditions in farm labor camps in his book *Factories in the Field* and described unbearable conditions of farm employment. This so angered the Association of Farmers that it passed a resolution describing McWilliams as "California's Agricultural Pest Number One, outranking pear blight and the boll weevil" (Bean and Rawls, 1983:401). Steinbeck's *The Grapes of Wrath* and other novels also showed the extreme poverty of rural labor in one of the world's most affluent states.

The history of rural California is also filled with conflict over development. Lumbering interests competed with an emerging ethic that would preserve parks in Yosemite, Kings Canyon, and the most spectacular redwood groves along the coast. Mining interests, especially hydraulic mining companies working large gold deposits in the northern Sierra Nevada range, competed with farmers and city dwellers, who suffered as silt clogged downstream rivers and caused massive floods. Agriculture competed for water with downstream users and ultimately fishery protection. Many once-abundant species became scarce or nearly extinct. All rural industries in one way or another have felt the pressure of urban interests and environmental constraints.

Even growth itself was a source of conflict. Since statehood, California's population doubled every 20 years until 1970, when it exceeded 20 million persons. From 1970 to 1990 population grew by an additional 10 million persons. This rate of population growth is one of the longest sustained population explosions of any industrial region in the world. As a consequence of that growth, the state's population, infrastructure, and economy were at the cutting edge of innovation and efficiency because every 20 years at least half of the developed state was the newest the country had to offer in technology, machinery, and life-style*(Bradshaw, 1976).

Interestingly, this dynamic growth shaped rural communities as well as urban ones. Agriculture, mining, and forest-products technology were continually upgraded as the state's development continued, leading to expanded production and new products. Labor-saving technology did not lead to widespread depopulation of rural communities, with minor exceptions such as some lumber mill towns and migrant farm-labor communities. The large increase in California's population and its new technology kept most rural places stable as higher-value crops were introduced, making California the specialty crop leader, and as industry responded similarly with more high-value-added production.

Nonetheless, rural California became dependent on urban-based firms and markets, and it did not share equally in either the wealth or the power of the state. Rural areas were kept busy supplying a rapidly urbanizing California with all the resources it needed. The California Water Project diverted massive flows of water from the northern mountains to the arid south, competitive markets kept wages and investment low in agriculture and related rural industries, and industrial concentration eliminated both farms and product-manufacturing facilities from rural communities. In this way, rural California shared much of the fate of other rural regions, in that resource dependency is highly correlated with poverty (Blakely, 1991).

Rural areas, however disadvantaged, still had a special relation to urban areas that would conflict with rural economic self-sufficiency. Urban interests wanted to preserve the abundant, bounty of California that was supplying urban California with so many resources. In the 1960s, with the emergence of the environmental movement, the public became outraged at more than urban smog; urban inhabitants began to fear that rural resources on which they depended were also being threatened. For example, massive public concern led to policies that addressed the declining water quality in the San Francisco Bay and the Sacramento Delta, the decline of the San Joaquin Valley water table and resulting land subsidence, the loss of unique forest areas to logging, the overuse of recreational and wild areas, the development of the coast which blocked access to views and beaches, and the conversion of farmland to residential tracts. For the most part, these policies reflected urban culture's effort to preserve the resources it needs, not rural culture. This conflict remains unresolved.

The interdependence of growth and rural culture can be illustrated by developments in Watsonville and the El Pajaro Valley in southern Santa Cruz County, some seventy-five miles south of San Francisco. This area is on the rural edge of the expanding Bay Area, but it figures minimally in the regional consciousness. Most people were not aware that the 17 October 1989 earthquake that damaged homes and bridges in San Francisco and Oakland actually caused worse damage to the small towns like Watsonville located within miles of the quake's epicenter. These towns were so isolated and destroyed that no one knew how extensive the damage was for several days. While the media focused on the expensive homes damaged in San Francisco, thousands of destroyed rural homes went unnoticed, and their occupants camped in the town square.

Watsonville and its neighboring rural communities are really caught between too little and too much urban attention. Once a sleepy little agricultural city bypassed by growth and fortune, Watsonville longed for modernity. Agriculture has been successful in a region known for some of the world's most fertile soils and an attractive microclimate for specialty crops such as artichokes and summer lettuce. Agricultural employment and wages have been good, but the gap between the field and packing shed workers who are largely Latino and the rest of the community (largely of European origin) has continued to grow. Watsonville's industrial base started to diversify in the 1980s from packing agricultural products to light manufacturing and electronics. Indeed, the relative proximity of Watsonville to Santa Clara County some twenty-five miles east has produced intense pressure both for industrial sites that can utilize low-wage assembly labor and for lower-cost housing for people who commute an hour or more across the hills to Silicon Valley jobs. This new urban pressure threatens the agricultural base with development on prime land and adds further tensions to the bifurcated community.

Housing is symptomatic of the bifurcation caused by urban growth. The local low-wage workers and their families are crowded into older houses. It is not uncommon to find multiple families living in the main house, another family living in the garage, and a third in a backyard shed, connected by hoses and extension cords. The extent of the need for low-income housing in Watsonville is so great that it would be almost impossible under current federal and state programs to construct enough new low-price housing to meet the needs of these people, and any enforcement of standards for existing housing would displace many low-income families. Yet market pressures for new housing development are so intense that the vacancy rate is practically zero. New housing is purchased as fast as it can be constructed, and commuters are buying and renovating many existing units because the price is much lower than housing in the city of Santa Cruz or Santa Clara County. As a consequence, the newcomers are driving up the price of all housing in Watsonville and eliminating many rental units. The dilemma is that new housing development is needed to relieve pressure on the existing housing market, especially for the indigenous population, but new housing will be quickly absorbed by outsiders. Construction of new housing units will thus lead to a rapidly increasing population base with almost no improvement in the availability of units for the workers in agriculture and the traditional rural industries, and probably with a significant loss for them. Development will also dramatically reduce agricultural land and jobs in related industries, further limiting opportunities for less-advantaged people. In short, there are two development problems in Watsonville: a more traditional rural problem of poverty and displacement from resource industry jobs, and a new problem of preserving a rural heritage and rich farm land in the face of rampant urban growth.

Watsonville is not alone in facing bifurcated development. Small towns and cities throughout rural California and the rest of America are experiencing the overlay of urban growth and well-being on rural poverty, hiding from view the rural problems and the policies that might help them. Furthermore, the dilemma plays out at a regional level, with boom-town-type growth occurring alongside lagging resource communities in forest, fishing, mining, and manufacturing areas as well as agriculture. Growing rural communities and small cities continue to struggle with problems of balancing their new popularity and wealth with developing an opportunity structure for the indigenous population and preserving their communities' rural character, which made them attractive in the first place. This dynamic of bifurcation is played out in five important trends.

Trends Shaping California's
Forgotten Communities

California's rural areas have not experienced the population deple-tion characteristic of most other rural states. The rural population has remained relatively constant, with major increases in the 1970s (Bradshaw and Blakely, 1979). This stability does not mean that all communities have grown, because some have not,[4] or that all rural communities have been affluent and stable. Simply, it means that among the list of California's rural problems, huge population loss has not been a major concern.

Population Growth

Recent population data indicate that California's rural areas are growing at a rate considerably higher than that of the state as a whole, but more slowly in the late 1980s than in the 1970s. The most recent estimates show a rural revival in the 1990s.

California has fifty-eight counties, many of which are very large and awkward mixes of urban and rural development. As such, most data do not capture the extent of low-density development outside the sphere of influence of large cities.[5] Although exact statistical portraits of rural California are difficult without additional new census data, we can proceed to give a reasonable overview by taking as the rural base of California the thirty-three counties that were classified as nonmetropolitan in 1975; five of these counties are now metropolitan (see Map 10.1). The rural counties in California grew by 35 percent during the 1970s, a decade of rural reverse migration throughout the nation. However, during the 1980s the growth rate of rural counties in California slowed slightly to 29 percent. In both cases the rural coun-ties had a higher growth rate than urban ones—during the 1970s urban areas grew by only 17 percent, increasing to 25 percent during the 1980s. Thus, during the 1970s rural growth was especially fast and urban growth was slow. But by the 1980s the difference between the two had narrowed considerably—rural areas continued to grow at a brisk pace, while the urban areas resumed historic growth rates (see Map 10.2). Also, during the 1980s California's most remote counties experienced essentially no growth; although they did not lose popula-tion, the northern timber counties failed to gain as they did during the 1970s.

The most recent estimates show that the 1990s may begin a pattern of growth more similar to the 1970s than to the 1980s. Between

Map 10.1 California's Thirty-three Rural Counties (1970 non-SMSAs)

Rural

1970 SMSA

1990 and 1991 the rural counties grew 3.92 percent, an annual rate faster than that of the 1970s. The major metropolitan counties in California grew by 2.58 percent during this same period. Although it is difficult to make trend predictions based on only one year, there are signs of rural growth well in excess of urban growth. Seven of the top ten counties ranked by population growth during the year were largely rural counties: Del Norte, Madera, Calaveras, El Dorado, Amador, Mariposa, Placer, and Mono (California Department of Finance, May

Map 10.2. Population Increase in California Counties, 1980–1990

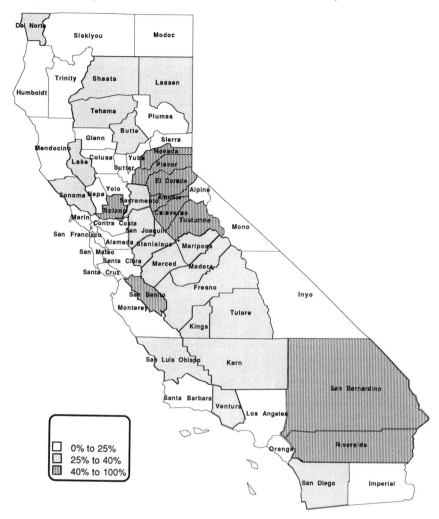

Legend:
- 0% to 25%
- 25% to 40%
- 40% to 100%

1991). The only large urban counties included were Riverside, San Bernardino, and Solano. In contrast, the ten slowest growth-rate counties included San Francisco, Los Angeles, San Mateo, Santa Clara, and Alameda—counties that account for nearly half the state's population.

Whereas various rural areas are growing in the early 1990s, they are not necessarily the same rural counties that were growing so rapidly a decade ago. For example, Lake County grew at the fastest rate of any county in the early 1980s and is now ranked twenty-fifth in population growth rate. Many urbanizing counties with a strong rural orientation have slowed their population growth by initiative or growth control. Santa Cruz, Napa, Marin, and Monterey have strong growth control programs and would be expected to grow faster in the absence of such measures.[6]

While growth dominates the discussion of California's demographic change, the more remote and forested counties have slow overall rates of growth and development. For example, 1980–90 census data show that the northern tier of counties had generally slow growth, with the exception of Del Norte County, which had a one-shot infusion of population due to completion of a large state prison—a measurable impact due to the small population base in the county (23,460). The remoteness of these areas and their dependence on forest industries continues to suppress growth.

The parts of the state with the strongest rural and agricultural roots will be the fastest growing economic regions through the 1990s (California Department of Finance, April 1991). Map 10.3 shows the state population projections for 1990–2005. Along with exurban Los Angeles, growth will be concentrated in the central Sierra and Central Valley. Slow growth is anticipated for the already urbanized areas and the most remote rural counties.

Data from the Center for the Continuing Study of the California Economy (CCSCE) show that the fastest projected job growth in the state from 1986 to 1995 will be in the Mountain region (30.32 percent), the Sacramento region (28.9 percent), the San Diego region (28.5 percent), and the San Joaquin region (25.1 percent), compared to a state growth rate of 20.7 percent. Existing urban areas as well as the more remote rural regions (e.g., North Coast at 14.1 percent) are projected to be below the state average in job growth (CCSCE, 1988:90). For the most part economic growth tends to follow population growth in rural areas, though this relationship is not as empirically established as one would desire. However, the projections for job growth support the trend of continued exurban pressure on California's rural areas.

Population growth in rural areas of the state has vastly more local impact and significance than its share of the state population growth suggests. The total rural growth between 1980 and 1990 was some 528,446 persons out of a state growth of over 6 million and well below the 636,000-person increase in San Diego County alone. Yet in some small towns populations doubled, new housing developments circled what used to be the town, property values rose speculatively, schools had to be constructed, sewage treatment plants upgraded, and stoplights installed. Although minor in urban areas, these accommoda-

Map 10.3. Projected Population Increase in California Counties, 1990–2005

Source: California Department of Finance, Demographic Research Unit Report 91 P-1, *Interim Population Projections*, April 1991.

tions to growth in small rural towns stretched capacity, resulted in conflict, and set in motion development agendas foreign to small-town politics and administration.

New Diversity in Rural Areas

California also has the most diverse population in the United States with the exception of Hawaii. Although there are differences, rural communities are beginning to share the overall trends of increasing ethnic diversity in California. In 1970 groups with Spanish surnames or of Hispanic origin and non-Caucasian racial groups made up 22 percent of the state's population, but by 1985 they constituted more than 37 percent. Accurate data are hard to obtain, but illegal migrants may make up 6 percent of the state's total population, and may be at least a third of the migratory stream entering the state (Fay and Fay, 1990:39–42). Refugee settlement and resettlements in California now total about 500,000; in 1988, 35,500 settled in California—45 percent of the national refugees for that year. Projections indicate that by 2010 today's minorities will be a majority (California Department of Finance, 1988); Bovier and Martin estimate, based on trend analysis, that minority groups could be 62 percent of California's population by 2030 (1985:13). Although these patterns clearly depend on international economic and political conditions, as well as U.S. immigration policies, there is little doubt that the Latino and Asian populations will continue faster growth because they have a much higher birth rate than the rest of the population and immigration is not likely to stop.

The largest numbers of immigrants settle in the Los Angeles area, but significant numbers settle in rural communities. Still, the rural population of California is dominantly white, leading many to suspect that a motive for the migration to rural areas rests in "white flight." While California as a whole in 1990 was 57.2 percent non-Hispanic white, the rural areas were 73.3 percent white, with the vast majority of the minority population being Hispanic. This is changing rapidly, however.

One of the most interesting patterns is the growth of refugee groups in Central Valley communities. For example, Merced County has the largest per capita refugee population of any county in the United States. Some have come directly from Laos, but the largest number have come as secondary migrants from other areas of the United States. It is estimated that there are 10,880 refugees in Merced County (total population of 178,000), and in the town of Merced refugees constitute 15 percent of the population. Nearly 70 percent of Merced County's refugees are Hmong tribespeople, former hill-country residents of Laos. English language skills are so limited that one of four students in the Merced City School District is classified as "limited English proficiency." Few have skills that could be translated into jobs. Nearly 90 percent of the Hmong were on welfare in 1988, swelling county welfare rolls to unmanageable proportions, and assimilation was hampered by their tight clan structure.[7] Customs such as squirrel hunting provoked local antagonism; indeed the challenge for social service workers was to help integrate people from a thirteenth century culture into twenty-first-century California (Speizer, 1985).

The Hispanic population has been an important part of rural California for decades. In California, Rochin and Castillo noted that in 1980 there were twenty-one communities with over 70 percent Hispanic-origin residents. The highest community was West Parlier in Fresno County with 98.2 percent Hispanic-origin population. In these highly "Latino" communities the median age is only 22.7 years compared to a median of 26.6 years in similar-size communities with low Latino populations and a statewide median of 29.9 years (Rochin and Castillo, 1990:8). These communities also are places with high proportions of single, young, migrant workers who live in very large households. The Latino communities, which are called "rural colonias," are located largely in the rich agricultural areas of the state and believed to have higher incidence of poverty with poorer access to social services than urban Latino neighborhoods. Finally, Rochin and Castillo show that the number of dominantly Hispanic communities is increasing, and within each the number of Hispanics is growing very rapidly, lending support to a "Networking Hypothesis, i.e, communities with relatively high numbers of Latinos attract more Latinos" (Rochin and Castillo, 1990:2).

The elderly population is increasing the diverse social mix of rural California. Motivated by lower housing prices and pleasant safe communities, retirees are taking their social security and pension incomes with them as they move from urban homes to rural communities. This has led to a greatly increased elderly population in rural areas. In 1990 the rural counties' population over age 60 had increased to 17.6 percent. This is well above the state total, where only 14.2 percent were over 60 years old. Data from the California Department of Finance project that 22 percent of the population will be over 60 by 2020, and figures for rural areas will undoubtedly be higher. Rural retirees are a visible and important social force, and they press for community responsiveness to their needs for services just as other groups press for jobs and schools. In small rural communities the retirees may be the most politically skilled and active groups, creating conflict with long-time residents.

The origins of the people in rural California provide one roadmap of the difficult challenge facing less-advantaged people today. At the same time, the overlays of different people and their economic ties provide another map because with each group and each cultural perspective lies a different vision of the future. The diversity of cultures is in fact much less than the diversity of visions about what the community should be, what uses should be made of the natural environment, who should be allowed in and for what reason, and what should be restricted. Between the newly arrived professionals, retirees, commuters, farm workers, and Hmong refugees there is not only a gap in experience and opportunity, but a vast gulf of vision. A critical problem is comprehending this diversity and developing it into a community rather than allowing it to fragment and evolve into conflict.

Declining Role of Traditional Rural Industries

Rural communities are growing in part because people want to live in less-congested rural environments, but location decisions are closely coupled with increased opportunities in some expanding sectors of the rural economy. Although the composition of rural economies is incredibly complex and diffuse, the broadbrush picture is one of the declining relative importance of traditional rural industries such as foresty and agriculture. With the continuing deteriorioation of opportunity and income in primary industries, greater economic bifurcation is accelerated as new industries either exploit the displaced labor or introduce high-profile growth industries linked to urban or international markets rather than to local labor markets or suppliers.

California Agriculture. The agricultural industry in California remains the nation's largest, and eight of the top ten agricultural counties are in California. One-third of the crop land is planted for export, and the state supplies some 50 percent of the nation's fresh vegetables. California agriculture has expanded during the postwar period due to increased acerage coming under irrigation, and this has led to stable or increasing employment. In addition, labor savings from mechanization have been more than offset by the persistent conversion from commodity crops to more labor-intensive specialty crops such as berries, fruits, nuts, and gourmet vegetables (see Rosenberg et al., 1990:30). The change in agricultural employment has generated a modest increase in the absolute number of employees, but they are declining in proportion to the very rapidly expanding work force. Production agricultural employment increased from 208,000 employees in 1972 to 262,000 in 1980 as new land was irrigated and more specialty crops were planted (see Figure 10.1). Since peaking in 1980, employment in agricultural production decreased to a low of 220,000 in 1986, though it bounced back to 239,000 in 1988. At the same time, agricultural services have shown a steady employment increase, going from about 60,000 workers in 1972 to 137,000 workers in 1989. As a consequence, total agricultural employment has increased from 268,000 in 1972 to 355,000 workers in 1988, though employment reached nearly this level in 1980 and dipped in the middle years of the decade. The changing levels of agricultural employment during the 1980s are partially due to how workers are counted; some of the production work has been shifted to contract labor, which is counted as agricultural services. For example, in 1986 contract labor supplied 65,000 workers in 1986 (California Governor, 1991).

As a component of the total economy, changes in agricultural em-

Figure 10.1 Agricultural Employment in California, 1972–1990 (in thousands)

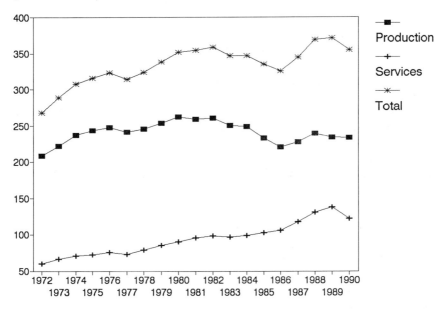

ployment have become increasingly dwarfed by other changes in the economy. Data from the California Employment Development Department (1972; 1986) indicates that agriculture, forestry, and fishery employment dropped from 3.9 percent of total statewide employment in 1972 to 3.3 percent in 1986. Similarly, in the Central Valley, where the greatest number of farmworkers are employed, the share of employment dropped from 15.7 percent in 1972 to 11.7 percent in 1986. During this period, average farm employment levels increased in the Central Valley by about 20,000 workers, from 165,000 to 186,000; however, employment in other industries added 521,000 new jobs, mostly in trade and service industries. These other industries created twenty-six times as many new jobs as agriculture created, and the *new* jobs during this thirteen-year period in the Central Valley were three times as many as the *total* of agricultural, forestry, and fishery jobs at its peak (Bradshaw and Willoughby, 1989).

Data from the Center for the Continuing Study of the California Economy show major projected job changes by industry. In rural areas the expansion of jobs and economic vitality is closely associated with the diversification of the rural economic base, especially in services. From 1979 to 1995, according to CCSCE projections for "basic industries" in the "rest of the state" outside major urban areas, resource-based jobs will decline by 13,200, while diversified manufacturing jobs will increase by 13,600; basic services will increase by 78,600 jobs. Total job growth in the rest of the state region will be some 538,000 new jobs, a growth of 31.1 percent. Government employment, which provided a significant boost to rural economies during the 1970s, is projected to grow at a rate of 29.5 percent, slightly below that of the total (Center for the Continuing Study of the California Economy, 1988:90, 186, 187).

Resource Industry Communities. One of the most significant aspects of decline in resource industries is felt by communities that are almost singly dependent on one firm or industry. For example, substantial rural small-town employment losses have occurred in forestry, and the number of mills has been reduced from nearly 1,000 in the 1950s to less than 100 today (California Department of Forestry, 1988:190–91), a loss magnified by the fact that a majority of these closed mills were major employers in their respective communities. Today seventy of the remaining mills are in sixty small towns that remain vulnerable to further mill closures. In 1972 California employed 52,000 workers in lumber, which increased to nearly 60,000 by 1976; a decade later lumber employment remained at 60,000, though this industry is strongly affected by the business cycle's effect on housing starts. A significant consequence of industry consolidation is that larger mills are located in more central urban communities. In addition, this static employment is a smaller proportion of a growing employment base. In 1972 employment in the lumber industry was 0.7 percent of total state employment; by 1986 it had fallen to 0.5 percent (computed from California Employment Development Department, 1972; 1986).

In fact, most of California's dynamic rural growth appears to be the exurban economy of the advanced industrial society—professional services, wholesaling, clerical, and small manufacturing. New employment in the service industries accounts for the largest share of employment expansion in rural areas. Some jobs are in personal services that reflect a purely local transfer of income from one person to another, but the majority are in industries that draw some or most of their income from outside the local area. For example, trucking, utilities, wholesale trade, insurance, tourism, and retirement services bring outside money into rural areas. In most cases manufacturing is not the driving force in rural development, but it is usually one component.

Restructuring the Rural Economy

The restructuring of the rural economy parallels that of the overall development of California with a strong emphasis on service industries and relatively high technology firms. In rural areas, the process of bifurcation shapes the restructuring that is taking place in the economy, as new firms, industries, and business relationships add to and overlay the old. Most of the growing segments are tied to global or urban needs and markets, and the new rural businesses, human capital, and linkages are not a natural outgrowth of the rural. For example, a Japanese company recently built a new tomato product processing plant in Los Banos that makes specialty sauces and drinks both for export and for the American market. While its input comes from a nearby cannery that produces bulk-canned tomatoes, foreign capital and management and a worldwide market are driving the industrial restructuring with a high value-added specialty product. The plant and its jobs are a welcome addition to the local economy, but rural isolation has clearly given way to increasing interdependence with global economic forces (Furukawa, 1991).

Some branch plants and manufacturing industries are locating in rural communities to take advantage of lower production costs and available labor, but on average manufacturing accounts for only about 20 percent of California rural employment, and most of this is concentrated in lumber or food processing (see Belzer and Kroll, 1986). Most theories of rural development assume that traditional manufacturing plants in mature industries provide the economic base for rural communities; manufacturing production plants relocate from cities where innovation takes place to rural areas where they can gain a competitive advantage from low labor costs in the routine mass production of goods (see, for example, Moriarty, 1980). This is happening at a very slow pace in rural California, however, with few large plants relocating in the state; most relocate out-of-state or to foreign countries. Industrial expansions, however, do produce new plants and jobs for rural communities.

Self-employment is often necessary because there are few large employers; the fact is that large numbers of migrants and others living in rural areas find that they must create their own jobs or else they will have nowhere to work. More centrally, as David Birch has pointed out (1987), small business is increasingly responsible for most job gains and product innovation. Rural small firms, frequently founded by rural residents, are the backbone of the economy in most California rural communities. In some cases the small firms make use of natural resources found in the area, and they often provide services both locally and for a wider market. In a survey of five rapidly growing rural communities, Bradshaw and Blakely (1981) showed that over 50 percent of recent (one- to five-year) migrants into the communities started their own business or were in the process of doing so. These businesses included a wide range of industries and skills, and their failure rate was surprisingly low.

Government is a major employer in many rural communities. Several rural communities have over 25 percent employment in government, including military bases, forest service, state government facilities (including prisons), schools, and local government facilities. Indirectly, the expanding number of social security recipients who can locate anywhere they like has led to extensive retirement migration to small towns where people enjoy both lower costs of living and an attractive life-style (Bradshaw and Blakely, 1988). However, the reduction of federal and state funding to local programs since the mid-1970s has substantially reduced the role of government employment as a stimulus for rural population growth and economic development.

Ties to the Global Economy. Economic growth, and with it population growth, is increasingly dependent on national and international patterns, and these determine regional dynamics. The electronics industry in Silicon Valley, electronics and aerospace in Orange County, and numerous other growth nodes have shaped regional fate, and with it the fate of surrounding rural areas (Storper and Walker, 1989). The fate of local communities is often determined by how a region competes internationally as much as by how it sets zoning or taxes, or how it struggles for economic development.

International markets determine the price received for agricultural products and for lumber. This is well understood because of large fluctuations in the demands for California rice, cotton, and other crops. Much of the Third World has become self-sufficient in basic commodity crops, and some developing countries are even exporting agricultural products. Within the developed world, fresh fruits and vegetables are now available year round, taking advantage of different seasons and growing conditions at the extreme corners of the earth, reducing the domestic consumption of frozen and canned produce. California's agriculture has long been attentive to export opportunities, and some $3.34 billion worth of products were exported in 1987, up from $2.84 billion in 1986 (American Farmland Trust, 1989:59). But this was well below the peak export of $4.3 billion recorded in 1981 and was the clearest evidence for the deep financial problems faced by farmers throughout the nation, including California.

What is happening now is that other countries and areas are competing for this export market, and as production in other parts of the world increases and markets diversify, some California producers will fail to find good markets for their crops. A variant on this dynamic is the expanding number of Japanese food firms that are producing and packing in California for export to their own country; higher trade quotas for food exports to Japan may not affect the open market as much as many hope. In addition, imports are starting to erode markets that were once locally controlled. One indication of this is the expansion of fresh fruit and vegetable production in Mexico and South America for California consumption. Imported produce is also being used in canning and frozen-food packing. For example, packing houses in Watsonville now receive a substantial amount of their broccoli from Mexico. Frozen broccoli from Mexico imported to the United States was a negligible 6.1 percent in 1980 (compared to the California share at 92.4 percent); by 1987 the Mexican share had increased to 32.4 percent while the California share had dropped to only 51.6 percent. The net result in Santa Cruz and Monterey counties alone has been the loss of at least 5,000 jobs (Ferriss and Sandoval, 1991).

International markets are also determinate in forestry. At present there is a bitter conflict over the shipment of logs to Japan and other foreign countries (rather than cut lumber) and over the differential between domestic lumber prices and that of Canada where government subsidies give Canadian companies an unfair advantage, according to U.S. industry claims.

Rural isolation has given way to intense global interdependence—reaching firms in the most remote rural communities. In Trinidad, along the northern California coast, International Cable News is produced, giving the programming for satellite television broadcasts received by cable stations and private dishes throughout the world. In a remote Mendocino County valley, a small specialty dental-equipment manufacturing company makes products that are sold worldwide. Lawyers and investors in small towns deal with international issues by phone, and travel is not that much more difficult from a small town than from many suburban locations. Blakely has argued that rural development must proceed by "building a new future for rural Americans as partners in the emerging global economy" (Blakely 1991:70). The globalization of the economy directly affects rural communities by restructuring the way wealth is generated—less from natural resources, and more from the manipulation of money. In addition, a new breed of professionals is operating in rural areas not bound by past urban institutional forms. These professionals are already working in a global economy from rural locations, participating in the information economy. Although participation in the global economy may build new forms of community based on life-style rather than place, Blakely argues that rural communities can benefit from finding their role in the emerging world order (Blakely, 1991:68–69). Participation in the global economy, however, is another aspect of the bifurcation that is affecting rural California. Global interdependence is an increasingly complex dynamic that is centered in urban rather than in rural business practices, and international ties come slowly to rural industry. Most of the expertise in global business comes not from local businesses but from outsiders bringing their contacts with them.

Rural Areas Are Poor and Getting Poorer

Despite the economic vitality of much of rural California and the general strength of its agricultural industry, poverty is concentrated in rural areas (and center-city neighborhoods), and it is increasing. For example, in Stanislaus County the Department of Social Services estimates that they provide some form of assistance to 20 percent of the population in that county. This does not include an additional 10 percent who receive Social Security or disability. At the same time, the economy of the county has never done better; population is increasing at rates that cause alarm among many who want to protect the agricultural land and the rural character of their county. From a "jobs" perspective, major new employment efforts would tend to fuel the forces of residential growth. The problem is that the rural poor are often working but earning too little, are unable to work, or can find only seasonal work.

Taking as a base the twenty-eight nonmetropolitan counties in 1989 and the five that were reclassified at the time of the 1980 census (total thirty-three rural versus twenty-five urban; see Map 10.1), we can see from the following indicators that rural California is in need of economic development: sixteen of the thirty-three rural counties had unemployment rates in 1990 of over 10 percent, whereas only three of the twenty-five urban counties had unemployment rates this high, at a time when the total state unemployment was 5.6 percent. The three urban counties (Fresno, Kern, and Stanislaus), with nearly double the state unemployment rate, were all urban farm counties (California, Department of Finance, 1990: Table C-2). Moreover, all of the thirty-three rural counties had median household incomes below $20,000, whereas only twelve of the twenty-five urban counties had median household income that low (Fay and Fay, 1990:247).

According to the most recent data from the California Department of Equal Opportunity, there were 176,752 California rural poor in 1987, and the rural poverty rate of 19.66 percent was 62 percent higher than the urban rate of 12.11 percent (California Department of Equal Opportunity, 1988:10). The total rural poor are about the same as the number of Californians working in production agriculture (or about 60 percent of the total working in agriculture).[8]

In California there is a strong correlation between resource-industry domination within the economy and poverty. The highest poverty rates are in the counties with the largest agricultural or forestry bases. This is the result of many factors, including the declining ability of agriculture to sustain the economic base of rural communities. In addition, high unemployment in many industries, seasonality, and low wages create conditions under which large families, even with dual wage earners, might not earn enough to be above the poverty line. These conditions appear to be mitigated in communities with a larger number of small family-size farms. MacCannell (1986) has replicated the classic work of Walter Goldschmidt (1978), who argued that rural poverty increases and community vitality decreases as the size of farming operations increase. MacCannell found higher poverty in agricultural areas with large-size farms relying on hired labor, as well as higher incidence of: "agricultural pollution, labor practices that lead to increasing social inequality, restricted opportunity to obtain land and start new enterprise, and the suppression of the development of a local middle class and the businesses and services demanded and supported by such a class" (1986:2). MacCannell reports that in the Westlands Water District poverty levels are three and four times that of the state level, reflecting the pressures toward low wages in large corporate farming operations. Not only is income low, but housing conditions are poor and social services, such as health care, are unavailable. The improvement of income levels, especially at the lowest rungs of the job ladder, is thus critical for dealing with rural poverty.

The most disturbing fact about the present rural poverty problem is that it includes a diverse and growing group of people whose needs are vast. Among these are the homeless. The gap between wages and financial resources available to rural poor and the price of housing has continued to grow. Housing costs are exceeding by a large margin the resources available to low-income groups in rural communities, forcing poor people to live in parks, under bridges, in cars, and wherever they can find a little shelter. A *Los Angeles Times* story reported that "Monterey County officials found 200 farm workers living in hand-dug, hillside caves and plastic lean-tos north of Salinas. In northern San Diego County, workers sleep in holes scooped out of the brush not far from $300,000 homes" (Corwin, 1991). Some rural homeless are taken care of by social service programs that provide beds in shelters or locate inexpensive motel rooms. Single poor men find few rooms in hotels, and in Modesto the two hotels that used to serve this population have both closed. Urban renewal has eliminated hundreds of residential rooms in poor sections of many rural farm towns. Public policy and planning are thus not only unable to respond to the rural homeless problem, but they may inadvertently cause it. Families in distress also have vast needs. Nearly half of all rural children are poor, and among the black population nearly three-quarters are poor. In many cases these children never had a stable family life, and for others divorce imposed hardship. Aid to Families with Dependent Children is by far the largest program supporting poor people, generally single women and their children. Nor are cities the only places where people with various psychological problems are found as outcasts; they are prevalent in many small communities as well. State assistance programs that eliminated centralized care facilities and turned these people back to their communities have generally not met their needs.

The process of bifurcation has perpetuated poverty conditions in generally affluent rural California and has produced two vastly different opportunity structures within rural communities. New growth communities and affluent newcomers are able to take advantage of one set of opportunities, while poor rural communities and the indigenous rural base that remains in growth communities have limited ability to participate in the overall development taking place in modern society.

Policy Agenda for Rural Areas in the United States

The challenges and prospects of the twenty-first century pose a dilemma for California's rural communities. Is it possible to simultaneously assist the traditional rural base in small towns and rural places while accommodating and controlling the exurban growth that is taking place? First, to assist rural areas it is necessary to generate a statewide growth agenda that meets the needs of rural communities for balanced growth rather than for bargain-seeking urban spillover. Second, the major policies to assist rural areas survive against urban encroachment should be rural *development* policies, not restrictions that lead to land preservation at the expense of rural economies. Third, rural development efforts need to be specially targeted to disadvantaged rural residents, including minorities, refugees, children, and other poor groups. Rural Californians have many resources that are highly valued—land and open space, a hardworking labor force, and solid communities which need to be enhanced rather than overrun by urban sprawl.

Statewide Growth Agenda

If state projections are even remotely correct, California will add some 10 million people within the next twenty to twenty-five years, reaching 40 million people by 2005 (California Department of Finance, April 1991). This new growth is the same total as the 10 million population that California had in 1950, a population explosion that covered the first 100 years of statehood, including the boom during and after World War II. During this period all the major cities were laid out, the statewide physical infrastructure was built to support urban growth, and plans were made that charted preeminence in both social and economic spheres. Then, in the 1960s, a bold master plan for public higher education, an extensive network of highways, and a far-reaching water system were designed to serve a growing state. By 1970 the population reached 20 million, but few foresaw the sustained urbanization that has developed in California.

However, the planning process did not continue into the 1970s and

1980s, and the infrastructure has not been maintained, let alone expanded to meet the needs of a much larger population. And there is no design, even vaguely articulated, that is far-reaching enough to look to where the projected 10 million new Californians will locate, what water they will drink and pour on their lawns, where they will work and how they will get there, and what industries will employ them. Planning and local politics have tended to be dominated by fiscal issues and by opposition to unwanted developments, including low priced housing,[9] whereas areas that can easily absorb growth are bypassed. The state has a responsibility to see that growth is not permitted to overrun rural communities and economies, forcing rural people to the fringe. As columnist Dan Walters recently wrote: "It's simply ludicrous that certain areas of the state should be trying to cope with overdevelopment while others suffer from underdevelopment. Left to their own devices, private interests and local governments can not resolve that imbalance. It's the Governor and the Legislature which should be imposing some broader development policy on the state" (Walters, 1989).

The state population will inevitably expand into many rural areas. Some urban density increases will be possible, but present urban areas have nearly covered all buildable land and usually resist higher densities. Consequently, the Central Valley is ripe for expanded growth, and it is already feeling the pressure caused by high growth rates. Most critically, the standoff grows each year between developers with strong interests in developing specific parcels of land and public interests who want to resist every possible encroachment. Thus, each new development becomes highly uncertain; standards for negotiating development are established on a site-by-site basis after extensive and expensive legal maneuvering; and the planning process is buckling under the weight of challenges it was not designed to manage. Although we cannot accurately identify where the future growth will concentrate, state or regional policy has no agenda by which the growth could be channeled into areas which either need or desire it, or where it will do the least harm and the most good. Bifurcation is the inevitable result of poor planning.

Although growth is now a statewide issue, the tools to manage it are all in the hands of county and city officials who have generally failed to consider the statewide and regional implications of their actions. The major force driving planning for growth in California is what Dean Misczynski has called the "fiscalization of land use," by which land use decisions are increasingly "driven by public facility and public financing concerns" (Misczynski, 1986:73). Since the property tax reductions imposed by Proposition 13 in 1978, California has relied on new developers to pay high "development fees" that provide funds for a large part of the needed infrastructure, such as roads, sewers, and schools. These new developments are viewed positively by rural community leaders, who see them as the major source of short-term new financing for needed community projects. However, even these funds are limited in that they must provide for the facilities needed by the new development, not the overall community. Thus, public facilities can be repaired or expanded, but the benefit substantially must go to the newcomers. This leaves the poor areas underfinanced in contrast to the new, richer areas, which have paid for their own facilities. As Misczynski points out, linking poor areas with worn-down and inadequate facilities would be "anathema to commonly held views about 'good' land use and public policy" (Misczynski, 1986:104). Rural planning increasingly favors new development as a tool that will provide community facilities, but unfortunately, the new facilities will be for those in new neighborhoods.

As a consequence of fiscalization, communities compete for growth and new development, especially large developments from which substantial development fees can be extracted. Fragmentation of land use is rampant, and regional influences are not managed. Development interests cite the need for new exurban housing to reduce existing pressures on the state's urban areas, but the growth is uneven. Rural housing is built for commuters because urban areas want the industrial tax base without allowing for adequate housing, especially low-income housing. For example, the Association of Bay Area Governments estimates that by 2010 about 200,000 Bay Area jobs will be created for which there will be no housing supply, forcing commuting from outside the region. Today, for example, commuters from small towns like Patterson, on the east side of the Central Valley, drive for as much as two hours each way to urban jobs so they can live in a single-family detached house with a yard. These newcomers are attracted by lower house costs, but they are isolated from community life, their "latch key children" are unattended after school, and they rarely shop in local stores (Blakely and Bradshaw, 1991).

In this planning environment, growth management has become the major concern aimed at stopping the worst land uses which often displace thousands of acres of prime farm land. However, policy tools are almost exclusively restrictive, and rarely promote an integrated development agenda. The result is a haphazard pattern of development—stopped in one place and ballooning out in another. The problem with this development pattern is that it promotes bifurcation by isolating poorer rural areas from the fiscal benefits of growth, and it saddles growing places with an overlay of outsiders who compete but do not contribute. California's development problem is thus more than just the management of growth; it requires, as a first and higher priority, an enhanced opportunity structure for the indigenous rural population, rather than the accommodation of urban commuters who want a rural bedroom community surrounded by well-watered lawns. The farmworkers and loggers, the small shop owners, and the old industry have little to gain from the newcomers except increased competition for land and community resources.

A dual policy strategy is needed to manage growth so it does not contribute to further bifurcation. First, urban areas must balance their housing resources with job creation, thus reducing the pressure for urban workers to "capture" rural communities and turn them into long-distance commuter suburbs. The second strategy is more important in that economic development resources should be shifted to assist small communities to build their own economic capacity that will utilize the skills and resources of the indigenous population. Newcomers must arrive as partners to those who preceded them and must contribute to their well-being, rather than as exploiters of the human, community, and natural resources of the rural communities in the path of urban growth. The techniques of rural local development are well known but are often forgotten in areas about to be overrun by urban growth.

Rural Development, not Land Preservation

The incentive for residential development in farm and wildland areas is so high primarily because the economic return from the natural resource industries is lower than the return from residential development. Most of the mechanisms in place today to protect farm, forest, or rangeland from conversion have done little to assure that the economic return to the farmer or forest owner is adequate to keep the land in its present use. Thus, the major emphasis needs to be on protecting the rural beneficial use rather than just the land—e.g., *to protect farming rather than farmland.* Land near growing urban areas is a particular problem because it assumes a speculative value far in excess of its productive value. In order for agricultural and forest zoning to work, land owners and purchasers must believe that the land will not be rezoned, thus removing all speculative value. Research has shown that the speculative value of land can be reduced by firm zoning policies (see Nelson, 1987; Doherty, 1984).

Even if land owners are willing to sustain farming or forestry on their lands, the traditional methods of working the land cause conflict with the newcomers when adjacent lands are developed for residential purposes (Healy and Short, 1981). For example, ranchers complain that pet dogs from adjacent housing developments frequently chase or kill their livestock, as well as carry disease. Crops have been vandalized and farm equipment stolen. On the other side, urban residents complain about aesthetic damage from logging operations, tractor noise, pesticide drift, farm odors, and dust—side effects of normal operations which are largely unavoidable. These conflicts between urban uses and rural industrial uses not only produce bad feelings but also constrain the possible economic activities on the land. It is ironic that many of the same people who complain about farming or logging are against any conversion of these lands for more development because of its "open space" quality. This problem means that land desired for agricultural or forestry use needs to be viable for its intended use, not just a museum of the past or an open-space, "park-like" buffer.

A number of strategies can alleviate the tensions between competing pressures on farm and forest land (see Schiffman, 1989). One strategy is to promote "right to farm" legislation that assures the farmer's rights by obtaining acknowledgement from an urban neighbor (as part of the deed) that the farmer has the right to use normal practices. Similar programs assure forest owners that they have the right to harvest trees. To some extent this resolves some legal conflicts between land uses, but right-to-farm legislation fails to resolve differences between neighbors that are often based on poor planning and the failure to allow an adequate buffer. In some more progressive areas, a buffer strip is required whereby the developer either purchases land or obtains use rights to a strip of land on which either reduced-impact farming or minimal farming is allowed. The buffer is sometimes a public green belt used for recreation or other purposes. The major limitation to obtaining buffers is that they are expensive and require substantial planning, but they are effective in maintaining stronger rural industries near urban growth.

More supportive programs go further toward overcoming the pressures toward bifurcation than just assuring that farmers and timber owners can go about their normal business. Property taxes based on the agricultural value rather than the speculative value of the land help reduce some of the financial constraints. For example, in California the Williamson Act has given farmers reduced taxes in most rural counties, and timber owners can benefit from Timber Production Zones where taxes are reduced until harvest. The most farsighted programs actually mobilize urban interests to promote the well-being of the farm and lumber opportunities nearby so that the land has productive value. Various forms of low-cost or nonfinancial assistance to farmers in the rural urban interface may increase the viability of these operations.

For example, in California cooperative purchasing and marketing ventures have started with Farmers' Markets that provide direct sales and increased income. Regional produce festivals (e.g., Gilroy's Garlic Festival and Patterson's Apricot Days) give producers exposure and income, leading to better contracts. Several areas have used "buy local" campaigns and have stocked grocery stores with local produce. Even in lumber areas, local furniture manufacturing and local marketing of wood can be effective in generating a higher-value-added product. Meeting local markets also means producing specialty crops that can be sold to restaurants and packers, such as baby salad greens and fresh vegetables. Many of these specialty products can be successfully exported worldwide, as has happened with many California fruits and vegetables. The key to improved marketing is usually local initiative and regional cooperation.

Higher-value-added production and better marketing require additional technical assistance and managerial skills. Some of the areas of technical assistance that are promising include value-added, on-farm processing; new industrial crops such as guayule (rubber), kenaf (pulp-fiber), and jojoba (oils); integrated poultry, fish, and energy production; horticulture and flowers; hydroponics; and of course, integrated pest management and organic farming methods. These practices lead to both high-value-added and sustainable agriculture that can operate more successfully near urban areas.

Both owners and field supervisors will also require training and information to be able to compete with new products and technology in markets beset by higher stakes and more uncertainty. The expertise required can be provided by many sources, including the state cooperative extension programs. Most extension advisors, however, fail to understand the particular challenges and needs of producers closest to urban areas. They also need to work with rural development specialists to develop a program that will assist people who most need new technological and managerial skills. Seed and chemical suppliers, consultants, and nonprofit organizations will supplement the traditional extension role.

In sum, rural areas often spend considerable effort to attract outsiders to their community without developing their existing economic base. As a result, bifurcation is extended rather than countered. In California improved local rural communities have usually resulted when community leaders have chosen to focus on the existing capacity of their communities, have developed educational and assistance programs, and have supported collaborative programs. By contrast, where the existing leadership has not developed the existing capacity, the gap has grown between urban and rural well-being.

Development Assistance Targeted to the Rural Poor

Since the poor, and especially the large ethnic minority population, constitute such a large presence in rural California, any effort to counter bifurcation needs to direct development assistance primarily toward disadvantaged groups in such a way that the assistance does not, in fact, stimulate a separate community or economy.

When left on their own, rural communities and the rural interests in growing small towns often lack the capacity to set or to be part of the development agenda. Although many are aware of the prevalence of rural deprivation in terms of income, jobs, social programs, and community control, dominance and control of economic and policy dynamics by urban organizations or interests leads to ineffective efforts for rural development. Some type of intervention is usually necessary for rural interests to develop in competition with this urban domination. Those using the basic community development model in rural areas have responded to this situation by providing both leadership development and economic development assistance (see Christenson and Robinson, 1989). A strategy to assist rural areas does not necessarily entail substantial infusions of money, but it should selectively target (a) less advantaged, stagnating rural communities that have been bypassed by growth and modernization, and (b) the less advantaged social groups within all rural communities that need particular assistance (Bradshaw, 1990).

Stagnating communities. Rural communities that are very small; have limited budgets; have large numbers of poor, minority, or unskilled workers; are facing declining industries and plant closures; and are not very geographically attractive need special assistance in contrast to communities that are in the path of growth. California's counties are too large to be effective targets for development assistance, since in even the well-off counties there are many depressed rural communities. Major development assistance must not be diverted to communities that will share in the inevitable growth taking place in California. Within rural communities the pattern of local development must involve the joint efforts to bring in outside resources and to develop indigenous leadership as well as the capacity to articulate the community interests so that development actually benefits the community first.

Rural programs too often are small versions of urban programs not specially suited to rural needs. Because of the low density and small scale of rural efforts, programs often fail when they are not specially attentive to rural needs. Urban administrative rules often result in high costs for rural programs. For example, rural hospitals, like all hospitals, are required to have a separate maternity delivery room not used for other operations. These rooms are rarely used in rural hospitals since most births now take place in "alternative birthing rooms," and there are fewer births due to demographic patterns. These rooms should be made into multipurpose surgical units in rural hospitals, improving the economic viability of the hospital (Bradshaw, 1987).

Hospitals, community colleges, public utilites, and to some extent the various service-providing units in local government have a special role in rural economic development that goes beyond their primary mission. These organizations are the largest untapped reservoirs of rural talent for development, and their organizational structure and staff both should be utilized for local economic development leadership. Community colleges, for example, have shown a significant interest in taking a leadership role in economic development that goes beyond simply offering courses to willing 19-year-old students. In the most progressive programs, rural colleges have been leaders in helping the community develop an economic development strategy, articulating ways the community can participate in generating economic opportunities, training leaders, establishing small business centers, providing technical assistance to existing businesses, and even helping in the creation of new businesses. These functions can be carried out by any major rural institution because they have the skills and organizational capacity to be effective; the missing ingredient is usually leadership (see Myers, Peterson, and Bradshaw, 1987).

Inadequate infrastructure for industrial development is a pervasive problem in stagnating rural communities. The construction of industrial parks is one of the most common efforts to deal with the infrastructure problem because industrial developers generally believe that developed industrial parks are necessary to attract new industry and jobs. Rural industrial parks were built throughout California with federal economic development grants in the 1970s, but Belzer and Kroll (1986) reported that in the forest region about 90 percent of the parks still have no major tenants. In fact, research throughout the country has shown that rural industrial parks generally fail to attract tenants and are an ineffective rural infrastructure program (Blakely and Bradshaw, 1982).

Targeted infrastructure programs that repond to the needs of existing or prospective industry, however, can help stagnating rural communities. California adopted a Rural Renaissance program in 1986 that included at least $30 million in loans and grants for what became known as the Rural Economic Development Infrastructure Program (REDIP). Unlike grant money that went to build rural infrastructure that may never be used, the REDIP loans and grants are for public works projects targeted to a specific business on a specific site. Projects targeted in this way have a much greater chance of benefiting rural communities compared to the industrial park approach, because they are linked to businesses that have already negotiated to expand or locate in the rural community. The Department of Commerce, which administers the REDIP program, reports that it has committed a substantial proportion of the money and that there are many good projects involved that deserve funding. But with recent state budget problems, new funding for Rural Renaissance projects has been eliminated.

There is increasing evidence that a major targeted rural development strategy is to secure the location of public or private facilities that are unwanted in urban areas, such as prisons, toxic waste disposal or combustion plants, and heavily polluting or dangerous factories. These facilities, which are not popular near large cities, can provide thousands of jobs in rural communities. A large prison has been a major economic benefit to Del Norte County in California, for example, leading to major population growth due to prisoners, their families, and the staff working at the prison. Rural communities now compete actively for these facilities. Small communities have also responded positively to waste disposal plants, although they often involve serious environmental problems that were not adequately understood or reviewed by the community prior to their location. A cogeneration incinerator and a tire disposal facility in Stanislaus County have both been the subject of continuing controversy. These facilities must be carefully evaluated, and rural communities need to have their interests protected through state or regional assistance.

In brief, the key to successful rural community assistance is to focus on how to make existing rural institutions and businesses more effective and efficient; how to support industries that are in the community and need better infrastructure; and how to gain the maximum local benefit from new plants, public facilities, and employment opportunities. These community level programs need to be accompanied by programs aimed at disadvantaged persons within rich or poor communities.

Disadvantaged rural populations. An effective rural development strategy needs to be directed to the rural poor to provide particular assistance to those who are forgotten as concerns over growth and new industry overshadow the people who lack the connections, resources, and skills to participate in it. To a large extent the problems of minority populations, refugees, displaced farmworkers, the sick and elderly, and children living in poverty are problems that must be solved at a national level by directing more of the resources of society to their problems. Moreover, even when these programs are available in rural areas they are spread very thin. Today, in the aftermath of the Los Angeles riots, increased attention to the problems of poverty and race has taken on an urban orientation, but rural conditions remain markedly worse in spite of all the attention to the urban disorder. There remains much that can be done in rural communities, however, to assist those who need it the most.

Jobs and increased employment are the most pressing needs in rural communities. To the extent that economic development programs are oriented toward the needs of the rural poor, gains can be expected. For example, a barrier to more stable farm employment for full-time farm workers is better information on where jobs are available and what skills are needed. In the past this has largely been an informal process dominated by a few labor contractors, and alternatives have been blocked by the availability of information in accessible language. However, a newsletter to major farm worker organizations in California has provided a Spanish-language alternative, sent by fax to a hundred or more community organizations where farmworkers can get the information they need.

In Merced an innovative job creation program has been initiated to help Hmong refugees start their own business. The County Office of Economic and Strategic Development started a program for Hmong persons to be trained in business skills, to prepare a business plan, and to get funding to start their own businesses. The program is still in its early phase, but two groups have already graduated from a multi-language training program; they prepared plans for businesses, and at least four new businesses are being started with some program-arranged financing. Within this community the new businesses are providing a model of hope; other Merced County groups have found the model so appealing that they have requested training and business-creation programs as well.

Farm labor is a particularly important target group in California. Often the victims of poor management and inadequate living conditions, California's farm workers are being pushed further and further from the mainstream of California community life. As in the example at the beginning of this paper of the tensions faced by farmworkers in

Watsonville, housing, health, and low income from part-year work are major problems. Today, many of the improvements of the last two decades are being reversed since a very large surplus of labor seems to be available, making innovative farm worker programs unnecessary from the farmers' point of view (Rosenberg et al., 1990). Large parts of the state's farm work needs are met by casual employment in spite of successful testing of improved farm labor practices. Mamer and Randall list five types of programs that can stabilize and increase farm worker income:

1. Strengthening employer-employee ties through systematic call-back agreements, benefits packages, and other incentives.
2. Minimum employment guarantees that were required under the Bracero Program, terminated in 1964, in which employment was guaranteed for a certain percent of the season.
3. Off-season employment for seasonal farm workers in other types of work. However, there are very few instances in which employers or employee groups have been successful in structuring off-season jobs.
4. Mechanization and crew stabilization in which machinery utilization has led to longer employment for a smaller crew, such as in cotton.
5. Miscellaneous approaches such as farm worker cooperatives (Mamer and Randall, 1991:54).

In farm work, as in other rural industries, the economic development problems are so substantial that a single-pronged approach is not viable. Several key aspects to a successful program would include as a first step the delivery of services and training in a culturally appropriate way; e.g., in a decentralized location and with translation if the recipient does not speak English. Second, the delivery of services with a long-term aproach to self-sufficiency, which usually means training and skill development. Third, linking the skills of workers to meaningful employment opportunities which often need to be created with public assistance. Finally, supporting the growth of successful rural programs and businesses, which are generally more beneficial than transplated urban programs.

There is no quick solution to the challenge of meeting the needs of California's rural poor. Given the opportunities of growth in the state, it is easier to focus on those who have more urban connections and capacity, forgetting the least advantaged. However, there is reason to hope that long-term solutions can be found in generating employment opportunities by using the local development techniques that have been successful in the past.

The bifurcation of California's rural communities means that the future will involve both supporting the sectors linked to the advanced industrial society and developing the sectors lacking access to the opportunities and resources of modern society. Because of the growth of the first, which is inherently attractive and positive, the plight of the latter is often forgotten because it is a "problem." However, the hope of California's forgotten communities lies in policies that integrate the underdeveloped sector with the growing one through targeted projects that enrich both human resources and organizational access of less-advantaged people. Thus, in spite of bifurcation, development strategies can benefit both the newcomers with their network of urban resources, and the rural people, who inherited the rural environment.

Notes

Research for this paper was supported by the University of California, Division of Agriculture and Natural Resources, and the Central Valley Project of the Agricultural Issues Center, University of California at Davis.

1. Data for 1979–1988 (Center for the Continuing Study of the California Economy, 1988:5).

2. U.S. Immigration and Naturalization Service data; see Fay and Fay, 1990:40.

3. Data are per capita personal income by county, 1989, calculated from *Survey of Current Business*, April 1991:41.

4. For example, between 1980–1990 all counties had an increase in population, and only four cities in nonmetropolitan counties showed decline (1990 U.S. Bureau of the Census).

5. In this analysis counties will be classified not by their current status as metropolitan statistical areas, but by their long-term role as rural or minor metropolitan areas. For example, Butte County was made a Standard Metropolitan Statistical Area (SMSA) after the 1980 census; the largest city is Chico, which now has 40,000 persons, but unincorporated areas include over two-thirds of the county population. In spite of the well-established urban core, most of the county is still rural, and we have considered it as such. Even this does not solve all data problems; for example, Fresno County is a SMSA dominated by the city of Fresno with 350,000 persons, but it also is the nation's largest agricultural county and has 160,000 persons living in unincorporated areas. This rural population in an urban county is a larger part of California's rural landscape than the total population of many rural counties without a large city.

6. Growth control measures are generally more intensively used in the urban fringe areas (see Bradshaw, Willoughby, and Blakely, 1991).

7. Data provided by Karen Prentiss, Office of Economic and Strategic

Development, Merced County, and Lao Family Community, Inc., from "Profiles of the Highland Lao Communities in the United States," U.S. Department of Health and Human Services, November 1988.

8. This comparison shows that the California rural poor population represents a large loss in human resources, not that the poor should work in agriculture.

9. Edward Blakely made this point in a speech to the Agricultural Issues Center, University of California at Davis, 1990. Many expressed concern that planning is dominated by strategies referred to as "NIMBYism" ("Not In My Back Yard"), and government has been largely paralyzed by the task of dealing with such changes.

References

American Farmland Trust. 1989. *Risks, Challenges and Opportunities: Agriculture, Resources, and Growth in a Changing Central Valley.* San Francisco: American Farmland Trust.

Bell, Charles G., and Charles M. Price. 1984. *California Government Today.* Homewood; Ill.: Dorsey Press.

Belzer, Dena, and Cynthia Kroll. 1986. *New Jobs for the Timber Region: Economic Diversification for Northern California.* Berkeley: Institute of Governmental Studies, University of California.

Birch, David. 1987. *Job Creation in America: How Our Smallest Companies Put the Most People to Work.* New York: Free Press.

Blakely, Edward J. 1989. *Planning for Local Economic Development.* Newbury Park, Calif.: Sage.

———. 1991. "The Emerging Global Economy and Rural Communities: A New Perspective." Pp. 59–71 in Kenneth E. Pigg (ed.), *The Future of Rural America: Anticipating Policies for Constructive Change,* Boulder, Colo.: Westview Press.

Blakely, Edward J., and Ted K. Bradshaw. 1982. *New Challenges for Rural Economic Development.* Working Paper 400. Berkeley: University of California, Institute of Urban and Regional Development.

———. 1991. "Room for Whom?" Pp. 1–11 in Harold O. Carter and Julie Spezia (eds.), *People Pressures: California's Central Valley.* Davis: University of California, Agricultural Issues Center.

Bouvier, Leon F., and Philip Martin. 1985. "Population Change and California's Future." Washington, D.C.: Population Reference Bureau.

Bradshaw, Ted K. 1976. "New Issues for California: The World's Most Advanced Industrial Society." *Public Affairs Report* 17:1–8.

———. 1987. "Trends in Rural Economic Development," *California Hospitals* (July–August):12–13.

———. 1990. "The Elusiveness of Rural Development Theory and Policy: Domestic and Third World Perspectives Joined." *Sociological Practice* 8: 58–71.

Bradshaw, Ted K., and Edward J. Blakely. 1979. *Rural Communities in Advanced Industrial Society: Development and Developers.* New York: Praeger.

———. 1981. *Resources of Recent Migrants for Economic Development*. Davis: University of California. Division of Agriculture.

———. 1982. "The Changing Nature of Rural America." Pp. 3–17 in William P. Browne and Don F. Hadwiger (eds.), *Rural Policy Problems: Changing Dimensions*. Lexington, Mass.: Lexington Books.

———. 1988. "Unanticipated Consequences of Government Programs on Rural Economic Development." Pp. 235–54 in David L. Brown, J. Norman Reid, Herman Bluestone, David A. McGranahan, and Sara M. Mazie (eds.), *Rural Economic Development in the 1980's: Prospects for the Future*. Rural Development Report no. 69. Washington, D.C.: Economic Research Service, U.S. Department of Agriculture.

Bradshaw, Ted K., and Kelvin W. Willoughby. 1989. "Trends in Changing Employment Patterns in the Central Valley." *Central Valley Briefs*, Davis: University of California. Agricultural Issues Center.

California Department of Economic Opportunity, Advisory Commission. 1989. "California's Unfinished Battle: The War on Poverty." Sacramento: California Department of Economic Opportunity.

California Department of Finance. 1990. *California Statistical Abstract*. Sacramento: California Department of Finance.

California Department of Finance, Demographic Research Unit. 1988. "Projected Total Population for California by Race/Ethnicity, July 1, 1970 to July 1, 2020." Report 88-P4. Sacramento, February.

———. 1991. "Interim Population Projections for California State and Counties, 1990–2005." Report 91 P-1. Sacramento, April.

———. 1991. "Population Estimates for California Cities and Counties, January 1, 1990 and January 1, 1991." Report 91 E-1. Sacramento, May.

California Department of Forestry, Forest and Range Resources Assessment Program. 1989. *California's Forests and Rangelands: Growing Conflict over Changing Uses*. Sacramento: California Department of Forestry, Forest and Range Resources Assessment Program.

California Employment Development Department. 1972. *California Employment and Payrolls*. October–December 1972. Report 127. Sacramento: California Employment Development Department.

———. 1986. *California Employment and Payrolls*. Sacramento: California Employment Development Department.

California. Governor. 1991. *Economic Report of the Governor*. Sacramento.

Carter, Harold O., and Carole F. Nuckton, (eds.). 1990. *California's Central Valley—Confluence of Change*. Davis: University of California. Agricultural Issues Center.

Center for the Continuing Study of the California Economy. 1988. *California Economic Growth*. Palo Alto, Calif.: Center for the Continuing Study of the California Economy.

Christenson, James A., and Jerry W. Robinson, Jr. 1989. *Community Development in Perspective*. Ames: Iowa State University Press.

Corwin, Miles. 1991. "The Grapes of Wrath Revisited." *Los Angeles Times*, 29 September:1.

Doherty, J. C. 1984. *Growth and Growth Management in Countrified Cities*. Alexandria Va.: Vert Milon Press.

Fay, James S., and Stephanie W. Fay, (eds.). 1990. *California Almanac*. 4th ed. Santa Barbara, Calif.: Pacific Data Resources.

Ferriss, Susan, and Ricardo Sandoval. 1991. "Lowering the Barriers." *San Francisco Examiner*, 22 December: E-1.

Furukana, Arleen. 1991. "State and Local Government Involvement in Industrial Development: A Case Study Kagome U.S.A." Berkeley: University of California, Department of City and Regional Planning.

Goldschmidt, Walter. 1978. *As You Sow.* Glencoe, Ill.: Free Press, 1947; Montclair, N.J.: Allanheld, Osmun, 1978.

Healy, Robert G., and James L. Short. 1981. *The Market for Rural Land: Trends, Issues, Policies.* Washington, D.C.: Conservation Foundation.

MacCannell, Dean. 1986. "Agribusiness and the Small Community." P. 2 in *Technology, Public Policy, and the Changing Structure of American Agriculture: Background Papers*, vol. 2. Washington, D.C.: Office of Technology Assessment.

Mamer, John, and Joan Randall. 1991. "Farm Employment in the Central Valley: Everything Old Is New Again," Pp. 47–63 in Harold O. Carter and Carole F. Nuckton (eds.), *People Pressures: California's Central Valley.* Davis: University of California. Agricultural Issues Center.

McWilliams, Carey. [1949] 1976. *California: The Great Exception.* Reprint. Santa Barbara, Calif.: Peregrine Smith.

Misczynski, Dean J. 1986. "The Fiscalization of Land Use." Pp. 73–106 in John J. Kirlin and Donald R. Winkler (eds.), *California Policy Choices*, vol. 3. Los Angeles: University of Southern California, School of Public Administration.

Moriarty, Barry. 1980. *Industrial Location and Community Development.* Chapel Hill: University of North Carolina Press.

Myers, Bill, Gary Peterson, and Ted Bradshaw. 1987. "Community Colleges Are Job Creation Vehicles in Small Towns." *Small Town* 17(6):26–28.

Nelson, Arthur C. 1987. "How Regional Planning Influences Rural Land Values." Pp. 263–76 in William Lockeretz (ed.), *Sustaining Agriculture near Cities.* Ankeny, Iowa: Soil and Water Conservation Society.

Parker, Edwin B., Heather E. Hudson, Don A. Dillman, and Andrew D. Roscoe. 1989. *Rural America in the Information Age: Telecommunications Policy for Rural Development.* Lanham, Md.: University Press of America.

Rochin, Refugio I., and Monica Castillo. 1990. "Latinos and Rural Colonias of California." Paper presented at the meeting of the National Association of Chicano Studies, University of California, Davis.

Rosenberg, Howard R., Roger E. Garrett, Ronald E. Voss, and David L. Mitchell. 1990. "Labor and Competitive Agricultural Technology in 2010." Pp. 27–50 in Harold O. Carter and Carole F. Nuckton (eds.), *Agriculture in California: On the Brink of a New Millennium.* Davis: University of California. Agricultural Issues Center.

Schiffman, Irving. 1989. *Alternative Techniques for Managing Growth.* Berkeley: University of California. Institute of Governmental Studies Press.

Sokolow, Alvin D. 1991. "County-City Competition for Land and Taxes: State Rules and Local Strategies in California's Central Valley." Paper presented to the meeting of the American Political Science Association, Washington, D.C.

Speizer, Irwin. 1985. "The Hmong Take Root." *Planning* (September):12–13.

Storper, Michael, and Richard Walker. 1989. *The Capitalist Imperative.* New York: Basil Blackwell.

U.S. Bureau of the Census. 1980. *Census of Population.*
———. 1990. *Census of Population.*
———. Population Estimates Branch. 1991. "1990 CPH-L-79 Population and Housing Units by Urban and Rural." Memorandum, 30 September 1991.
Walters, Dan. 1989. "The Plight of 'The Other California.'" *Oakland Tribune,* 15 November.

11 | Forgotten Places Redux
William W. Falk and Thomas A. Lyson

WHEN WE FIRST THOUGHT of putting together a book dealing with America's lagging rural regions, it was with the hope that our effort would bring attention to parts of the United States that are largely forgotten. The chapters in the book provide vivid testimony to the aspiration we had. Indeed, every place discussed—from the rural Northeast to the timber region in the Northwest—is out of the mainstream of everyday life in America. These places are much like the areas covered in William Least-Heat Moon's (1982) book *Blue Highways*—interesting side trips but hardly major stops for most Americans.

Here we wish to focus again on the largely forgotten quality of these areas in the theoretical context of spatial inequalities. Space itself is a largely forgotten or overlooked dimension to life in the United States. We need to reconsider this oversight, not only by social science researchers but by policymakers as well. At a time when expressions such as "global economy," "global politics," and "global community" are in vogue, it seems particularly relevant to discuss the role that space plays in our everyday lives.

Uneven Development and the Lack of Opportunity

It is clear the areas examined in this book truly are what the economist Wilbur Thompson (1965) has called "economic backwaters," out of the economic mainstream of American life. Although it could be argued that this is true of nearly all rural areas, we would argue that it is particularly true of the areas discussed here.

The pristine, pastoral, bucolic qualities of the rural Northeast serve to mask the deep economic division there. In the *Beans of Egypt, Maine,* Carolyn Chute (1985) showed through fiction that yes, even Maine has poverty and that those living in it are little different from those living under similar conditions elsewhere in the country. Of course, no part of the United States has been more romanticized and depleted in fictional accounts than the South. Whether going with the wind (Mitchell, 1961), migrating (Steinbeck, 1939; Morris, 1970), living a life in decay and change (Welty, 1946; Percy, 1971), or focusing on the plight of rural blacks who move to urban areas (Baldwin, 1953; Ellison,

1952; Wright, 1945), the themes have been similar—social change bringing foreign ideas and painful adjustments to the lives of southern folk, many or all of whom were living in poverty. Indeed, the "blue grass," "country," and "blues" music forms in our culture are rooted in the everyday experiences of rural people in general, and southern people in particular—and social change (as evinced by marital discord, job loss, and so on) is part of the fabric that makes up these music forms. The fictional or biographical accounts of the Northeast and the South are paralleled by works focusing on Appalachia (Caudil, 1963), the Ozarks (Minick, 1975), the Southwest (McMurtry, 1979), California (Steinbeck, 1939), and the Northwest (Kesey, 1965; Robbins, 1990). Again, what is common to many of these works is their focus on the downtrodden, those somehow left out of a fair share of the "good life."

What we see in these fictional accounts is a kind of sociology brought to life—actors whose everyday lives are in some ways circumscribed and delimited by the conditions within which they find themselves. A large, amorphous group of people, crossing race, ethnic, and geographic lines, share a lack of skills and opportunities.

The residents of the rural regions profiled here represent an entire stratum of society, a class, which is to some degree trapped (see Duncan, 1992). This is not to say that this class is helpless, or that it represents a distinct culture of poverty, or that it cannot escape its confines. It is to say, however, that people in this stratum live in a kind of economic twilight zone. This class is the most negatively affected by economic downturns and the least positively affected by economic upturns. In good times or bad, it is *sui generis*, a class unto itself. It lacks economic, political, and social power. It can, on occasion, be mobilized, but such mobilization is unusual and episodic only. In general, it is this group which Marx had in mind when he referred to "a large reserve army of the unemployed." As "a large reserve," it is the residual group we have discussed; its largely detrimental and widely perceived negative qualities bind it together. This group takes different forms in different places but its one common element is a lack of full participation in economic life. Casualties of uneven development, "the reserve" often become "the poor."

Given these conditions, we can easily see the relationship between an area's lack of development and the presence there of rural poverty. The two dimensions go hand-in-glove. After all, uneven development is really a characterization of some geographical feature: whether within a neighborhood, a town, a city, a county, a state, a region, a nation, or the world, not all areas are economic equals. And any measures of this are driven by curiosity about how unequal or uneven these areas are. Thus, by whatever measure (education, income, births, deaths, etc.), the intent is the same: to know how alike any two or more areas are.

What our contributors have repeatedly shown is that by virtually all measures, the quality of life and standard of living in many rural areas of the United States lag behind those in the highly urbanized parts of the nation. We found precisely this when examining the urban south (see Falk and Lyson, 1988; Lyson, 1989); prosperity characterizing one (urban) place is quickly found to be absent in another (rural) place. Indeed, as Lyson (1989) has shown, the gap between the prosperous and poor parts of the South actually widened in the 1980s. Thus, the degree of "unevenness" which exists may be getting larger not smaller.

Theory In, Theory Out

The theoretical work in social science that deals with uneven development is driven mostly by a set of competing paradigms, ranging from modernization theory to dependency theory to world systems theory. Some variation on each of these themes is found in the chapters of this book.

Modernization theory has become passé in many circles because of its largely conservative economic premise that the surest way for an area to prosper economically is to emulate more developed areas by having the same kinds of economic activities and the same kinds of social institutions (to include, of course, capitalism) that characterize developed areas. In recent years, this position has been widely rejected by many scholars, in favor of newer, alternative paradigms. Key among these are two: dependency theory and world-systems theory.

Dependency theory views uneven development as a reflection of the contradictions of capitalism. Capitalists are always seeking ways to create surplus value. One way they do this is by exploiting undervalued factor costs (i.e., labor, land, etc.) in less developed, "peripheral" regions of the world. Regional economic inequality, then, is a built-in and persistent structural feature of the world economic order as "core" economic centers dominate less-developed peripheral regions. According to dependency theory, lagging and exploited regions have little opportunity to advance to core status because they lack the capital resources to do so.

World-systems theory differs from dependency theory by taking a more historical approach to uneven development. It focuses on the historical dynamics of the evolving world economic system and its implications for nation states. It, too, takes as fundamental that capitalists always act in ways to maximize profits. Consequently, they must always look for economic advantage wherever it can be found. This inevitably leads to their awareness of and emphasis on the mobility of capital—capital as unrestricted to any place or investment. In a lawlike way, they seek maximum return, ignoring where or in what they have invested. Thus, of necessity, as capital is moved around, it creates some pockets of wealth (which even a conservative economist like Olson [1982] admits are transitory) and some pockets of poverty. This, unfortunately, is life in the marketplace where, for every winner, there must be at least one loser.

The dependency and world-systems models help us to better understand the unevenness of development which has been described in this book. Local and regional economies in the Northeast were financially crippled by the flight of industry to the rural South in the early part of this century. Subsequently (especially in the 1980s), industry started to look overseas where it could exploit the same qualities it had found in the South years earlier. In an ironic twist, the South was suddenly being beaten at its own game: historically cheap land, labor, and taxes were even cheaper overseas, and industry accordingly went there.

We can extend this argument and analysis to the other areas covered in our book. In every case, large geographic areas have become economically vulnerable as the rules of the economic game have changed in a global economy. Throughout this book, these "large geographic areas" are often referred to as *regions*, a concept which bridges many terms unique to social science disciplines and, to some degree, (we believe) helps to integrate them.

The Transcending Nature of Region

Region was made part of the sociological vocabulary by two men— Howard Odum (1936) and Rupert Vance (1932). Working separately but as intellectual colleagues and neighbors (Odum at the University of North Carolina at Chapel Hill; Vance at Duke University), both men argued that region could be used as a conceptual and analytical tool for understanding the social and economic organization of large geographic areas. In sociology's pursuit for normativeness, the region concept helped to focus attention on commonality across political borders. Thus sociologists obfuscated the borders of towns, cities, and counties with region to determine how these smaller areas coalesced into larger ones.

For Odum and Vance, as for other human ecologists who followed in their tradition, certain common traits had to be found for a region to exist—such as contiguity, demographic characteristics, economic bases, natural resources, and geographic characteristics. Although regional analyses were somewhat popular in sociology for several decades, the regional approach had virtually disappeared by the late 1960s (see Reed and Singal, 1982).

Recently, however, a regional approach seems to be regaining popularity. This seems especially true among some geographers (for whom region remained an important concept), but also among certain political economists. Foremost among them is Ann Markusen. Markusen has defined region in this way: "[An] historically evolved, contiguous territorial society that possess a physical environment, a socioeconomic, political, and cultural milieu, and a spatial structure distinct from other regions and major territorial units" (1987:17). We are attracted to Markusen's definition in part because it is more wholistic than other, earlier definitions. Too, because of its political economic theoretical grounding, it is sensitive to issues of history, culture, and politics. Again, these things point to its more inclusive orientation.

Markusen's conception of region fits nicely with every chapter in this book, since all of the forgotten places discussed share similar circumstances—as smaller, less advantaged places located in the context of a much larger, more advantaged place (i.e., the United States). It takes little imagination to use Markusen's concept with dependency and world-systems theory. When we do this, the places included in our book become akin to colonies; they serve at the pleasure of places located elsewhere and are dependent upon them. Thus, we have core-and-periphery relations between regions, with some regions (for us, rural areas of the United States) inevitably lagging behind *and*, importantly, dependent upon others (large urban areas of the United States).

Regional Planning and Industrial Policy

It is the characteristics common to regions that allow for and facilitate planning. Although planning may occur at the most local level (down to and including individual streets within neighborhoods), in general, an abstract plan of some kind must be drawn up. Such a plan is akin to a cognitive map, a grid on which the parts to a place are arranged and configured—housing here, schools there, industry here, hospitals there, and so on. Indeed, knowing the kinds of services that are necessary for populations to exist has always been the forte of planners who wished to optimize locational and development strategies as much as possible. But, as the chapters in this book have shown, huge imbalances in population and in needs exist. The distribution between workers and jobs is not always a perfect one. Jobs do not always go where the people are, nor do people necessarily go where the jobs are.

In America, lacking an industrial policy, the movement of people and jobs has always been based on free-market principles, laissez-faire capitalism. The rules for starting, developing, and moving businesses have always had a certain fluidity, mostly to favor those investing private capital. Thus, we have witnessed in this century huge migration streams of industry from the North to the South, and more recently from the South (and elsewhere in the United States) to overseas. This is consistent with our history and commitment to laissez-faire principles. In effect, we subscribe to the principle of letting capital go where it may be maximized; but this is very narrowly determined as profits, pure and simple. Thus, the shoe industry in the Northeast moved overseas; when the steel industry declined and eventually became almost moribund (because reinvestment in it would have cost too much), it, too, went overseas; the textiles industry moved from the Northeast to the South, and more recently many textiles plants have joined the overseas exodus.

What is important for us is that the industrial actions and policies adopted by industrialists (albeit with some influence or, as industrialists would say, "interference" from the federal government) become a de facto industrial policy for the country as a whole. Storper and Walker (1989) refer to these kinds of decisions as "windows of locational opportunity." If these are primarily profit-driven and -determined decisions, then regions of the country will inevitably be characterized by radical differences in development. And, indeed, Storper and Walker demonstrate these to be the consequences of what they call "the capitalist imperative."[1]

Unlike the United States, all other industrialized countries actually have a coherent industrial policy. Such a policy is meant to help guide industrial development—encouraging certain actions at some times, while discouraging others but always mindful of the need to balance among people, economic opportunities, and job creation. For example, Japan helps industries to phase out products or services for which markets no longer exist and to develop new products or services to replace them. This helps to support business and, importantly, provides a steadier, more predictable source of employment than is found in the United States. All of the European countries have similar practices and policies.

As we have shown elsewhere, the debate about industrial policy in the United States decidedly favors free-market principles (see Falk and Lyson, 1991)—thus barring a more democratically determined industrial policy. At the same time, not unexpectedly, it would be fair to say (as we have also shown) that conservative economists favor prevailing practice, whereas more liberal economists do not. Moreover, U.S. economists stand largely in opposition to their counterparts in Europe and elsewhere overseas (reviewed in Falk and Lyson, 1991).

The net effect to the de facto industrial policy approach found in the United States is to exacerbate regional differences—to have some highly successful places (the bicoastal economy, the most urban parts of the Midwest, South, and Southwest) and other economically lagging places (nearly everywhere else including virtually all rural areas). The sharp interregional differences point to the difficulty of any form of social planning. Again, unlike that of most other countries, much of our planning consists of reacting to events beyond our control rather than of dealing with consequences of our own making—hence the ad hoc quality of planning. The dominant ethos in American political culture is truly the Jeffersonian formulation, "that government which governs least governs best." It is only on selective issues that most Americans wish to see this approach abandoned. And thus far, there has been little movement for a more planned economy (the central requisite of an industrial policy).

Lacking planning, we are left with "forgotten places." They remain forgotten because they are simply not perceived as very central to the lives of people in other regions. Even during the height of the "farm crisis" in the early 1980s, most Americans remained aloof from and apathetic to the everyday problems of farmers (see Lyson, 1987). Phrased differently, farmers, living in places that are mostly forgotten, were themselves largely forgotten, no matter how serious their plight. Of course, it was our sense of this that led to this book, and the authors of the various chapters have aptly demonstrated how this plays itself out in different regions of the country.

Outer Spaces, Inner Circles

In William Domhoff's (1971) powerful book, *The Higher Circles*, he shows how the most important decisions about governing America

264 | WILLIAM W. FALK & THOMAS A. LYSON

(whether politically or economically) are made by a relatively few actors located largely on the East Coast (government in Washington, finance in New York). Their decisions help to perpetuate certain class relations in American society. If we abandon the Marxian class division between owners and workers and substitute instead a distinction between those with and without power, then we have a summary of Domhoff's view. This serves to keep some in power, others out of it. In this way, the truly crucial decisions about political and economic life can be controlled by small interest groups.

This process helps to further explain the forgotten quality of the areas we have covered in this book. As a rule, rural areas are not only out of the economic mainstream, but they are also out of the political mainstream. They are more *affected by* than *influential upon* important political decisions at the national level. And even when decisions are of direct importance to many rural residents (such as the recent case in Oregon in which it was decided to "save the owl" rather than to cut timber), local politicians appear to be largely impotent at influencing outcomes. Again, the debate takes on a national, translocal quality, even though it is local people and a local industry at stake. In the popular, long-lasting television series, "Star Trek," characters are occasionally "beamed" into another dimension. It takes a kind of decomposing/recomposing for them to leave one place and get to another. It would not be overstretching to suggest that a similar experience would be necessary for most Americans and for most politicians at the federal level to get in touch with the forgotten places we have included in this book. Whether the rural Northeast or the rural Northwest, the Black Belt South or the Rio Grande Valley of Texas, these places exist much like outer space. They are totally alien to most Americans and rarely, if ever, on their minds. That these rural areas languish and lag behind most urban places of the country is not defined by most people as a problem. Or, as the sociologist C. Wright Mills might have said, "these are private troubles, not public problems." Alternately, they are the province of the victims not the victimizers.

The "rational choice" approach to "private troubles" favored by most Americans places responsibility for individual action on the individual: One may choose to do or not to do certain things. And one of these things is to move to where jobs may be more plentiful, hence more likely to be found. This is, in effect, our population policy. "Go West, young man" is more than just Horace Greeley's exhortation to search for work; it is a type of national credo for us, since we are always searching and vigilant for opportunity wherever it might be found. But as planning, as industrial policy, as a way of dealing with the imbalance between one region and another, it is poor philosophy and practice.

As we complete this book, the world is in a peculiar state of chaos. Economic and political alignments that have existed since the early 1900s are crumbling. The Soviet Union, for long our archenemy, has suddenly become our ally. Its communist politics and economics are being thrown aside to be replaced by some as-yet-to-be-determined political-economic system. It may be that this new system will owe much to democracy and capitalism. Indeed, democracy has been the watchword for the most recent Soviet revolution.

Yet, while the former Soviet Union goes through the pangs of change from one form of government and economy to another, and capitalism and democracy come in for praise in many quarters as a "better" system, the United States finds itself in the throes of its own revolution—but this time highlighting the difficulties of uneven development and (in Los Angeles and other major cities) the urban poor. Thus what has been cast as virtuous for one place has been shown worldwide (via CNN) to have certain defects affiliated with it. And what has driven the uneven development that has arisen in Los Angeles and other major cities in the United States? The same kind of problems described throughout our book—lack of jobs, lack of quality education, lack of hope.

For us, uneven development and lack of opportunity are best understood in large geographical contexts, via the use of a regional approach. We used this approach for our book, and the same thing could be done for other places as well. For example, in the former Soviet Union, one finds historically based cultural divisions which—although suppressed by political ideology for generations—have quickly resurfaced, once allowed to do so. Estonia, Latvia, Lithuania, and other "republics" have asserted their identities as free-standing countries. In effect, these were always unique parts (viz., regions) within the Soviet Union, demonstrating that political repression never fully prevented cultural identity from forming.

Indeed, we could readily apply Markusen's conceptualization of region to the Soviet Union as well as to the United States. Like the United States, the Soviet Union has immense territorial *and* cultural diversity, as the republics noted above indicate. And, for us, the republics are much akin to the "forgotten" places in our book. The political ferment we now see and read about reflect the pent-up anger and frustration which has been simmering there for generations. In effect, people living in these republics are saying that they are tired of being forgotten, of being out of the mainstream; they want the right to act on their own behalf—feeling, of course, that in the end their lot in life will be improved because of it. In the United States, such a revolutionary movement is unlikely. Here, though, similar frustrations exist.

The theoretical tenets of dependency and world-systems theory come into play whether examining the Soviet Union or the United States. In either case, some parts of the country are made dependent upon other parts, and those areas providing raw material are most vulnerable to forms of economic exploitation. In a capitalist economy such as ours, this is part and parcel of "doing business." Costs (especially labor and material) are minimized wherever possible so that profits may be maximized. There is no sense that this equation is morally or economically wrong. It is merely how things are done. And, as is well known, similar economic principles were used throughout the Soviet Union, even during its most rigidly communist days. As George Orwell wrote in *Animal Farm*, "Some are more equal than others."

In the United States, equality has always been regarded as an individual attribute—as in "all men are created equal." The metaphor has been a race; everyone was to start from the same point without handicap. Of course we know that the metaphor was flawed. Some (especially minorities and women) start the race with decided handicaps that in most cases they are never able to fully overcome. These "handicaps" are, sociologically speaking, structural constraints—patterns of behavior such as racism, sexism, ageism, and so on. They are normative systems that come to exist and that act as constraints, facilitating achievement for some, precluding it for others.

The same kinds of barriers are evident when we examine regional development. Some areas fare better than others. *If* principles of equality held, how could we explain these differences? Why do some areas prosper while others languish?

We have argued elsewhere (Falk and Lyson, 1991) that industrial policy in America is decidedly urban in tone. Although the United States has no comprehensive industrial policy, what thought has been given to the issue has focused almost exclusively on urban areas. Rural areas, by contrast, have an industrial policy (if we may call it that) based on propping up farmers through government subsidies; this is coupled with a de facto population policy which has, for a hundred years, encouraged out-migration in search of employment. Farm support policy has become vulnerable and subject to criticism, since more and more farms are based on corporate models, thus calling into question the need for government subsidies in an arena normally guided by free-market principles. However, allowing rural areas to atrophy and die and their populations to move elsewhere are practices that continue.

Yet despite the harsh tone to our comments here, some rural areas overcome all odds. They thrive even in times of economic hardship. Research documenting such success has recently appeared in a number of places (see, for example, Flora and Flora, 1990; John et al., 1988). Common to these studies is the finding that no matter how phrased, human capital and ambition—as they exist in key individuals and come to characterize entire communities—can be made to work for the betterment of a place.

We have argued that industrial policy must be debated at the national level. But Flora and Flora, and John et al. would argue, quite correctly, that industrial policy may be debated at the national level, but it must be implemented at the local level. In this way, such initiatives as venture capital, revenue sharing, and perhaps some form of set-asides could be used to spur economic growth in rural areas (just as similar programs are now being touted by the Bush Administration for urban areas). Regardless of whether policies and practices are advocated at national or local levels, whether for rural or urban areas, in the United States or abroad, the intent is the same: To help reduce the degree to which uneven development exists and to improve the lot in life of the general population.

Although the title of our book gives emphasis to forgotten places, we must not forget, *ever*, that the real victims of being forgotten are the people who live in these places. They are easily forgotten, we believe, because so little is understood about them. They represent a part of our population that is less and less engaged in farming, either directly or indirectly. They are an ill-defined, largely unknown residual group of rural folk, many of whom are poor. For these people, the issues are: What kinds of opportunities will they have if they wish to continue to live locally? What policies exist to encourage or enhance their participation in the nation's economic life? What should we be doing (in rural or urban places, at the national or more local levels) to provide less uneven development? Perhaps more fundamentally, should we be doing anything to minimize uneven development or is uneven development to be part of our cultural and historical legacy?

Notes

1. We are well aware that the position of Storper and Walker and countless other writers who share their view contrasts sharply with that of neoclassical economists who argue that the system always seeks to balance itself. For them,

the disadvantages experienced in one locale should, theoretically, be offset by advantages experienced elsewhere. There is no moral or social imperative here to consider the detrimental aspects of what occurs in the disadvantaged places. Some places prosper, while others decline; such is the ebb and flow of economic life.

References

Baldwin, James. 1953. *Go Tell It on the Mountain.* New York: Knopf.

Caudil, Harry. 1963. *Night Comes to the Cumberlands.* Boston: Little, Brown.

Chute, Carolyn. 1985. *The Beans of Egypt, Maine.* New York: Ticknor and Fields.

Duncan, Cynthia M. 1992. *Rural Poverty in America.* Greenwood Press.

Domhoff, William. 1970. *The Higher Circles: The Governing Class in America.* New York: Random House.

Ellison, Ralph. 1952. *Invisible Man.* New York: Random House.

Falk, William W., and Thomas A. Lyson. 1988. *High Tech, Low Tech, No Tech: Industrial and Occupational Change in the South.* Albany, N.Y.: State University of New York Press.

Falk, William W., and Thomas A. Lyson. 1991. "Rural America and the Industrial Policy Debate." Pp. 8–21 in Cornelia B. Flora and James A. Christianson (eds.), *Rural Policies for the 1990s.* Boulder, Colo.: Westview Press.

Faulkner, William. 1964. *Absalom, Absalom!* New York: Random House.

Flora, Cornelia Butler, and Jan Flora. 1990. "Developing Entrepreneurial Rural Communities." *Sociological Practice* 8:197–207.

John, DeWitt, Sandra S. Beatie, and Kim Norris. 1988. *A Brighter Future for Rural America? Strategies for Communities and States.* Washington, D.C.: National Governors' Association.

Kesey, Ken. 1965. *Sometimes a Great Notion.* New York: Bantam Books.

Lyson, Thomas A. 1987. "Who Cares about the Farmer?" *Rural Sociology* 51:490–502.

———. 1989. *Two Sides to the Sunbelt: The Growing Divergence between the Rural and Urban South.* New York: Praeger.

Markusen, Ann. 1987. *Regions: The Economics and Politics of Territory.* Totowa, N.J.: Rowman and Littlefield.

McMurtry, Larry. 1979. *The Last Picture Show.* New York: Penguin Books.

Minick, Roger. 1975. *The Hills of Home: The Rural Ozarks of Arkansas.* San Francisco: Scrimshaw Press.

Mitchell, Margaret. 1961. *Gone with the Wind.* New York: Macmillan.

Moon, William Least-Heat. 1982. *Blue Highways.* Boston: Little, Brown.

Morris, Willie. 1970. *North toward Home.* New York: Dell Publishing Company.

Odum, Howard W. 1936. *Southern Regions of the United States.* Chapel Hill: University of North Carolina Press.

Olson, Mancur. 1982. *The Rise and Decline of Nations.* New Haven, Conn.: Yale University Press.

Percy, Walker. 1971. *Love among the Ruins.* New York: Farrar, Straus & Giroux.

Reed, John Shelton, and Daniel J. Singal (eds.). 1982. Pp. ix–xxi in *Regionalism and the South: Selected Papers of Rupert Vance.* Chapel Hill: University of North Carolina Press.

Robbins, Tom. 1990. *Another Roadside Attraction.* New York: Bantam.

Steinbeck, John. 1939. *Grapes of Wrath.* New York: Viking Press.

Storper, Michael, and Richard Walker. 1989. *The Capitalist Imperative.* New York: Basil Blackwell.

Updike, John. 1981. *Rabbit Run.* New York: Knopf.

Vance, Rupert. 1932. *Human Geography of the South.* Chapel Hill: University of North Carolina Press.

Welty, Eudora. 1946. *Delta Wedding.* New York: Harcourt, Brace & Company.

Wilson, William J. 1987. *The Truly Disadvantaged: The Inner City, the Underclass, and Public Policy.* Chicago: University of Chicago Press.

Wolfe, Tom. 1988. *Bonfire of the Vanities.* New York: Bantam.

Wright, Richard. 1945. *Black Boy.* New York: Harper & Bros.

About the Contributors

Ravindra Amonker has been a professor of sociology at Southwest Missouri State University in Springfield for twenty-five years. He specializes in demography. He has written many articles on the Missouri Ozarks and is currently writing a book on the demography of Missouri.

Marie Ballejos was a graduate student at Texas A&M when her chapter was written. Her interests include Mexican Americans, women, and demography.

Dwight Billings is professor of Sociology at the University of Kentucky. He has published widely on topics related to development in the South and in Appalachia. He is author of *Planters and the Makers of a New South.* Currently he is directing a restudy of a small Appalachian community, Beech Creek, that was first studied in 1940 and again in the mid-1960s.

Ted Bradshaw is a research sociologist at the University of California at Berkeley. He has written widely on his investigations into how rural communities will fare in postindustrial societies and is also author of *Rural Communities in Advanced Industrial Societies.*

Rex Campbell is a professor of rural sociology at the University of Missouri. He has studied and written about Missouri's people for more than thirty years. His current research focuses on demographic changes in small towns and rural development, particularly in rural Missouri.

James Elias is a planning consultant assisting community development and environmental organizations in the Rocky Mountain region. He was a graduate student at the University of Oregon when his chapter, sections of which were taken from his master's thesis, was written.

William Falk is professor and chair of the Department of Sociology at the University of Maryland, College Park. His current work focuses on uneven development in the American South, with particular attention to historically black counties. His recent publications include articles on this topic in *Social Problems* and *Rural Sociology,* and he is working on a book on this topic as well.

Michael Hibbard is chair of the Department of Planning, Public Policy and Management at the University of Oregon. He is the author of more than thirty articles and research reports on various aspects of socioeconomic development in resource-dependent communities. His work has appeared in the *Journal of the American Planning Association, Social Service Review,* and the *Community Development Journal.*

Stanley Hyland, associate professor of anthropology and chair of the Department of Anthropology at Memphis State University, is experienced in applied research on grassroots community action, especially related to housing, weatherization, and community leadership. He is founder of the Center for Voluntary Action Research at Memphis State and former director of the Lower Mississippi Delta Development Corporation.

Sue-Wen Lean recently completed her Ph.D. in sociology and social demography at Michigan State University. Her research focuses on the migration of social capital as it affects the development of rural regions in Third World contexts as well as the United States.

A. E. Luloff is associate professor of rural sociology in the Department of Agricultural Economics and Rural Sociology at Pennsylvania State University. He is interested in the impacts of rapid social change, and his teaching and research focus on community development and planning in nonmetropolitan areas.

Thomas Lyson holds a teaching and research position in the Department of Rural Sociology at Cornell University. His research interests include rural development, industrial restructuring, and sustainable agriculture. He is also director of the Farming Alternatives Program at Cornell.

Mark Nord is a Ph.D. candidate in the Department of Agricultural Economics and Rural Sociology at Pennsylvania State University. His research focuses on natural resources and rural poverty. He has worked in the field of international development in Indonesia and Central America. Most recently he directed the poverty alleviation program of the Mennonite Central Committee in Bangladesh.

Bruce Rankin is a Ph.D. candidate in sociology at the University of Maryland. He is currently exploring the relationship between inner-city poverty, neighborhood characteristics, and achievement at the Center for the Study of Urban Inequality at the University of Chicago. He has published articles on historically black counties in the South in *Social Problems* and *Rural Sociology.*

Rogelio Saenz is an associate professor at Texas A&M University. His research interests center on economic development issues in Texas and on issues related to race and ethnicity in the United States.

Harry Schwarzweller is professor of sociology at Michigan State University. He has been the principal investigator on a project studying changes in rural life in Michigan's Upper Peninsula. His other research interests deal with agricultural change in Australia and the United States. His books include *Mountain Families in Transition*.

John Spencer lived in the Missouri Ozarks for fifteen years before completing his doctorate in rural sociology at the University of Missouri. He is currently working on a regional development project and writing a book about rural social economy.

Clarence Talley is an assistant professor of sociology at the University of Kentucky. His primary research interest is the relationship between race, residence, and uneven development, especially in the South.

Ann Tickamyer is professor of sociology at the University of Kentucky. She has published widely on poverty, Appalachian development, gender stratification, and labor markets. Her articles have appeared in the *American Sociological Review, Rural Sociology,* and the *American Sociologist.*

Michael Timberlake is professor of sociology in the Department of Sociology, Anthropology and Social Work, Kansas State University. He is currently working with sociologists Bonnie Dill and Bruce Williams on a study of poor rural communities in the Mid-South. He also conducts research on the political economy of international development and underdevelopment.

Index